Christianity in the
Later Roman Empire:
A Sourcebook

Bloomsbury Sources in Ancient History

The Bloomsbury Sources in Ancient History series presents a definitive collection of source material in translation, combined with expert contextual commentary and annotation to provide a comprehensive survey of each volume's subject. Material is drawn from literary, as well as epigraphic, legal and religious, sources. Aimed primarily at undergraduate students, the series will also be invaluable for researchers, and faculty devising and teaching courses.

Christianity in the Later Roman Empire: A Sourcebook

David M. Gwynn

Bloomsbury Sources in Ancient History

B L O O M S B U R Y

LONDON · NEW DELHI · NEW YORK · SYDNEY

Bloomsbury Academic

An imprint of Bloomsbury Publishing Plc

50 Bedford Square	1385 Broadway
London	New York
WC1B 3DP	NY 10018
UK	USA

www.bloomsbury.com

Bloomsbury is a registered trade mark of Bloomsbury Publishing Plc

First published 2015

British Library Cataloguing-in-Publication Data
A catalogue record for this book is available from the British Library.

ISBN: HB: 978-1-44112-255-1
PB: 978-1-44110-626-1
ePDF: 978-1-44118-039-1
ePub: 978-1-44113-735-7

Library of Congress Cataloging-in-Publication Data
A catalog record for this book is available from the Library of Congress.

Typeset by Refinecatch, Bungay, Suffolk
Printed and bound in India

Contents

Introduction

Few periods in western history have witnessed so dramatic a transformation as the years that separate the third and seventh centuries AD. In the year 300, the Later Roman empire ruled unchallenged over the ancient Mediterranean world. From Spain and Gaul to Syria and Egypt, it was a world that had been shaped by the culture and religion of classical Greece and Rome since before the birth of Christ. Following the crucifixion of their Saviour, the early Christians had spread their message across this empire and beyond. But the Christians were as yet just a small if significant minority, expanding with each generation but still regarded with suspicion. No one alive at the turn of the third and fourth centuries could possibly have foreseen what the future held in store.

The fourth century was a time of revolution for Christianity and the Later Roman empire alike. The Great Persecution, unleashed by the emperor Diocletian in 303, failed to break the Church and in 312 Constantine became the first Roman emperor to convert to the Christian faith. Constantine's reign brought new privileges and responsibilities for the Church, and in the decades that followed Christianity established itself as the dominant religion of the empire. Christian doctrine and liturgy, which had remained largely fluid in earlier centuries, underwent a process of formation and canonization, while the Church's rising wealth and social prominence brought major changes in Christian society and culture. By AD 400 the Later Roman empire was fundamentally a Christian Roman empire.

Yet these years of Christian triumph also marked the beginning of the empire's 'Decline and Fall', as Germanic invaders crossed the frontiers and settled on Roman territory. At the Battle of Adrianople in 378 the Goths defeated and killed the eastern emperor Valens, and over the course of the fifth century one by one the western provinces of the empire fell away from imperial control. The Gothic army of Alaric sacked Rome in 410, Britain was abandoned and eventually occupied by the Anglo-Saxons, while the people known as the Vandals crossed Gaul and Spain to invade Roman North Africa. The Franks emerged in northern Gaul and began to conquer the land to which they would give their name, and in 476 the last western Roman emperor, Romulus Augustulus, was deposed. In the east the Later Roman empire survived, centred upon the new imperial capital of

Constantinople. But western Europe was now a mosaic of constantly shifting tribes and kingdoms.

For the Christians of east and west, the fifth and sixth centuries brought both challenges and opportunities. Across the eastern empire theological debates raged over the humanity and divinity of Christ, creating divisions within the Church that have never fully healed. The attempted 'reconquest' of the lost western provinces by the emperor Justinian in the sixth century caused the destruction of Vandal North Africa and the Ostrogothic kingdom of Italy, but failed to restore the old empire. In the west, the Christian Church was now the only institution that bound the former Roman territories together, and the bishops of Rome had taken over many of the roles that the emperors once played. By the beginning of the seventh century, the world of the Later Roman empire had given way to the dawn of medieval Christendom.

The purpose of this volume is to gather into a single accessible collection the sources that illustrate this crucial historical period. The years of crisis and transformation inspired generations of great writers, among them Eusebius of Caesarea, Athanasius of Alexandria, Julian 'the Apostate', Ambrose of Milan, John Chrysostom, Jerome and Augustine. Their works and many others illuminate famous episodes such as Constantine's conversion and the Sack of Rome and allow us to explore the evolution of Christian doctrine and liturgy, the rise of asceticism and the cult of the holy man, and the place of Christianity in an ever-changing world.

Chapter 1 traces the initial rise of Christianity from the death of Christ to the end of the third century. This was followed by the onslaught of the Great Persecution (Chapter 2), and the dramatic and much-debated conversion of Constantine (Chapter 3). The emperor's patronage transformed Christian wealth and social prestige, and laid the foundation for the imperial Church (Chapter 4). Christianity's growing prominence, however, also increased the stakes involved in internal Christian disputes. The Donatist Schism in North Africa (Chapter 5) was the first Church controversy to draw the attention of a Christian emperor and provoked the first persecution of Christians by a Christian ruler. Still more significant, and on a far wider scale, were the fourth-century theological debates over the doctrine of the Trinity (Chapter 6). Often referred to incorrectly as the 'Arian' controversy, these Trinitarian debates spanned the ecumenical councils of Nicaea (325) and Constantinople (381) and influenced the Christian faith adopted by the Goths and other Germanic peoples.

Christianity's transformation into the favoured religion of the empire led to pressure for greater uniformity in organization and practice to replace the relative diversity of the early Church. The fourth century thus saw the formal definition of the canon of Scripture and the increasing use of set formulas for the church liturgy and the celebration of the eucharist (Chapter 7). Baptismal practices evolved to cope with the flood of converts now embracing Christianity, and new festivals like Christmas shaped the emerging Christian calendar. The ecclesiastical hierarchy underwent a similar process of definition (Chapter 8). The changing roles that bishops had to play reflected the changing status of the Church in the empire and the Germanic kingdoms, while the bishop of Rome was an ever more influential figure in the post-Roman west. The relationship of Church and State did not always run smooth (Chapter 9), but the bond between emperor and bishop survived in the east and influenced later western concepts of the divine right of kings. Yet for some Christians, the Church's new wealth and prestige left them seeking a stronger expression of their faith. The ascetic movement of the fourth century spread the ideals of solitary and communal monasticism throughout east and west with vast consequences for Late Roman and medieval society (Chapter 10).

By the end of the fourth century, Christianity had become the majority religion of the Later Roman empire. This process of 'Christianization' was by no means straightforward, and the interaction between Christianity and traditional Graeco-Roman religion changed not only the empire but Christianity itself (Chapter 11). Christianity's connection with classical Graeco-Roman culture was particularly controversial, and concerned a number of the leading writers of the age (Chapter 12). Two prominent religious minorities likewise faced new challenges in a Christian Roman empire. Christianity's relationship with Judaism fluctuated from conflict to toleration and back, while the dualist religion of Manichaeism was subjected to almost unceasing persecution (Chapter 13). And although hardly a minority, the place of women in society also changed for both better and worse, as Christian values combined with the prevailing patriarchal worldview of ancient Rome (Chapter 14).

Christian influence extended throughout all walks of life. The emergence of ascetic holy men and women was one of the characteristic features of Late Roman Christianity, from desert monks and stylites on their pillars to female emulators of the Virgin Mary (Chapter 15). These holy men and women further contributed to the growth of pilgrimage and the cult of relics, which originally centred upon the Holy Land and the miraculous discovery of sacred sites and treasures such as the True Cross (Chapter 16). Beyond the empire's borders, the fourth to seventh centuries saw Christianity expand far beyond the Mediterranean. Missionaries reached Ethiopia in the south and the Germanic tribes across the river Danube, while Gregory the Great of Rome sent his mission to Anglo-Saxon England and eastern Christians were received with honour at the court of imperial China (Chapter 17). Within the empire, the Gothic invasions and the Sack of Rome prompted Augustine of Hippo, one of the most remarkable figures of western history, to embark upon his monumental work: the City of God (Chapter 18).

The contrasting fates of the eastern and western halves of the Later Roman empire are brought into stark focus by the conflicts that they faced in the fifth and sixth centuries. In the east the empire survived largely unscathed until the seventh-century Islamic Conquests. Yet eastern Christianity was racked by controversy over the human and divine natures of Christ and the doctrine of the Incarnation. The divisions that emerged around the teachings of Cyril of Alexandria and the councils of Ephesus (431) and Chalcedon (451) have remained to the present day, and the questions at stake still strike at the heart of the Christian message (Chapter 19). While the eastern Christians were debating Christology, the western Romans were fighting for their lives. The western empire fell one piece at a time, and in its place rose the kingdoms of Vandal North Africa, Gothic Italy and Spain, Merovingian Francia and Anglo-Saxon England. Religious turmoil was a threat in many of these kingdoms, for the Goths and Vandals had converted to a form of Christianity regarded as heretical by the Roman church. Over time, however, the catholic Christianity of Rome and the Franks prevailed and the Church's authority extended throughout the otherwise fragmented west (Chapter 20). Medieval Christendom was united not by a single empire but by the Christian religion.

In each of the chapters, the sources collected are embedded in a narrative that sets the context and explains their significance. All the material is intended to be accessible to students of both history and religious studies while also being of benefit to scholars, and every chapter concludes with a short bibliography offering guidance for further reading. The sources themselves are extremely diverse, from traditional Greek and Latin to Syriac, Coptic, Armenian and Chinese. Many of the full texts are available in English in excellent translation series, including Penguin Classics, the Loeb Classical Library, the Nicene and Post-Nicene Fathers, and most recently Liverpool Translated Texts which has opened a number of less well-known works to a wider readership. Alongside the translations that I have made myself, I would like to express my profound thanks to all the publishers who have granted permission for the republication of material in this sourcebook. Their generosity made the wide scope attempted here possible, and is acknowledged gratefully throughout the volume.

This project was originally inspired by Michael Greenwood, to whom go my deepest thanks for his initial support and encouragement. Dhara Patel and Charlotte Loveridge at Bloomsbury have been consistently helpful (not to mention patient) and I am again most grateful for all their assistance.

David M. Gwynn
Royal Holloway
University of London

Acknowledgements

Sincere thanks are due to the following publishers for permission to reproduce copyright material. The specific works cited are acknowledged in the bibliographies at the end of each chapter.

Brepols Publishers
Cambridge University Press
Edinburgh University Press
The Edwin Mellen Press
Equinox Publishing Ltd
InterVarsity Press
Liturgical Press
Liverpool University Press
Oxbow Books Ltd
Oxford University Press
Penguin Books Ltd
Princeton University Press
Routledge
University of California Press

Chronological Table

284–305 Diocletian and the Tetrarchy

c.302 Manichaean Rescript

303–313 Great Persecution

306–337 Constantine

312 Battle of the Milvian Bridge

313 The Donatists appeal to Constantine

314/15 Lactantius, *De Mortibus Persecutorum*

325 Council of Nicaea

324/5 Final edition of Eusebius of Caesarea's *Ecclesiastical History*

327 Helena's pilgrimage to the Holy Land

330 Dedication of Constantinople

337–361 Constantius II

339 Eusebius of Caesarea, *Life of Constantine*

c.340 Ulfila begins his mission to the Goths

c.350 Cyril of Jerusalem, *Catechetical Lectures*

356 Death of Antony

c.356 Athanasius of Alexandria, *Life of Antony*

361–363 Julian 'the Apostate'

361–363 Julian, *Letters, Misopogon, Rescript on Christian Teachers*

364–375 Valentinian I and 364–378 Valens

367 Athanasius of Alexandria, *Festal Letter* 39 on the canon of Scripture

c.370 Death of Faltonia Betitia Proba, *De Laudibus Christi*

374–397 Ambrose (Milan)

c.375 Epiphanius of Salamis, *Panarion*

378 Battle of Adrianople

379–395 Theodosius I

381 Council of Constantinople

382 Jerome begins the Vulgate Bible

383/4 Jerome, *Letter* 22

384 Altar of Victory Debate

After 384 Optatus of Milevis, *Against the Donatists*

386 'Conversion' of Augustine

c.386 Libanius, *Pro Templis*

386/7 John Chrysostom, *Homilies against the Jews*

390 Massacre of Thessalonica

391–392 Anti-pagan laws of Theodosius I

395–408 Arcadius and 395–423 Honorius

395 Ambrose of Milan, *On the Death of Theodosius I*

395–409 Paulinus of Nola, Poems in honour of St Felix

395–426 Augustine of Hippo, *De Doctrina Christiana*

397 Death of Martin of Tours

397 Augustine of Hippo,
Confessions

398–404 John Chrysostom
(Constantinople)

404 Jerome, *Letter* 108

406 Vandals cross the river Rhine

408–450 Theodosius II

410 Alaric and the Goths sack Rome

411 Conference of Carthage

412–444 Cyril (Alexandria)

412–426/7 Augustine of Hippo,
City of God

418 Visigoths settle in Aquitaine

c.420 John Cassian, *Institutes*

428–431 Nestorius (Constantinople)

429–439 Vandal conquest of North Africa

431 First Council of Ephesus

433 Formula of Reunion

438 *Theodosian Code* published

439 Death of Melania the Younger

440–461 Leo the Great (Rome)

c.440 Salvian of Marseille, *On
the Governance of God*

448 Trial of Eutyches

449 Second Council of Ephesus

449 *Tome of Leo*

451 Council of Chalcedon

451 *Acts of Chalcedon*

c.455–c.489 Sidonius
Apollinaris, *Letters*

459 Death of Symeon the Stylite

c.481–c.511 Clovis king of the Franks

> c.484 Victor of Vita, *History of the Vandal Persecution*

492–496 Gelasius (Rome)

493–526 Theoderic king of Ostrogothic Italy

507 Battle of Vouille

> 525 Dionysius Exiguus' chronology

527–565 Justinian

533–554 'Reconquest' of North Africa and Italy

537 Dedication of Hagia Sophia

> c.538 Cassiodorus, *Variae*

> c.540 Gildas, *The Ruin of Britain*

542/3 Jacob Baradeus ordained bishop of Edessa

> c.545 *Rule of St Benedict*

553 Council of Constantinople

> 560s Cassiodorus, *Institutions of Divine and Secular Learning*

586–601 Reccared king of Visigothic Spain

589 Reccared converts his kingdom to catholic Christianity

590–604 Gregory the Great (Rome)

> c.590 Gregory the Great, *Pastoral Rule*

> 594 Gregory of Tours, *History of the Franks*

597 Mission of Augustine to England

610–641 Heraclius

610 Muhammad receives the first revelations of the Qur'an

626 Siege of Constantinople by the Persians and Avars

634–698 Islamic conquest of Syria, Egypt and North Africa

635 Mission of Olopun to China

711 Islamic invasion of Spain

731 Bede, *Ecclesiastical History of the English People*

768–814 Charlemagne

800 Charlemagne crowned emperor in Rome

829–836 Einhard, *Life of Charlemagne*

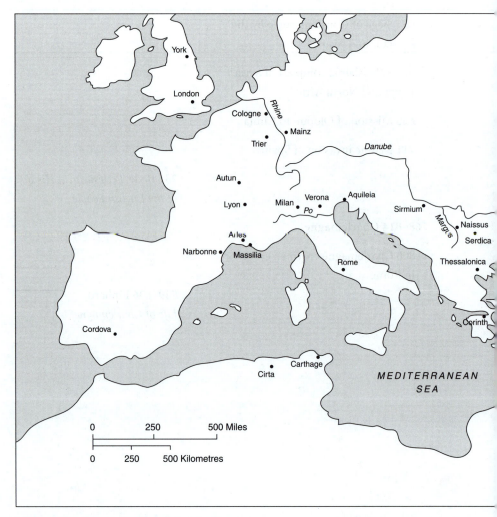

1 Map of the Roman Empire of Constantine

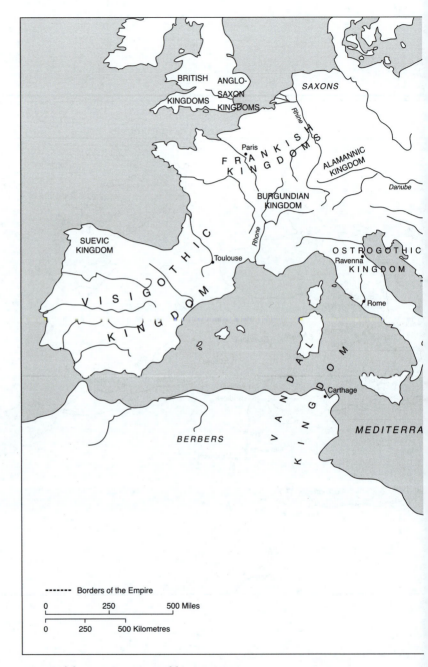

2 Map of the Late Roman world in AD 500

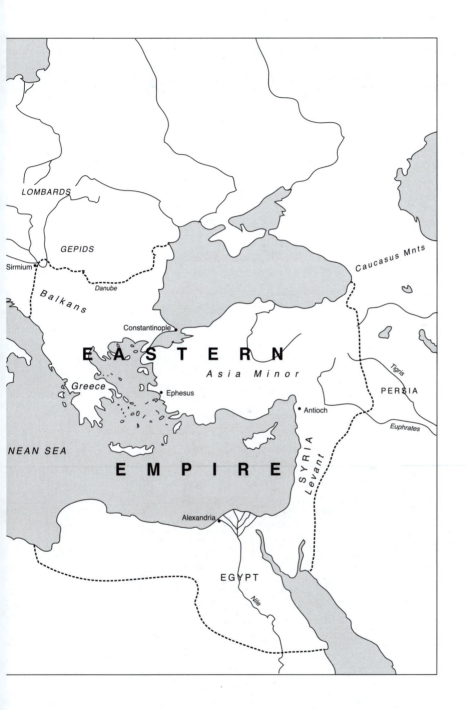

1

Christianity and Rome

> Jesus stood before the governor; and the governor asked him, 'Are you the King of the Jews'? Jesus said, 'You say so'. But when he was accused by the chief priests and elders, he did not answer. Then Pilate said to him, 'Do you not hear how many accusations they make against you'? But he gave him no answer, not even to a single charge, so that the governor was greatly amazed. Now at the festival the governor was accustomed to release a prisoner for the crowd, anyone whom they wanted. At that time they had a notorious prisoner, called Jesus Barabbas. So after they had gathered, Pilate said to them, 'Whom do you want me to release for you, Jesus Barabbas or Jesus who is called the Messiah'? For he realized that it was out of jealousy that they had handed him over. While he was sitting on the judgement seat, his wife sent word to him, 'Have nothing to do with that innocent man, for today I have suffered a great deal because of a dream about him'.
>
> Now the chief priests and the elders persuaded the crowds to ask for Barabbas and to have Jesus killed. The governor again said to them, 'Which of the two do you want me to release for you'? And they said, 'Barabbas'. Pilate said to them, 'Then what should I do with Jesus who is called the Messiah'? All of them said, 'Let him be crucified'! Then he asked, 'Why, what evil has he done'? But they shouted all the more, 'Let him be crucified'! So when Pilate saw that he could do nothing, but rather that a riot was beginning, he took some water and washed his hands before the crowd, saying, 'I am innocent of this man's blood; see to it yourselves'. Then the people as a whole answered, 'His blood be on us and on our children'! So he released Barabbas for them; and after flogging Jesus, he handed him over to be crucified.
>
> (Matthew 27.11–26)

The early history of Christianity is inseparable from the history of the Roman empire. Jesus Christ was born in the time of Augustus, the first emperor of

Rome (31 BC–AD 14). He was crucified during the reign of Augustus' successor Tiberius (AD 14–37), at the command of Pontius Pilate the Roman governor of Judaea. The ancient Mediterranean world in which the Christian message began to be proclaimed was already ruled by the power of Rome. Yet while it is easy to imagine the early Christians locked in unceasing conflict with that imperial power, the Roman empire also offered an environment within which the new religion could flourish. Missionaries travelled along Roman roads and gathered followers in Greek and Roman cities, protected by the peace enforced by the Roman legions. It was against this background that the Christian Church initially took shape across the centuries that separated Christ from Constantine, the first Christian emperor (306–337). In the years that followed Constantine's conversion in 312, Christianity became the dominant religion of the Later Roman empire and of the western Germanic kingdoms that emerged following Rome's fall.

This sourcebook is devoted to the transformation of Christianity into a true world religion in the Late Roman period between the fourth and seventh centuries AD. Before we can turn to these complex years, however, it is necessary to sketch if only in outline Christianity's gradual expansion from the death of Christ to the end of the third century and the relationship of those early Christians with the Roman empire in which they lived.

Christianity was slow to attract direct imperial attention. Pilate is depicted as a relatively sympathetic figure in Matthew's Gospel, who believed in Christ's innocence but sacrificed him to maintain public order and placate a bloodthirsty mob. The earliest persecutions of Christians were inspired by the hostility of Jews and local communities rather than the imperial authorities, and when an emperor did act against Christianity it was for personal rather than ideological motives. After the city of Rome was devastated by the Great Fire of 64, the unpopular Nero (emperor 54–68) faced accusations that he had orchestrated the disaster.

> To get rid of the report, Nero fastened the guilt and inflicted the most exquisite tortures on a class hated for their abominations, called Christians by the populace. Their originator, Christus, had been executed in Tiberius' reign by the procurator of Judaea, Pontius Pilate. But the wicked superstition, though temporarily checked, broke out again not only in Judaea where the evil had begun but even in Rome where all things hideous and shameful from every part of the world find their centre and become popular. First those who confessed

> themselves Christians were arrested. Then, on their information, a multitude of others were condemned, not so much for the crime of arson as for hatred of the human race. Mockery of every sort was added to their deaths. Covered with the skins of beasts, they were torn by dogs and perished, or were crucified, or were doomed to the flames and burnt to illuminate the night when daylight failed.
>
> (Tacitus, *Annals* 15.44.3–6)

There is little evidence that this Neronian persecution extended beyond Rome itself, although in Christian tradition Nero claimed two major victims in the apostles Peter and Paul. The Roman historian Tacitus, who wrote his *Annals* almost fifty years after Nero's death, certainly had no love for Christians but did not regard them as responsible for the Great Fire. By the early second century Christianity had spread throughout much of the Roman world, and it is Tacitus' friend Pliny the Younger who provides our most valuable insight into official Roman attitudes towards the emerging Church. As governor of Pontus-Bithynia on the Black Sea in c.112, Pliny reported on his treatment of Christians to the emperor Trajan (98–117).

> I have never attended investigations of Christians. Thus I do not know the nature of their crimes, the extent of the punishments usually imposed upon them, or how far an examination concerning them should be pressed. I am likewise uncertain whether any distinction should be made between them because of age or if young and old should be treated alike; whether a pardon ought to be given to those who retract their beliefs or if someone who has once been Christian gains nothing by renunciation; and whether punishment attaches to the mere name of Christian regardless of their crimes or to the crimes associated with the name. In the meantime this is the course that I have taken with those who were brought before me on the charge of being Christians. I asked them if they were Christians, and if they confessed, I repeated the question a second and third time with threats of punishment. If they persisted, I ordered them to be led away for execution; for I was convinced that whatever admission they made their stubbornness and unbending obstinacy ought to be punished.
>
> (Pliny the Younger, *Letter* 10.96, to Trajan)

Trajan in reply endorsed Pliny's actions.

You have adopted the right procedure, my dear Pliny, in investigating those persons accused before you with being Christians. It is impossible to lay down a general rule for all such cases. They are not to be sought out. If they are brought before you and convicted they must be punished, but those who deny that they are Christian and prove this by worshipping our gods shall be pardoned for their repentance no matter how suspect their past conduct may be. Anonymous pamphlets, however, must play no part in any accusation, for they create a most dangerous precedent and are quite foreign to the spirit of our age.

(Trajan to Pliny, preserved as Pliny the Younger, *Letter* 10.97)

The exchange between Trajan and Pliny set a precedent for imperial policy concerning Christians that endured for more than a hundred years. Christianity remained illegal, and a self-professed Christian might be executed without any other charge. But Christians were not to be hunted down. There was no systematic persecution before the mid-third century, and the outbreaks of violence that occurred were primarily inspired by local hostility not state intervention. Popular anti-Christian prejudice was fuelled by the suspicious rumours known to Tacitus and Pliny and refuted by a number of Christian apologists. Stories circulated of Christians practising incest and cannibalism and enjoying nocturnal orgies (possibly based on a misconception of the eucharist). Early in the third century, the apologist Minucius Felix gave an account of the alleged perversions attributed to his fellow Christians.

To say that a man who had suffered capital punishment for a crime and the death-dealing wood of the cross are objects of their veneration is to assign fitting altars to abandoned wretches and the manner of worship that they deserve. The story about the initiation of young novices is as detestable as it is notorious. An infant covered over with dough, that it may deceive the unwary, is placed before the one who is to be stained with their rites. The young initiate, encouraged to strike apparently harmless blows on the surface of the dough, secretly stabs the infant to death. Thirstily – O horror! – they lick up its blood and eagerly divide its limbs. By this victim they are bound together; with this consciousness of wickedness they are pledged to mutual silence. Such sacred rites are more foul than any sacrilege. What takes place at their banquets is so well known that all men speak of it everywhere, as is attested by a speech of our countryman of Cirta. On a solemn day they assemble at the feast, with all their children, sisters, mothers, people of every sex and of every age. There, after much feasting, when the fellowship has grown warm and the fervour of incestuous lust has grown hot with drunkenness, a dog that has been tied to a lamp is tempted, by throwing a small piece of offal beyond the length of its tether, to bound forward and leap. Thus the tale-telling light is overturned and extinguished, and in the shameless darkness the embraces of abominable lust are exchanged and all by complicity if not by action are involved in incest.

(Minucius Felix, *Octavius* 9.4–7)

The circulation of such stories in the early centuries AD reflected the uncertainty that surrounded the new religion, but actual violence against Christians was rare and localized. The reluctance of the emperors to take direct action, allied with the relative stability of the Roman empire during this period, gave the Christian movement the opportunity to expand. Yet why would potential converts be attracted to an illegal cult which venerated an executed criminal and whose adherents faced death for proclaiming their faith? Christianity promised salvation in heaven and communal support and charity in the present. The polytheistic Graeco-Roman religion that the majority of the empire's population followed did share the ideal of a blessed afterlife. But the Christian vision of salvation through Christ for those who believe (and the punishment facing the unrighteous) was far stronger and lay at the heart of their faith. In the words of Irenaeus of Lyon (c.130–c.200):

The Church, though dispersed throughout the whole world, even to the ends of the earth, has received from the apostles and their disciples this faith: in one God, the Father Almighty, who made the heaven and the earth and the seas and all things that are in them; and in one Christ Jesus, the Son of God, who became incarnate for our salvation; and in the Holy Spirit, who proclaimed through the prophets the dispensations and the advents, and the birth from a virgin, and the passion, and the resurrection from the dead, and the incarnate ascension into heaven of the beloved Christ Jesus our Lord and His future manifestation from heaven in the glory of the Father to sum up all things and to raise up anew all flesh of the whole human race, in order that to Christ Jesus, our Lord and God and Saviour and King, according to the will of the invisible Father, 'every knee should bow, of things in heaven, and things in earth, and things under the earth, and that every tongue should confess' [Philippians 2.10–11] to Him, and that He should execute just judgement towards all; that He may send spiritual wickednesses and the angels who transgressed and became apostates together with the ungodly and unrighteous and wicked and profane among men into the everlasting fire; but may, as an act of His grace, confer immortality on the righteous and holy and those who have kept His commandments and have persevered in His love, some from the beginning and others from their repentance, and may surround them with everlasting glory.

(Irenaeus of Lyon, *Against Heresies* 1.10.1)

The hope that Christianity offered to believers after death was balanced by the support that they received in life. The Christian message was open to all regardless of gender and social class, and converts gained a new sense of purpose, a code by which to live in the present and a feeling of community and belonging. Ancient Graeco-Roman society had no strong tradition of caring for the poor and unfortunate. Christians travelling across the vast Roman empire could look to fellow Christians for hospitality, and the Church offered charitable aid even to non-believers in times of crisis. This made a major impression in a world where plague, famine or war might threaten at any time, and the emphasis on welfare and caring for others for their own sake is one of Christianity's greatest legacies to modern times. At the end of the second century the North African Christian Tertullian (c.160–c.225) wrote:

We are a body bound together by a shared religious feeling, by unity of discipline, and by the common bond of hope. We meet together as an assembly and congregation so that, offering up prayer to God with united force, we may wrestle with Him in our supplications. This violence God delights in. We pray also for the emperors, for their ministers and for all in authority, for the welfare of the world, for the prevalence of peace, for the delay of the final end. We assemble to read our sacred writings, should any peculiarity of the times make us look to the future or the past. Whatever the case may be, with the sacred words we nourish our faith, we animate our hope, we reaffirm our confidence; and no less by inculcation of God's precepts we reinforce our teaching. Likewise during our gatherings exhortations are made, rebukes and sacred censures are administered. With great gravity is the work of judging carried on among us, as befits those who feel assured that they are in the sight of God; and it is a most notable foretaste of the judgment to come when anyone has sinned so grievously as to be severed from us in prayer, in the congregation and in all sacred intercourse. Those who preside over us are proven elders, obtaining that honour not by purchase but by established character. There is no buying and selling of any sort in the things of God. Though we have our treasure chest, it is not made up of entrance money, as of a religion that has its price. Once a month, each person if they wish puts in a small donation; but only if they wish and only if they are able: there is no compulsion, all is voluntary. These gifts are, as it were, the trust funds of piety. For they are not taken and spent on feasts and drinking bouts and eating-houses, but to support the poor and to bury them, to supply the needs of boys and girls destitute of means and parents, and of the old now confined to the house, and of those who have suffered shipwreck.

(Tertullian, *Apology* 39.1–6)

Even the periodic outbreaks of violence that Christians suffered proved paradoxically a source of strength. The willingness of Christians to face death as martyrs ('witnesses') to their faith again had no strong parallel in traditional Graeco-Roman religion and aroused considerable respect. Tertullian once more rebuked potential persecutors for their folly.

Nothing is accomplished by your cruelties, however exquisite. It is rather a temptation that draws men to us. The more we are cut down by you, the more we grow in number; the blood of Christians is seed.

(Tertullian, *Apology* 50.13)

In 177, twenty years before Tertullian wrote his *Apology*, one of the greatest attacks on a local Christian community took place in Lyon in Gaul. Some forty-eight Christians were killed, including the bishop Pothinus, and many others suffered injury and imprisonment. Irenaeus, who was in Rome delivering a message at the time of the assault, succeeded Pothinus as bishop. The heroism of those who were martyred is celebrated at length in a letter sent by the surviving Christians of Lyon and nearby Vienne to the churches of the east, which was preserved by the ecclesiastical historian Eusebius of Caesarea.

The severity of our trials in this region, the fury of the heathen against the saints and the sufferings of the blessed martyrs, we cannot recount accurately nor indeed could any report do them justice. The adversary fell upon us with all his might, giving us a foretaste of the unrestrained activity which will accompany his future coming. He endeavoured in every manner to train and equip his adherents against the servants of God, not only shutting us out from houses and baths and markets, but forbidding any of us to be seen in any place whatever. But the grace of God led the resistance against him, delivering the weak and setting them firm pillars able through patience to endure all the wrath of the evil one. And they joined battle with him, undergoing all manner of shame and injury, and regarding their great sufferings as no serious matter they hastened to Christ, revealing truly that 'the sufferings of this present time are not worth comparing with the glory about to be revealed to us' [Romans 8.18]. First of all, they endured nobly the injuries heaped upon them by the populace: clamouring, blows, dragging along the ground, robberies, stonings, imprisonments and all the things which an angry mob delights in inflicting on its enemies. Then they were taken to the forum by the tribune and the authorities of the city, they were examined in the presence of the whole multitude, and having confessed they were imprisoned until the arrival of the governor.

(*Letter of the churches of Vienne and Lyon*, quoted in Eusebius of Caesarea, *Ecclesiastical History* 5.1.4–8)

Through the courage of the martyrs, the strength of communal spirit and the promise of salvation, Christianity survived and prospered. By the middle of the third century, although still illegal in the eyes of the emperors and subject to slanderous stories and occasional violence, Christian communities had spread throughout the Roman empire. Sadly, there is far too little evidence to provide an accurate estimate of early Christian numbers. For the period between the apostles and the conversion of Constantine, we possess just one explicit numerical statement recording the clerical establishment of a Christian community. At the time of bishop Cornelius (251–253), the church of Rome maintained:

Forty-six presbyters, seven deacons, seven sub-deacons, forty-two acolytes, fifty-two exorcists, readers and door-keepers, and more than fifteen hundred widows and persons in distress, all of whom are nourished by the grace and loving kindness of the Master.

(Cornelius of Rome, quoted in Eusebius of Caesarea, *Ecclesiastical History* 6.43.11)

We cannot generalize easily from one solitary example, particularly from the imperial city which always represented an exceptional case. The figures confirm that the Christian community of Rome in the 250s was considerable, perhaps 30,000 to 50,000 in total, while the emphasis upon charity is reflected in the concern for widows and others in need of welfare. Outside Rome we can identify from texts many urban centres which possessed Christian communities. But the earliest churches were simply converted houses which leave almost no physical trace to reveal their size and the size of their congregations (the only early house-church so far excavated in detail comes from Dura Europus in modern Syria, on the Roman frontier with Persia). Even without precise figures, however, Christianity in the mid-third century was clearly growing significantly in both numbers and public prestige. And it was at this time that the Roman state first began the empire-wide persecution of the Church.

In Roman history the years between 235 and 284 are often described as the 'third-century crisis'. The empire faced invasions from the rising Sassanian Persian empire to the east and Germanic tribes to the north, combined with repeated civil wars and socio-economic collapse. Some contemporaries placed the blame for these disasters on the Christians. They were called 'atheists', who denied the traditional gods and so brought down divine wrath on the empire. Nevertheless, the first emperor said to have ordered a systematic persecution of Christians did not originally intend to attack the Church. Desperate to gain divine favour, the emperor Decius (249–251) ordered that his subjects display their piety by offering public sacrifice to the gods. It was the refusal of Christians to comply that led to outright persecution, although not all the faithful shared the convictions of the martyrs as one bishop lamented.

All were terrified, and many of the more eminent came forward immediately in their fear while others in public positions were compelled to do so by their business and still others were dragged forward by the mob. As their names were called they approached the impure and impious sacrifices. Some of them were pale and trembling, as if they were not about to sacrifice but to be sacrifices themselves and offerings to the idols, so that they were jeered at by the multitude standing around because it was plain to everyone that they were afraid either to die or to sacrifice. Others advanced eagerly towards the altars, declaring boldly that they had never been Christians. Of these the Lord predicted most truly that they shall hardly be saved. Among the rest, some followed one or other of these groups, some fled, and some were seized. Of the latter some remained faithful until they faced chains and imprisonment, and some who had been imprisoned for many days nevertheless abjured the faith before they were brought to trial. Others, having for a time endured great tortures, finally retracted. But the firm and blessed pillars of the Lord, being strengthened by Him and having received vigour and might suitable and appropriate to the strong faith which they possessed, became admirable martyr-witnesses of His kingdom.

(Dionysius of Alexandria (bishop 247–264), *Letter to Fabius of Antioch*, quoted in Eusebius of Caesarea, *Ecclesiastical History* 6.41.11–14)

Decius was killed by Goths in 251, the first Roman emperor to die in battle with a foreign foe, and his edict lapsed into oblivion. Then in 257/8 a new attack on Christianity broke out under Valerian (emperor 253–260). This time the persecution specifically focused upon the Church itself. Christian property was seized and the clergy singled out for punishment. One victim was Cyprian of Carthage (bishop 249–258), whose martyrdom at the order of proconsul Galerius Maximus is recorded in semi-fictionalized form in a later work claiming to be the *Acta* (minutes) of Cyprian's judgement and execution.

Galerius, after briefly conferring with his judicial council, with much reluctance pronounced the following sentence: 'You have long lived an irreligious life, and have drawn together a number of men bound by an unlawful association, and professed yourself an open enemy to the gods and the religion of Rome; and the pious, most sacred and august emperors Valerian and Gallienus, and the most noble Caesar Valerian, have endeavoured in vain to bring you back to conformity with their religious observances. Whereas, therefore, you have been apprehended as principal and ringleader in these infamous crimes, you shall be made an example to those whom you have wickedly associated with you; the authority of law shall be ratified in your blood'. He then read the sentence of the court from a written tablet: 'It is the sentence of this court that Thascius Cyprianus be executed with the sword'.

Cyprian: Thanks be to God.

After this sentence the crowd of brethren cried: 'Let us also be beheaded with him'. Hence arose an uproar among the brethren, and a great crowd accompanied him. So Cyprian was led forth on to the land of Sextus, and there he divested himself of his mantle, and kneeled upon the ground, and bowed in prayer to the Lord. And when he had divested himself of his dalmatic and handed it to the deacons, he stood clad in his linen garment, and prepared to await the executioner.

(*Acta proconsularia S. Cypriani* 4–5)

Like Decius, Valerian seems to have sought to restore divine favour to the empire, and to Christian joy he met a similar doom. The emperor was captured by the Persians in 260, and after his death his skin was removed, dyed vermillion, and placed in a Persian temple as a reminder to Rome. The failure of the Decian and Valerianic persecutions and the terrible fates of the emperors responsible for them brought the Church a respite. For the last four decades of the third century Christianity was tolerated, although its legal status remained ambiguous. These years in fact witnessed particular Christian growth, celebrated by the ecclesiastical historian Eusebius of Caesarea who was born in c.260 and grew to adulthood during this period of peace, which ended abruptly with the Great Persecution of Diocletian.

It is beyond my ability to describe in a suitable manner the extent and nature of the glory and liberty with which the word of piety toward the God of the universe, proclaimed to the world through Christ, was honoured among all men, both Greeks and barbarians, before the persecution of my time. The favour shown to our people by the rulers might be brought forward as evidence, for they even committed the government of provinces to them and on account of the great friendship with which they regarded our doctrine, released them from anxiety in regard to sacrificing. Why need I speak of those in the imperial palaces and of the supreme rulers, who allowed the members of their households, their wives and children and servants, to speak openly before them of the divine message and way of life, and suffered them almost to boast of the liberty of their faith? Indeed, they esteemed them highly and preferred them to their fellow-servants. Such a figure was the famous Dorotheus, the most devoted and faithful to them of all and on this account especially honoured by them more than those who held the most prestigious offices and governorships. With him was the celebrated Gorgonius, and as many like him as had been esteemed worthy of the same distinction on account of the word of God. One could see that the leaders in every church were accorded the greatest favour by all officers and governors. And how can anyone describe those vast assemblies, and the multitude that crowded together in every city, and the remarkable gatherings in the houses of prayer? No longer satisfied with the ancient buildings, on this account they erected from the foundations large churches in all the cities. Envy did not hinder the progress of these affairs, which advanced gradually and grew and increased day by day. Nor could any evil demon slander them or hinder them through human counsels, so long as the divine and heavenly hand watched over and guarded His own people as being worthy.

(Eusebius of Caesarea, *Ecclesiastical History* 8.1.1–6)

Where did Christianity stand within the Roman empire at the end of the third century? Despite Eusebius' rhetoric, Christians were still a distinct minority of the population and perhaps made up 10–15 per cent of the empire's estimated 60 million inhabitants. The vast majority continued to worship the traditional gods and goddesses of ancient Greece and Rome. Most Christians came from the urban social classes, and Christianity was slower to penetrate the peasants in the countryside, the governing aristocracy, or the army. There was similarly a greater concentration of Christians in the Greek-speaking eastern regions of the empire, where Eusebius resided, than in the more distant Latin-speaking provinces such as Gaul and Britain. Perhaps most importantly, Christianity itself at this time was extremely diverse, to the point that some commentators prefer to speak of 'Christianities'. The early Christian message took many different forms, and essential elements such as the theology of God, the hierarchy of the clergy and the canon of Scripture remained controversial. Only after the conversion of the emperor Constantine would these characteristic markers of Christian identity be clearly defined as the Church expanded dramatically in size and influence. Even before Constantine's conversion, however, Christianity was already the fastest growing religious movement that the ancient Mediterranean world had ever known. From humble origins in Judaea, the followers of Christ had not only survived but thrived and so laid the foundation for Christianity to resist the Great Persecution, gain the favour of Constantine, and become the dominant religion of the Later Roman empire.

Further Reading

D. Boyarin, *Dying for God, Martyrdom and the Making of Christianity and Judaism* (Stanford 1999)

H. Chadwick, *The Early Church* (revised edition, London and New York 1993)

P. F. Esler (ed.), *The Early Christian World*, 2 volumes (London 2000)

E. Ferguson, *Backgrounds of Early Christianity*, 3rd edition (Grand Rapids 2003)

R. M. Grant, *Augustus to Constantine: The Thrust of the Christian Movement into the Roman World* (London 1971)

K. Hopkins, *A World Full of Gods: Pagans, Jews and Christians in the Roman Empire* (London 1999)

R. Horsley (ed.), *Christian Origins: A People's History of Christianity*, Volume I (Minneapolis 2005)

M. Humphries, *Early Christianity* (London 2006)

R. Lane Fox, *Pagans and Christians in the Mediterranean World from the Second Century AD to the Conversion of Constantine* (London and New York 1986)

P. McKechnie, *The First Christian Centuries: Perspectives on the Early Church* (Downers Grove 2001)

P. Rousseau, *The Early Christian Centuries* (London 2002)

J. Z. Smith, *Drudgery Divine: On the Comparison of Early Christianities and the Religions of Late Antiquity* (London and Chicago 1990)

M. Sordi, *The Christians and the Roman Empire*, translated by A. Bedini (London and Sydney 1986)

R. Stark, *The Rise of Christianity: A Sociologist Reconsiders History* (Princeton 1996)

R. L. Wilken, *The Christians as the Romans saw them*, 2nd edition (New Haven and London 2003)

2

The Great Persecution

The third century AD was a period of turmoil for the Roman empire. During these years of crisis and uncertainty, some began to question their faith in the traditional gods while others sought an explanation for what had brought down the gods' wrath. It was against this background that the first empire-wide attacks upon Christianity were unleashed under the emperors Decius and Valerian in the 250s. By the end of the century, however, the worst was over. The man chiefly responsible for restoring stability to the empire was Diocles, a Balkan peasant soldier who rose through the army ranks to become emperor in 284 and took the name Diocletian. His imperial reorganization saw authority divided between four rulers, the Tetrarchy, to oversee the recovery. But today Diocletian's reign is remembered less for the restoration of the empire than for the most dangerous attack that Christianity had yet faced: the Great Persecution.

Diocletian recognized that the empire was simply too large for one man to rule alone. In 286 he appointed a fellow Balkan soldier, Maximian, as co-Augustus to rule in the west while Diocletian ruled the east. Then in 293, a junior emperor or Caesar was assigned to each Augustus, Galerius to Diocletian and Constantius Chlorus to Maximian. The unity and harmony of the Tetrarchy was celebrated in panegyrical speeches and art, including the famous porphyry statue group of the embracing Tetrarchs now outside San Marco in Venice. Contemporary Christians were less charitable. Lactantius was a North African who became the Professor of Latin Rhetoric at Diocletian's capital of Nicomedia before the Great Persecution. His *De Mortibus Persecutorum* (*On the Deaths of the Persecutors*), probably written in 314–315, celebrated the gruesome deaths of those who persecuted the Church and is a crucial if highly biased source on the Tetrarchy. In Lactantius' words:

Diocletian was an author of crimes and a deviser of evils; he ruined everything and could not even keep his hands from God. In his greed and anxiety he turned the world upside down. He appointed three men to share his rule, dividing the world into four parts and multiplying the armies, since each of the four strove to have a far larger number of troops than previous emperors had had when they were governing the state alone. The number of recipients began to exceed the number of contributors by so much that, with farmers' resources exhausted by the enormous size of the requisitions, fields became deserted and cultivated land was turned into forest. To ensure that terror was universal, provinces too were cut into fragments; many governors and even more officials were imposed on individual regions.

(Lactantius, *De Mortibus Persecutorum* 7.1–4)

Contrary to Lactantius, the Tetrarchy succeeded in bringing prosperity back to much of the empire. The frontiers were secured, administration improved, and the economy revived. The Tetrarchy's stability depended heavily upon the strong personality of Diocletian, and after his abdication in 305 the system fell apart in an orgy of civil wars from which Constantine, the son of Constantius Chlorus, eventually emerged triumphant. But as long as Diocletian remained in power, the imperial government was in good hands. It was the treatment of his fellow Christians that inspired Lactantius' hostility.

Religion played an integral part in Diocletian's vision of the empire. Like the majority of his subjects, Diocletian believed strongly in divine providence, that the gods' will determined the course of worldly events. To restore prosperity to the empire, he therefore had to restore divine favour. Diocletian took the title Jovius to express his devotion to Jupiter Optimus Maximus, the greatest god of ancient Rome, while his colleague Maximian became Herculius. In 289 an anonymous orator praised Maximian accordingly:

When only divine help was sufficient for [the state's] restoration after its collapse in former times, and not even the help of one god sufficed; you came to the aid of the Roman name, as it faltered, at the side of the leader, with that same timely assistance as your Hercules once lent to your Jupiter.

(*Panegyrici Latini* X(2).4)

Initially, Diocletian and Maximian focused upon reviving the people's faith in the traditional cults. Over time, however, the Tetrarchy began to attack 'new' religions that might anger the old gods. The first to attract imperial attention were not the Christians but those who followed Manichaeism, a dualist movement founded by the Persian religious leader Mani in the mid-third century (see Chapter 13). Not only did the Manichees reject the existing Graeco-Roman gods, but as a Persian cult they were seen as a potential fifth column betraying the empire from within. In c.302 an edict was proclaimed against Manichaeism:

Excessive leisure sometimes provokes ill-suited people to cross natural limits and encourages them to introduce false and outrageous forms of superstitious doctrine, so that many others are persuaded to recognize the authority of their mistaken beliefs. In their foresight, the immortal gods have deigned to insist that the principles of virtue and truth be acknowledged and confirmed by the counsel and thoughts of many good, great and wise men. It is wrong to oppose or resist these principles; and no new belief should criticize the religion of old. It is highly criminal to discuss doctrines established and defined by our ancestors, which still have their acknowledged place and role. For this reason we are absolutely determined to punish the stubborn madness of these worthless people.

We have heard all those matters relating to the Manichaeans which in your wisdom you reported to us in our serenity – that against the older beliefs they establish new and unknown sects, wickedly intending to overthrow the doctrines confirmed for us long ago by divine favour; that recently they have advanced or emerged from their native homes in Persia – an enemy of ours – like strange and monstrous portents, and have settled in this part of the world, where they commit many evil acts, upsetting the peace of the people and seriously damaging towns. There is a danger that in time they will try, as usual, to contaminate with the Persians' criminal habits and insane laws the innocent, orderly and peaceful Roman people, and the whole empire as well, as if with the poison of an evil snake.

Because everything you in your prudence explained in your report about their religion demonstrates that what our laws see as their crimes are born of a wild and false imagination, we have set deserved and suitable penalties for these people. We command that the authors and leaders of these sects receive severe punishment and be burnt in the flames with their detestable books. We order that if they prove defiant, their followers suffer capital punishment, and their possessions pass to the imperial treasury. If those people who have crossed to that unknown, outrageous and disreputable belief, or to the Persians' belief, are in public office or are of any rank or higher social status, you must confiscate their estates, and send the offenders to the Phaeno [quarry] or to the Proconnesus mines. In your devotion, hurry to execute our orders and commands so that this iniquitous disease is completely cleansed from our most happy age.

(Manichaean Rescript, *Collation of the Laws of Moses and Rome* 15.3)

The denunciation of Manichaeism had ominous implications for Christianity. While the Christians did not share the Manichees' 'Persian' taint, they too stood accused of being a 'new' sect opposed to the ancient gods. Two eyewitness accounts of the Great Persecution have survived: Lactantius' *De Mortibus Persecutorum* and Eusebius of Caesarea's *Ecclesiastical History*. According to Lactantius, in c.299 the first violence against Christians broke out after an imperial sacrifice:

He [Diocletian] was once sacrificing cattle and looking in their entrails for what was going to happen, when certain of his attendants who knew the Lord and were present at the sacrifice, placed the immortal sign on their foreheads; at this the demons were put to flight and the rites thrown into confusion. The *haruspices* began to get agitated at not seeing the usual marks on the entrails, and as if they had not made the offering, they repeated the sacrifice several times. But the slaughter of victim after victim still revealed nothing; and finally their Tagis, the chief of the *haruspices*, whether through suspicion or on the evidence of his own eyes, said that the reason why the sacrifices were not yielding an answer was that profane persons were present at the sacred ceremonies. Diocletian then flew into a rage; he ordered that not only those who were attending the rites but all who were in the palace should do sacrifice, and that any who declined should be punished by whipping; he also sent letters to commanders ordering that soldiers too should be compelled to perform the abominable sacrifices, and that any who disobeyed should be discharged from military service.

(Lactantius, *De Mortibus Persecutorum* 10.1–5)

This episode preceded the general persecution by several years, and provides valuable evidence for the presence of Christians at Diocletian's court and among his soldiers. Eusebius too reported an initial attack upon the Christians in the army. For Eusebius, however, the persecutors were fulfilling the will of God. Like the Israelites in the Old Testament, the Christians fell into evil ways and brought divine anger upon themselves:

On account of the abundant freedom we fell into arrogance and sloth. We envied and reviled each other, and were almost as it were taking up arms against one another with words like spears. Leaders attacked leaders, laity formed factions against laity, and monstrous hypocrisy and dissimulation rose to the greatest height of wickedness. Thus while the multitudes still continued to assemble, the divine judgment with forbearance as is its wont began to gently and gradually restore order. With the Christians in the army the persecution began. But as if blind we made no effort to make the Deity favourable and propitious, and as if we were atheists we thought that our affairs went unheeded and ungoverned and so went on adding one wickedness to another. Those who were accounted our shepherds, casting aside the restraining influence of the fear of God, were excited to conflicts with one another and did nothing else than heap up disputes, threats, jealousy, enmity and mutual hatred.

(Eusebius of Caesarea, *Ecclesiastical History* 8.1.7–8)

Exactly who among the Tetrarchs drove the assault against the Christians has been a subject for debate. Diocletian was the senior emperor, and a strong supporter of traditional Roman religion. But he had tolerated Christianity for the majority of his reign, and both Lactantius and Eusebius place the chief blame on the Caesar Galerius who drove Diocletian to act. Whoever the instigator was, the Great Persecution began at dawn on 23 February 303.

A suitable and auspicious day was sought for carrying the business out, and the festival of the *Terminalia* on 23 February was chosen as best, so that a termination so to speak could be imposed on this religion. 'That day was the first which was the cause of death, the first which was the cause of ills' [Virgil, *Aeneid* 4.169–70] – ills which befell both them and the whole world.

(Lactantius, *De Mortibus Persecutorum* 12.1)

The first church attacked could be seen from the imperial palace at Nicomedia.

While it was still twilight the prefect came to the church with military leaders, tribunes, and accountants. They forced open the doors and searched for the image of God. They found the Scriptures and burnt them; all were granted booty; the scene was one of plunder, panic, and confusion. The rulers themselves from their vantage point (the church was built on high ground and so was visible from the palace) argued with each other for a long time whether the building ought to be set on fire. Diocletian won the argument by warning that a large fire might cause some parts of the city to go up in flames; for the church was surrounded on all sides by a number of large houses. So the praetorian guard came in formation, bringing axes and other iron tools, and after being ordered in from every direction they levelled the lofty edifice to the ground within a few hours.

(Lactantius, *De Mortibus Persecutorum* 12.2–5)

The prominence of this church in Diocletian's capital reflects the status that Christianity had achieved by this time, although Lactantius' report that the building's destruction took just a few hours suggests that the church was not a huge structure.

On 24 February (the following day) the first persecuting edict was published. All churches were to be destroyed and their sacred books and vessels seized, congregations were banned and Christians lost their official positions and social and legal privileges. A man named Euetius who tore the edict down was roasted to death as a martyr, and further edicts soon followed. The second persecuting edict a few months later ordered the arrest of all Christian clergy, while a third edict offered an amnesty to clergy who sacrificed to the gods but torture for those who refused. Finally, a fourth edict extended the order to sacrifice to everyone in the empire.

The texts of the persecuting edicts do not survive, although in tone and language they were probably very similar to the edict against the Manichees. More difficult to judge is just how effective the edicts actually were. Passing a law did not guarantee that the law could be enforced across the empire, and the Great Persecution's impact varied widely. Regional differences in the numbers and prominence of Christians were a factor, as were the attitudes of officials and the wider populace. In earlier centuries outbursts of violence against Christianity had largely depended on local hostility rather than imperial action, but by 303 Christians were no longer regarded as alien or dangerous by the majority of the population. Even at the level of the Tetrarchy there were differences in motivation, and this was revealed as the Persecution ran its course.

Eusebius described in detail the suffering he witnessed in his native Palestine and in Egypt, and celebrated the courage of those who faced martyrdom:

I was in these places and observed large crowds [of victims] in a single day. Some suffered decapitation, others were tortured by fire. So many [were killed] that the

> murderous axe was blunted and having been weakened broke into pieces, while the very executioners grew weary and relieved each other. And we beheld the most wonderful eagerness and the truly divine energy and zeal of those who believed in the Christ of God. For as soon as sentence was pronounced against the first, one after another rushed to the judgment seat and confessed themselves Christians. Paying no heed to the terrors and the varied forms of tortures, they declared themselves boldly and undauntedly for the religion of the God of the universe. They received the final sentence of death with joy, laughter and cheerfulness, so that they sang and offered up hymns and thanksgivings to the God of the universe till their very last breath.
>
> (Eusebius of Caesarea, *Ecclesiastical History* 8.9.4–5)

In the western parts of the empire the Persecution was more sporadic. Only the first persecuting edict of 303 was ever enforced in the west by Maximian or his Caesar Constantius Chlorus. Indeed, Lactantius and Eusebius deny that Constantius took any violent actions against the Christians of Britain and northern Gaul. Both authors wrote after the conversion to Christianity of Constantius' son Constantine, which must have influenced their judgements. But it seems probable that Constantius did do little to enforce the Persecution, not least because there were not many Christians in his regions to persecute. Under Maximian some executions occurred, most significantly in Roman North Africa where Christianity was particularly strong. Under the strain of persecution, conflict broke out within the African Church over how to handle those who lapsed and betrayed their faith. The resulting Donatist Schism endured for centuries and will be explored in more detail in Chapter 5. Through the records preserved in that Schism, however, we gain our clearest insight into the impact of the Persecution on local communities. At the Numidian town of Cirta in 303, the local priest and official set out to enforce the imperial will:

> Felix the permanent priest, curator of the public weal, said, 'Bring forth the Scriptures that you have, so that you may comply with the bidding of the emperors and their edict'. Catullinus brought forth one extremely large codex. Felix the permanent priest, curator of the public weal, said to Marcuclius and Silvanus, 'Why have you given only one codex?' Catullinus and Marcuclius said, 'We have no more, as we are subdeacons; but the readers have the codices'. Felix the permanent priest, curator of the public weal, said, 'Show me the readers!' Marcuclius and Catullinus said, 'We don't know where they live'. Felix the

permanent priest, curator of the public weal, said to Catullinus and Marcuclius, 'If you do not know where they live, tell their names'. Catullinus and Marcuclius said, 'We are not traitors. Here we are, have us killed'. Felix the permanent priest, curator of the public weal, said, 'Let them be taken into custody'.

(preserved in the *Gesta apud Zenophilum*, quoted in turn by Optatus, *Against the Donatists*, Appendix 1)

After the first wave of violence in 303/4, the Persecution continued at varying levels of intensity for almost a decade. The exact scale of human suffering inflicted by the Great Persecution is very difficult to assess. The imperial government was out to subdue rather than kill, so imprisonment and torture were the preferred weapons rather than execution, and the greatest impact was psychological rather than physical. This must not overshadow the heroic endurance of those who suffered, or the shock experienced by Christians like Lactantius and Eusebius who had grown up in the years of peace since 260. The failure of the Great Persecution was a triumph for the Christian spirit and the Church as a community which was simply too strong for the imperial authorities to break. In 311 even Galerius, by this stage the senior emperor, conceded defeat. To Lactantius' unconcealed delight, Galerius fell critically ill with a malady the Christians attributed to divine judgement.

A malign ulcer appeared on the lower part of his genitals and spread more widely ... As the marrow was assailed, the infection was forced inwards, and got a hold on his internal organs; worms were born inside him. The smell pervaded not just the palace but the whole city; and this was not surprising, since the channels for his urine and his excrement were now confused with each other. He was consumed by worms, and his body dissolved and rotted amid insupportable pain.

(Lactantius, *De Mortibus Persecutorum* 33.1–8)

Subdued by his illness, shortly before his death Galerius passed an edict of religious toleration:

Among all the other arrangements which we are always making for the advantage and benefit of the state, we had earlier sought to set everything right in accordance with the ancient laws and public discipline of the Romans and to ensure that the Christians too, who had abandoned the way of life of their ancestors, should return to a sound frame of mind; for in some way such self-will had come upon these same Christians, such folly had taken hold of them, that they no longer followed those usages of the ancients which their own ancestors perhaps had first instituted, but, simply following their own judgement and pleasure, they were making up for themselves the laws which they were to observe and were gathering various groups of people together in different places. When finally our order was published that they should betake themselves to the practices of the ancients, many were subjected to danger, many too were struck down. Very many, however, persisted in their determination and we saw that these same people were neither offering worship and due religious observance to the gods nor practising the worship of the god of the Christians.

Bearing in mind therefore our own most gentle clemency and our perpetual habit of showing indulgent pardon to all men, we have taken the view that in the case of these people too we should extend our speediest indulgence, so that once more they may be Christians and put together their meeting-places, provided they do nothing to disturb good order. We are moreover about to indicate in another letter to governors what conditions they ought to observe. Consequently, in accordance with this indulgence of ours, it will be their duty to pray to their god for our safety and for that of the state and themselves, so that from every side the state may be kept unharmed and they may be able to live free of care in their own homes.

(quoted in Lactantius, *De Mortibus Persecutorum* 34.1–5)

Galerius made no apology for the Persecution. The return of the empire to the standards of the ancients required the suppression of the Christians and their novel beliefs. Nevertheless, he acknowledged that his efforts had failed and peace had to be restored. Galerius concluded by asking the Christians to pray to their god for the good of the state, but Lactantius was pleased to report that the emperor's contrition failed to win divine mercy and he duly died in horrible pain.

The Persecution did not completely end with the edict of 311. When Galerius died, authority in the east was divided between Licinius and Maximinus Daia, and under the latter the attack on Christianity was temporarily renewed. Eusebius described the subsequent violence in the ninth book of his *Ecclesiastical History*, yet the danger was short-lived. Licinius crushed Maximinus Daia in c.July 313, and it was Licinius who issued the decree that put a final end to the Great Persecution: the so-called 'Edict of Milan'.

When I, Constantine Augustus, and I, Licinius Augustus, met happily at Milan and conferred regarding all matters which concerned the advantage and security of the state, we resolved that, among the various things which would benefit the vast majority of people, the most immediate need was to ensure reverence for the Divinity. Our intention is to grant both to Christians and to all others freedom to follow whatever religion they choose, in order that whatever Divinity there is in heaven may be appeased and benevolent towards us and towards all who have been placed under our authority. Therefore we have determined, in accordance with sound and correct reasoning, that this opportunity is to be denied to no one, whether they wish to follow the religious observances of the Christians or the religion that they hold most fitting for themselves, so that the supreme Divinity to whose worship we willingly devout ourselves may show in all matters His accustomed favour and benevolence towards us.

Therefore we wish your Devotedness to know that it is our pleasure to abolish all the conditions regarding the Christian name that were contained in letters previously sent to your office. All those measures which are utterly inauspicious and alien to our clemency should be repealed, and every person who shares the same desire to observe the religion of the Christians may do so freely and unconditionally without any anxiety or interference. We resolved that this should be communicated most fully to your Solicitude, so that you may know that we have granted to these same Christians free and absolute permission to practice their religion. And when you perceive that we have accorded this favour to these people, your Devotedness may understand that others too have likewise been accorded open and free permission to follow their own religion and worship as befits the peace of our times, so that every man may have freedom to practice whatever worship they have chosen. This has been done by us to ensure that we should not appear to have discriminated against any cult or religion.

We further decree in regard to the Christians that, if anyone should appear to have purchased either from our treasury or from another person those places in which they were previously accustomed to assemble, about which a definite rule had previously been laid down in the letters sent to your office, those same places must now be restored to the Christians without requiring any payment or price and without any delay or hesitation. Anyone who received such places as a gift shall likewise restore them as quickly as possible to these same Christians. Both those who purchased such places and those who received them as a gift, should they request anything of our benevolence, may apply to the deputy that provision be made for them by our clemency. But all these places must be handed over to the community of Christians through your care immediately and without delay.

And since the said Christians are known to have possessed not only the places in which they were accustomed to assemble but also other property belonging to their community – that is, to their churches not to individuals – you will command that all this property, in accordance with the law which we have stated above, should be restored without any hesitation or dispute to the said Christians, that is to their community and assemblies, observing of course the provision given earlier that those who restore this property as required without receiving a price may hope to gain compensation from our benevolence.

In all these matters you must offer the aforesaid community of Christians your most effective support, so that our commands may be fulfilled as quickly as possible and so that in this as in other matters the interests of public tranquillity may thus be provided by our clemency. In this manner we will ensure, as we have said before, that the divine favour towards us which we have already experienced in so many important affairs may continue for all time for our prosperity and the well-being of the state. And so that the terms of our gracious ordinance may be known to all, it is expected that you will publish what we have written everywhere through a proclamation of your own and bring it to the attention of everyone, so that this command of our benevolence may not be hidden.

(quoted in Lactantius, *De Mortibus Persecutorum* 48.2–12, see also Eusebius of Caesarea, *Ecclesiastical History* 10.5.2–14)

There has been considerable confusion over the authorship and significance of this document. Constantine and Licinius had met in Milan early in 313, before Licinius' defeat of Maximinus Daia, and formed an alliance sealed by Licinius' marriage to Constantine's half-sister Constantia. Unfortunately, the traditional title of the decree has therefore led many to assume that this text was jointly issued by both emperors, and the 'Edict of Milan' is frequently cited in debates over Constantine's beliefs and religious policies. In reality, the sole emperor responsible was Licinius, and the two surviving versions of the text preserved by Lactantius and Eusebius come from Licinius' domains. Licinius' decree reaffirmed Galerius' edict of toleration throughout the eastern provinces, and then went further by ordering the restoration of all property lost by the Church. The Christians of the west had no need for such a proclamation. They had already received far greater benefits from imperial patronage, following the conversion in 312 of Constantine, the first Christian Roman emperor.

Copyright Acknowledgements

Further Reading

T. D. Barnes, *Constantine and Eusebius* (Cambridge, Mass. and London 1981)

S. Corcoran, *The Empire of the Tetrarchs: Imperial Pronouncements and Government AD 284–324* (Oxford 1996)

E. D. Digeser, *The Making of a Christian Empire: Lactantius and Rome* (Ithaca and London 2000)

E. D. Digeser, *A Threat to Public Piety: Christians, Platonists, and the Great Persecution* (Ithaca and London 2012)

R. Lane Fox, *Pagans and Christians in the Mediterranean World from the Second Century AD to the Conversion of Constantine* (London and New York 1986)

R. Rees, *Diocletian and the Tetrarchy* (Edinburgh 2004)

V. Twomey and M. Humphries (eds), *The Great Persecution* (Dublin 2009)

S. Williams, *Diocletian and the Roman Recovery* (London 1985)

3

The Conversion of Constantine

In 306, in the city of Eboracum (modern York), Constantine was hailed emperor by his soldiers upon his father's death. Born in c.272/3 at Naissus in the Balkans, Constantine was the son of Constantius Chlorus, one of the original members of Diocletian's Tetrarchy. When Constantine came to power his authority was restricted to Britain, Gaul and Spain. Over the next twenty years he reunited the empire under his rule, defeating his western rival Maxentius outside Rome in October 312 and his eastern counterpart Licinius in 324. In the east, on the site of ancient Byzantion, he founded Constantinople ('the city of Constantine'), today Istanbul. Constantine died in 337, leaving the empire to his sons. But his greatest legacy was his conversion to Christianity, the first Roman emperor to embrace the new religion.

> Constantine, alone of all those who have ever wielded the Roman power, was the friend of God the Sovereign of all and was established as a clear example of a godly life to all mankind. God Himself, whom Constantine worshipped, has confirmed this truth by the clearest manifestations of His will, being present to aid him at the beginning, the middle, and at the end of his reign, and holding him up to the human race as an instructive example of godliness. Accordingly, through the manifold blessings that He conferred upon him, God distinguished Constantine alone of all the sovereigns of whom we have ever heard as at the same time a mighty luminary and most clear-voiced herald of genuine piety. God honoured the duration of his reign with three complete decades, and further extended the term of his mortal life to twice this number of years. And being pleased to make him a representative of His own sovereign power, He displayed him as the conqueror of the whole race of tyrants and the destroyer of those God-defying giants of the earth who madly raised their impious arms against Him, the supreme King of all.
>
> (Eusebius of Caesarea, *Life of Constantine* 1.3–5)

Constantine's conversion has been the subject of huge controversy. For Christians like Eusebius still reeling from the Great Persecution, the dramatic appearance of a Christian emperor was nothing short of a miracle. Some modern scholars have been more sceptical. Christian resistance to persecution had demonstrated the strength of the religion, and Constantine might have sought political advantage through alliance with the Church. Constantine was certainly ambitious, and we cannot sharply distinguish his political and religious motives. But he rose to power in the least Christian regions of the empire, at a time when Christianity still held limited influence among the aristocracy or the army. To understand Constantine's decision we must therefore look to the evidence of his contemporaries and the emperor's own writings.

We know very little of Constantine's early years or of his religious beliefs before he became emperor. He was a witness to the Great Persecution and so was obviously aware of the existence of Christianity. Yet there is no indication that he had any close familiarity with Christian beliefs, and following his accession in 306 he continued to patronize the traditional gods. In 310, an anonymous Gallic orator in the city of Trier delivered a panegyric in praise of Constantine. According to the orator, Constantine had recently experienced a religious vision:

Fortune herself so ordered this matter that the happy outcome of your affairs prompted you to convey to the immortal gods what you had vowed at the very spot where you had turned aside toward the most beautiful temple in the whole world, or rather, to the deity made manifest, as you saw. For you saw, I believe, O Constantine, your Apollo, accompanied by Victory, offering you laurel wreaths, each one of which carries a portent of thirty years. For this is the number of human ages which are owed to you without fail – beyond the old age of a Nestor. And – now why do I say 'I believe'? – you saw, and recognized yourself in the likeness of him to whom the divine songs of the bards had prophesied that rule over the whole world was due. And this I think has now happened, since you are, O Emperor, like he, youthful, joyful, a bringer of health and very handsome. Rightly, therefore, have you honoured those most venerable shrines with such great treasures that they do not miss their old ones any longer. Now may all the temples be seen to beckon you to them, and particularly our Apollo, whose boiling waters punish perjuries – which ought to be especially hateful to you.

(*Panegyrici Latini* VI(7).21)

This 'pagan vision' of Constantine is less well known than the Christian vision he experienced just two years later. A panegyrical oration is not a reliable historical source, but on first principles Constantine's vision of Apollo is no less plausible or implausible than his vision of the cross. The god Sol Invictus (the Unconquered Sun), with whom Apollo was closely associated, became a prominent figure on Constantine's coins from 310 onwards. At the very least, the orator in 310 clearly believed that Constantine would approve of a speech celebrating his relationship with the traditional gods. In 312 this changed.

When Constantine came to power in 306, rule over the western regions of the empire was divided between himself and Maxentius, the son of Diocletian's co-ruler Maximian, who ruled over Italy and North Africa. In 312, Constantine invaded Italy and advanced upon Rome. Maxentius' army was crushed at the Battle of the Milvian Bridge on 28 October and Maxentius drowned fleeing across the river Tiber.

> In the time of Moses himself and the ancient God-beloved race of the Hebrews, 'Pharaoh's chariots and his army He cast into the sea; his picked officers were sunk in the Red Sea. The floods covered them' [Exodus 15.4–5]. In just the same way, Maxentius also with his soldiers and bodyguards 'went down into the depths like a stone' [Exodus 15.5] when he fled before the power of God which was with Constantine.
>
> (Eusebius of Caesarea, *Ecclesiastical History* 9.9.5)

Constantine was now the sole western emperor. And he immediately began for the first time to pour money and privileges into the Christian Church. The precise motives for his decision will forever remain a matter of conjecture. Two contemporary accounts describe a divine sign that inspired Constantine's conversion shortly before his defeat of Maxentius. Unfortunately, the two accounts differ on numerous points of detail, while Constantine's own writings offer only the briefest allusion to his experience.

The earlier of our two contemporary accounts is that of Lactantius in his work *De Mortibus Persecutorum*. Lactantius wrote close to the events, in 314–315, and knew Constantine well (he tutored Crispus, the emperor's oldest son). Lactantius placed Constantine's divine sign on the eve of the Battle of the Milvian Bridge:

Civil war had already started between them. Although Maxentius confined himself to Rome on the strength of an oracular reply that he would perish if he went outside its gates, his campaign was being conducted for him by capable commanders. Maxentius had the larger forces, with both his father's army, recovered from Severus, and his own, which he had recently brought over from the Mauri and the Gaetuli. Fighting took place in which Maxentius' troops held the advantage until Constantine at a later stage, his courage renewed and ready for either success or death, moved all his forces nearer to the city of Rome and based himself opposite the Milvian bridge. The anniversary was at hand of the day on which Maxentius had taken imperial power, 27 October [actually the 28th], and his *quinquennalia* were coming to an end. Constantine was advised in a dream to mark the heavenly sign of God on the shields of his soldiers and then engage in battle. He did as he was commanded and by means of a slanted letter X with the top of its head bent round he marked Christ on their shields. Armed with this sign, the army took up its weapons.

(Lactantius, *De Mortibus Persecutorum* 44.1–6)

More famous is the description of Constantine's vision offered by Eusebius of Caesarea in his *Life of Constantine*. In his *Ecclesiastical History*, the last edition of which appeared in 324/5, Eusebius says nothing of the motives for Constantine's conversion. The *Life of Constantine* on the other hand, composed after the emperor's death in 337, provides a detailed account of Constantine's experiences. Eusebius explicitly insists that he received this account directly from the emperor, most probably at the Council of Nicaea in 325. According to Eusebius, before the campaign against Maxentius even began, Constantine searched for a God to aid him in his struggle:

While he was praying with fervent entreaty, a most marvellous sign appeared to him from heaven. The account might have been hard to believe had it been related by any other person. But since the victorious emperor himself long afterwards declared it to the present writer when I was honoured with his acquaintance and society, and confirmed his statement by an oath, who could hesitate to believe the report, especially since the testimony of subsequent events has confirmed its truth? He said that at about noon, when the day was just beginning to decline, he saw with his own eyes in the heavens the trophy of a cross of light, resting over the sun and bearing the inscription 'By this conquer' (*touto nika*). At this sight he himself was struck with amazement and so too were his whole army, which accompanied him on this expedition and witnessed the miracle. He said, moreover, that he doubted within himself what the meaning of this vision could be. And while he continued to meditate and debated over its meaning, night overtook him. Then, in his sleep, the Christ of God appeared to him with the same sign which he had seen in the heavens, and commanded him to make a likeness of that sign and to use this as protection in all engagements with his enemies.

(Eusebius of Caesarea, *Life of Constantine* 1.28–29)

In Eusebius' version, Constantine's vision and dream are placed before the campaign against Maxentius, not on the eve of battle as suggested by Lactantius. Some of the details provided are vague (there is no indication of where the expedition in question took place), but Eusebius, again unlike Lactantius, is emphatic that Constantine saw a cross. No conclusive judgement can be drawn on which account is superior. Nevertheless, the underlying story is common to both contemporaries. As his rivalry with Maxentius drew to a climax, Constantine was inspired by a vision and/or a dream to seek victory in the name of the Christian God. His victory affirmed his faith. From October 312 onwards Constantine never once wavered in his support for Christianity.

Constantine himself left no description of his conversion in his surviving writings. The only clear allusion occurs in a speech he gave at Easter in an unspecified year between 313 and 325, preserved at the end of Eusebius' *Life of Constantine*. Known as the *Oration to the Assembly of the Saints*, the speech denounces 'pagan' error and proclaims Constantine's faith in God and the Incarnation. The *Oration* offers valuable evidence for how Constantine understood Christianity and for the depth and sincerity of his beliefs. Near the mid-point of the speech, Constantine urges his audience to spread the faith to new converts just as he heard the call:

Let us for our part strive to fill the uninitiated with the good hope that is in such words, calling God to our aid in the endeavour. For it is no small work to have turned to piety the souls of those who hear us, should they happen to be good, and if they be evil and ignorant, to lead them to the opposite course, rendering them profitable instead of good for nothing. Rejoicing indeed in these same endeavours, and thinking it the work of a good man to hymn the Saviour, I dismiss all that the base sway of fortune imposed on my unfortunate predicament, reckoning repentance the most efficacious salvation. I fervently wish that this revelation had been granted to me long ago, if indeed the man is blessed who has been brought up from infancy gladdened in the knowledge of things divine and in the beauty of virtue.

(Constantine, *Oration to the Saints* 11)

This passing reference is all that Constantine has to say regarding his conversion experience. What the *Oration to the Saints* does make very clear, however, is Constantine's conviction that he was chosen by God and that it was his duty as emperor to perform God's will. In the final words of the *Oration*, Constantine returns to the subject of divine providence and the rewards in this world and the next received by those who honour the true God:

All human beings know that the most holy devotion of these hands is owed to God with pure faith of the strictest kind, and that all that has been accomplished with advantage is achieved by joining the hands in prayers and litanies, with as much private and public assistance as everyone might pray for on his own behalf and that of those dearest to him. They indeed have witnessed the battles and observed the war in which God's providence awarded victory to the people, and have seen God co-operating with our prayers. For righteous prayer is an invincible thing, and no-one who pays holy adoration is disappointed of his aim. For no place is left for disappointment, except where faith's part fails, since God is always present with goodwill to welcome human goodness. Thus it is human to lapse sometimes, but God is not to be blamed for human lapses. Those who pursue piety should, however, confess their gratitude to the Saviour of all for our own salvation and the good state of public affairs, and petition Christ for one another with holy prayers and litanies, that He may continue His benefits to us. For He is an unconquerable ally and defender of the righteous, He Himself is the best judge, the guide to immortality, the bestower of eternal life.

(Constantine, *Oration to the Saints* 26)

Divine providence and the duty of an emperor to ensure the proper worship of God were fundamental to Constantine's conception of Christianity. These convictions underlay the privileges that he gave to the Church and his intervention in internal Christian disputes, topics that will be discussed in subsequent chapters. Nor was Constantine alone in his beliefs. In 336, Eusebius of Caesarea delivered a panegyric at the *tricennalia* celebrations for the thirtieth anniversary of Constantine's reign. The contrast between Eusebius' oration (the *Laus Constantini*) and the anonymous panegyric of 310 reflects the dramatic changes across the intervening quarter of a century. Constantine no longer venerates false deities like Apollo, but rules by the will of the true God as Christ's representative on earth:

> The only-begotten Logos of God reigns as co-ruler with His Father from ages which have no beginning to infinite ages which have no end. Likewise His friend [Constantine], who derives the source of imperial authority from above and is strong in the power of his divine calling, rules the empire of the world for a long period of years. And as the Preserver of the universe orders the heavens and earth and the celestial kingdom according to His Father's will, so His friend, by leading those whom he rules on earth to the only-begotten Logos and Saviour renders them fit subjects of His kingdom. Again, He who is the common Saviour of mankind, by His invisible and divine power, drives away those rebellious spirits which once flew through the earth's air and fastened on men's souls, like the good shepherd drives savage beasts far away from his flock. And likewise His friend, armed against his enemies with standards from Him above, subdues and chastens the open adversaries of the truth by the law of combat. He who is the pre-existent Logos, the Preserver of all things, imparts to His disciples the seeds of true wisdom and salvation, and at once enlightens and gives them understanding in the knowledge of His Father's kingdom. His friend, acting like an interpreter of the Logos of God, seeks to recall the whole human race to the knowledge of God, proclaiming clearly so that all might hear and declaring with a powerful voice the laws of truth and godliness to all who dwell on the earth. The universal Saviour opens wide the heavenly gates of His Father's kingdom to those whose course leads there when they depart this world. The other, emulating the divine example, has purged his earthly dominion of every stain of impious error, and invites holy and pious worshippers within his imperial mansions.
>
> (Eusebius of Caesarea, *Laus Constantini* 2.1–5)

Eusebius believed that the Roman empire was destined to become Christian and to spread the Christian faith to the whole human race. Constantine was part of this providential plan. As the 'friend' and representative of God, the emperor was blessed with prosperity and victory on earth. In his turn, Constantine modelled his reign on the imitation of the kingdom of heaven. He ended persecution, suppressed 'impious error', and led his subjects towards the truth.

Eusebius' rhetoric may be exaggerated, but his presentation of Constantine as the ideal Christian ruler was hugely influential on medieval and Byzantine concepts of the relationship of Church and State and the divine right of kings.

At no point did Eusebius question the sincerity of Constantine's conversion. Constantine equally had no doubts that he was Christian. Yet Constantine was not baptized after his initial conversion in 312, or even twenty-four years later at the time of his *tricennalia*. This has troubled some modern commentators who have even challenged whether Constantine should be called Christian at all. However, Constantine's decision to postpone his baptism until just before his death was not unusual. Baptism in the early fourth century did not represent the ceremony of admission into the Church, to which Constantine belonged from 312 onwards. Rather, baptism represented the one unrepeatable cleansing of past sins, after which the recipient was expected to live by strict moral standards. Like many of his contemporaries, Constantine left his baptism as late as possible.

> Being at length convinced that his life was drawing to a close, he decided that the time had come at which he should seek purification from the sins of his past career, firmly believing that whatever sins he had committed as a mortal man, his soul would be purified from them through the power of the mystical words and the saving waters of baptism.
>
> (Eusebius of Caesarea, *Life of Constantine* 4.61)

The emperor was preparing for war with Sassanian Persia to the east in 337 when his final illness struck. Eusebius reports that Constantine desired to be baptized in the river Jordan in imitation of Christ. But he was unable to complete the journey and so received baptism in Nicomedia not far from Constantinople.

> Thus Constantine was the first of all sovereigns who was reborn and perfected in a church dedicated to the martyrs of Christ. Gifted with the divine seal of baptism, he rejoiced in spirit and was renewed and filled with heavenly light. His soul rejoiced in the fervency of his faith and was awestruck at the manifestation of the power of God. At the conclusion of the ceremony he arrayed himself in shining imperial vestments, brilliant as the light, and reclined on a couch of the purest white, refusing to clothe himself with the purple any more.
>
> (Eusebius of Caesarea, *Life of Constantine* 4.62)

Constantine died at Pentecost, on 22 May 337, and was buried in his mausoleum church of Holy Apostles in Constantinople. His prestige as the first Christian emperor made him the focus for numerous later legends. Perhaps the most famous of those legends addressed the problem of his baptism. Not only had Constantine delayed baptism until just before his death, but the bishop who performed the ceremony was Eusebius of Nicomedia, a man regarded by later generations as one of the greatest heretics of the fourth century. Over time an entirely new interpretation of Constantine's conversion and baptism emerged. Constantine, it was claimed, initially persecuted the Church and was punished by God with leprosy. Pagan priests informed the emperor that he could be cured if he bathed in the blood of children, but upon his refusal he received a vision of Peter and Paul and sought instruction from Pope Sylvester of Rome. Sylvester then baptized Constantine, in the process healing him of the leprosy, and in return Constantine granted to the Pope supremacy over all secular power. This is the legend immortalized in the so-called *Donation of Constantine*:

On the first day after I had received the mystery of holy baptism, and after my body had been cured of the blight of leprosy, I apprehended that there was no other god but the Father, the Son and the Holy Spirit, whom blessed Sylvester the Pope proclaims, the Trinity in unity and unity in Trinity. For all the gods of the nations, whom I have worshipped up to this time, are clearly proved to be daemons, the work of human hands. And furthermore, the reverend father explained to us most clearly what measure of power in heaven and earth that same Saviour of ours had conferred on His apostle the blessed Peter, when, finding that he showed faith in answering His question, He said, 'You are Peter, and on this rock I will build my church, and the gates of Hades will not prevail against it' [Matthew 16.18]. Take note, ye powerful, and attend with the ears of your heart, what the good master and Lord added, saying to His disciple, 'Whatever you bind on earth will be bound in heaven' [Matthew 16.19]. A marvellous thing indeed is this and a glorious one, to bind and loose on earth and have it bound and loosed in heaven. And inasmuch as, learning these things from the preaching of the blessed Sylvester, I also found that by the beneficence of the same blessed Peter I had been restored to perfect health.

We have deemed it expedient, in company with all our satraps and the whole senate of my nobles also, and furthermore the whole Roman populace which is subject to our imperial glory, that just as Saint Peter is seen to have been established as the vicegerent of the Son of God on earth, so the pontiffs also who are vicegerents to this chief of the apostles, should receive by a grant from us and our dominion a power of primacy greater than the mildness of our imperial Serenity is seen to possess on earth; thus we choose this same chief and his vicegerents to be our steadfast advocates with God. And, as is the case with our imperial power on earth, so we have decreed that his sacred church in Rome is to be honoured with reverence, and that to a greater degree than our dominion and earthly throne the most sacred chair of the blessed Peter is to be exalted in glory; thus we assign to him power and glory, imperial in dignity, strength and honour.

('*Donation of Constantine*' 10–11)

Already denounced as a forgery in the eleventh century and unanimously since c.1450, the *Donation* was probably composed in the late eighth century in the context of papal relations with the rising Frankish power of Charlemagne. Yet the popularity of such a legend is itself a reminder of Constantine's enduring significance as a model and inspiration for later Christian generations.

Copyright Acknowledgements

Constantine, *Oration to the Saints*
'*Donation of Constantine*'
Translated in M. Edwards, *Constantine and Christendom* (Liverpool 2003), by permission of Liverpool University Press

Lactantius, *De Mortibus Persecutorum*
Translated in J. L. Creed, *Lactantius: De Mortibus Persecutorum* (Oxford 1984), by permission of Oxford University Press

Panegyrici Latini
Translated in C. E. V. Nixon and B. S. Rodgers, *In Praise of Later Roman Emperors: The Panegyrici Latini* (Berkeley and Oxford 1994, © by the Regents of the University of California), by permission of the University of California Press

Further Reading

T. D. Barnes, *Constantine and Eusebius* (Cambridge, Mass. and London 1981)
N. H. Baynes, *Constantine the Great and the Christian Church* (London 1929)

J. Burckhardt, *The Age of Constantine the Great*, translated by M. Hadas (London 1949)

E. D. Digeser, *The Making of a Christian Empire: Lactantius and Rome* (Ithaca and London 2000)

H. A. Drake, *'In Praise of Constantine': A Historical Study and New Translation of Eusebius' Tricennial Orations* (Berkeley 1976)

T. G. Elliott, *The Christianity of Constantine the Great* (Scranton 1996)

J. Fried, *Donation of Constantine and Constitutum Constantini: The Misinterpretation of a Fiction and its Original Meaning* (Berlin and New York 2007)

R. Van Dam, *Remembering Constantine at the Milvian Bridge* (Cambridge 2011)

4

Constantine and the Imperial Church

When Constantine entered Rome after the Battle of the Milvian Bridge in 312, Christianity was still reeling from the physical and psychological terrors of the Great Persecution. Loss of life, confiscation of property and destruction of churches combined to further weaken Christianity's already restricted public profile. Yet victory at the Milvian Bridge secured Constantine's faith in the new religion as well as his authority over Rome's western provinces. In 324 he defeated his eastern rival Licinius and united the empire under his sole rule until his death in 337. The wealth and privileges that Constantine poured into Christianity across that twenty year span transformed the Church and its place in the Later Roman empire.

Constantine's first commitment was to restore Christian wealth lost in the persecution. Within a few months of his conversion, in late 312 or early 313, the emperor directed a letter to Anulinus, the proconsul of Roman North Africa.

> It is the custom of our benevolence, most esteemed Anulinus, to wish that those things which belong by right to another should not only be left unmolested but should also be restored. Therefore it is our wish that, when you receive this letter, if any such property once belonged to the catholic Church of the Christians in any of the cities or other places but is now held by citizens or by any others, then you will see to it that this property is restored immediately to the said churches. For we have already determined that those possessions which these same churches formerly held shall be restored to them. Since therefore your Devotedness perceives that this command of ours is most explicit, you must make haste to restore to them, as quickly as possible, everything which formerly belonged to the said churches, whether gardens or buildings or anything else.
>
> (Constantine, *Letter to Anulinus*, quoted in Eusebius of Caesarea, *Ecclesiastical History* 10.5.15–17)

The same restitution was extended to Christians throughout Constantine's western domains. But Constantine then went further, and far beyond the so-called 'Edict of Milan' issued by Licinius in the east. For the emperor also despatched another letter to North Africa in early 313, this time to Caecilian, the bishop of the provincial capital Carthage.

> Since it is our pleasure that something should be granted in all the provinces of Africa and Numidia and Mauretania to certain ministers of the lawful and most holy catholic religion to assist with their expenses, I have written to Ursus, the illustrious finance minister of Africa, and have directed him to make provision to pay to your Steadfastness 3,000 *folles*. When you have received this sum of money, you must command that it be distributed among all those mentioned above, according to the schedule supplied to you by Ossius. If you should discover that anything is wanting for the fulfilment of my purpose in regard to all of them, you must demand without hesitation whatever you find necessary from Heraclidas, our treasurer. I commanded him when he was present that if your Steadfastness should ask him for any money, he should see that it be paid without delay.
>
> (Constantine, *Letter to Caecilian*, quoted in Eusebius of Caesarea, *Ecclesiastical History* 10.6.1–3)

It is difficult to estimate the exact value of the 3,000 *folles* that Constantine granted to Caecilian. Evidently it was a significant sum, and was followed by the remarkable promise that the bishop could request any additional money that he desired. Caecilian was at this stage already embroiled in the Donatist Schism, into which Constantine would also be drawn (see Chapter 5). Indeed, the desire for imperial recognition and therefore access to this new source of patronage was one of the factors in escalating that Schism. Nevertheless, the wealth now available to bishops dramatically increased both their status in society and their capacity for charitable spending. This improved still further in 321 when Constantine gave legal permission to anyone who wished to leave their property to the Church upon their deaths. The law presupposes that such bequests were already being made, but they now became far more common and contributed to the massive expansion of Church wealth in the fourth century.

Every person shall have the liberty to leave at his death any property that he wishes to the most holy and venerable council of the catholic Church. Wills shall not become void. There is nothing which is more due to men than that the expression of their last will, after which they can no longer will anything, shall be free and the power of choice, which does not return again, shall be unhampered.

(*Theodosian Code* 16.2.4, AD 321)

Constantine's law on bequests was only one of a series of edicts that the emperor issued to reinforce the new significance of Christianity and Christian values. Some of those laws might surprise a modern reader. Constantine banned the facial branding of criminals, although not on grounds of cruelty.

If any person should be condemned to the arena or to the mines, in accordance with the nature of the crime in which he has been detected, he shall not be branded on his face, since the penalty of condemnation can be branded by one and the same mark on his hands and on the calves of his legs, so that the face, which has been made in the likeness of celestial beauty, may not be disfigured.

(*Theodosian Code* 9.40.2, AD 316)

It was also Constantine who decreed that Sunday should be kept free of legal disputes and craftwork. He did permit that slaves could be emancipated on a Sunday and that farmers might in necessity labour in their fields. But the principle of Sunday as the day of rest at the end of the working week was clearly laid down.

Just as it appears to us most unseemly that the Day of the Sun (*dies Solis*), which is celebrated on account of its own veneration, should be occupied with legal altercations and with noxious controversies of the litigation of contending parties, so it is pleasant and fitting that those acts which are especially desired shall be accomplished on that day. Therefore all men shall have the right to emancipate and manumit [i.e. to free slaves] on this festive day, and the legal formalities thereof are not forbidden.

(*Theodosian Code* 2.8.1, AD 321)

All judges and the people in the city should rest, and the work in all the crafts should cease, on the holy Sunday. But the people in the country may freely and lawfully apply themselves to the cultivation of the fields, as it frequently happens that the sowing of grain or the planting of vines cannot be deferred to a more suitable day, so that the benefit conferred by the providence of God may not perish with the opportunity of the moment.

(*Justinianic Code* 3.12.2, AD 321)

The public prestige that the Church now possessed was likewise reflected in the honours received by Christian clergy. Constantine granted a number of privileges to bishops that had previously been held by the priests of traditional Roman cults. The most valued of these was immunity from performing local civic duties, a privilege that the emperor justified in a letter addressed once again to proconsul Anulinus in North Africa.

It is clear from many circumstances that when true religion is neglected, in which is preserved the chief reverence for the most holy celestial Power, great dangers are brought upon public affairs, but that when lawfully restored and observed it confers the greatest prosperity to the Roman name and remarkable felicity to all the affairs of men through divine beneficence. Therefore it has seemed good to me, most esteemed Anulinus, that those men who with due sanctity and with constant attention to this law give their services to the worship of the divine religion should receive recompense for their labours. So it is my will that within the province entrusted to you, in the catholic Church over which Caecilian presides, those who give their services to this holy religion, and who are commonly called clergy, shall be entirely exempted from all public duties. Thus they may not through any error or sacrilegious negligence be drawn away from the service due to the Deity, but may devote themselves without any hindrance to their own law. For when they show the greatest reverence to the Deity, the greatest benefits are conferred to the state.

(Constantine, *Letter to Anulinus*, quoted in Eusebius of Caesarea, *Ecclesiastical History* 10.7.1–2)

Constantine's devout belief in divine providence comes across very strongly from this letter, as does his conviction that the Christian clergy played an integral part in the empire's social fabric. Unfortunately, he later had to qualify his generosity to prevent unscrupulous individuals entering the clergy under false pretences.

Exemption from compulsory public services shall not be granted by popular consent, nor shall it be granted indiscriminately to all who petition under the pretext of being clerics, nor shall great numbers be added to the clergy rashly and beyond measure. But rather, when a cleric dies, another shall be selected to replace the deceased, one who has no kinship with a decurion family and who has not the wealth of resources whereby he may very easily support the compulsory public services. Thus, if there should be a dispute about the name of any person between a municipality and the clergy, if equity claims him for public service and if he is adjudged suitable for membership in the municipal council through either lineage or wealth, he shall be removed from the clergy and shall be delivered to the municipality. For the wealthy must assume secular obligations, and the poor must be supported by the wealth of the churches.

(*Theodosian Code* 16.2.6, AD 326/329)

The collective impact of these Constantinian laws and privileges was to transform the wealth and status of the Church and to demonstrate publicly the favoured position that Christianity now held within the empire. This transformation also received physical expression, in the magnificent churches that Constantine began to build. His first church in the imperial city of Rome was the Basilica Constantiniana, known today as St John in Lateran. Completed in the early 320s, the church was over 300 feet in length and modelled on the traditional Roman basilica with a long central nave and aisles on either side. A similar design on an even grander scale was followed for the greatest of Constantine's Roman churches: the original St Peter's Vatican. Built on the site where the apostle Peter was believed to be buried, the outline of the Constantinian church can still be traced today underneath the current Renaissance structure. Over 600 feet from atrium to apse, the church's lavish decoration was described in detail in the *Liber Pontificalis*, the history of the early bishops of Rome.

Then the emperor Constantine built a basilica to St Peter the apostle, at the temple of Apollo, where he buried the tomb with St Peter's body in this way: the actual tomb he sealed on all sides with copper to make it immovable, 5 ft each at the head, the feet, the right and left sides, the bottom and the top; thus he enclosed St Peter's body and buried it. Above he decorated it with porphyry columns and other vine-scroll columns which he brought from Greece. He also built the basilica's apse-vault shining with gold-foil; and over St Peter's body, above the bronze in which he had sealed it, he provided a cross of finest gold weighing

150 lb, made to measure; on the cross itself is written in nielloed letters 'Constantine Augustus and Helena Augusta. He surrounds this house with a royal hall gleaming with equal splendour'.

He also provided 4 brass candelabra, 10 ft in size, finished in silver with silver medallions of the acts of the apostles, each weighing 300 lb;

3 gold chalices, with 45 prase and jacinth jewels, each weighing 12 lb;

2 silver metretae weighing 200 lb;

20 silver chalices each weighing 10 lb;

2 gold amae each weighing 10 lb;

5 silver amae each weighing 20 lb;

a gold paten with a tower of finest gold and a dove, adorned with prase and jacinth jewels and with pearls, 215 in number, weighing 30 lb;

5 silver patens each weighing 15 lb;

a gold crown in front of the body, which is a chandelier, with 50 dolphins, weighing 35 lb;

32 silver lights in the centre of the basilica, with dolphins, each weighing 10 lb;

on the right of the basilica, 30 silver lights each weighing 8 lb;

the altar itself, of silver chased with gold, weighing 350 lb, decorated on all sides with prase and jacinth jewels and pearls, the jewels 210 in number;

a censer of finest gold, decorated on all sides with jewels, 60 in number, weighing 15 lb.

(*Liber Pontificalis* 34.16–18)

After Constantine defeated his eastern rival Licinius in 324 and united the empire, he extended his patronage to the Christians previously under Licinius' rule. An edict was sent out across the east, and Eusebius of Caesarea quotes the document published in his own province of Palestine.

I am well aware that those who are sincere in the pursuit of the heavenly hope, and have fixed this hope in heaven itself as the firm and particular principle of their lives, have no need to depend on human favour. Indeed, they enjoy proportionately higher honours the more that they have separated themselves from the inferior and evil things of this earthly existence. Nevertheless, I deem it incumbent upon me to remove at once and most completely from all such persons the hard constraints laid upon them from time to time and the unjust injuries under which they have suffered although free from any guilt or just liability. It would be quite absurd if the courage and constancy of soul displayed by such men should be fully apparent during the reigns of those whose first object was to persecute them on account of their devotion to God, and yet that the glory of their character should not be more bright and blessed under the administration of a prince who is His servant. Therefore let all who have exchanged their country for a foreign land because they would not abandon that reverence and faith towards God to which they had devoted themselves with their whole hearts, and have in consequence at different times been subject to the cruel sentence of the courts; together with any who have been enrolled in the curial registers though in time past exempt from such office; let all these, I say, now render thanks to God the Liberator of all that they are restored to their hereditary property and their customary contentment. Let those also who have been despoiled of their goods, and have hitherto passed a wretched existence, mourning under the loss of all that they possessed, once more be restored to their former homes, their families and estates, and receive with joy the bountiful kindness of God.

(Constantine, *Letter to the provincials of Palestine*, quoted in Eusebius of Caesarea, *Life of Constantine* 2.29–30)

Constantine swiftly discovered that the Christians of the eastern Mediterranean, while more numerous than in the west, were far from unified. The theological questions that had divided the eastern Church will be explored in Chapter 6, but it was in response to those debates that Constantine summoned the first ecumenical council that met at Nicaea in Asia Minor in June–July 325.

[Constantine] summoned a legion of God, a world-wide council, and with respectful letters invited the bishops from every region to hasten to attend. He did not merely issue a bare command, but the emperor's good will contributed directly to its being carried into practical effect. For he allowed some the use of the public post, while he afforded to others an ample supply of pack-animals. The place selected for the synod was likewise appropriate to the occasion, the city of Nicaea in Bithynia which is named after victory. Thus as soon as the imperial injunction was generally made known, all with the utmost willingness hastened to come as though they would outstrip one another in a race. They were encouraged by the anticipation of a happy result, by the hope of enjoying the present peace, and the desire to behold something new and strange in the person of so admirable an emperor. When they were all assembled, it appeared evident that the proceeding was the work of God. Men who had been most widely separated, not only in spirit but also physically and by difference of territory, place, and province, were brought together and contained within the walls of a single city, forming as it were a vast garland of priests composed of a variety of the choicest flowers.

The most distinguished of God's ministers from all the churches which abounded in Europe, Libya, and Asia were assembled. And a single house of prayer, as though divinely enlarged, sufficed to contain them all together: Syrians and Cilicians, Phoenicians and Arabians, delegates from Palestine and others from Egypt, with Thebans and Libyans and those who came from between the rivers [Mesopotamia]. A Persian bishop too was present at the council, nor was even a Scythian found wanting to the number. Pontus and Galatia, Cappadocia and Asia, Phrygia and Pamphylia provided their chosen men, while those who dwelt in the remotest districts of Thrace and Macedonia, of Achaia and Epirus, were nevertheless in attendance. Even from Spain, one whose fame was widespread took his seat as an individual in the great assembly. The prelate of the imperial city was prevented from attending by extreme old age, but his presbyters were present and deputized for him. Constantine was the first prince of any age who bound together such a garland as this with the bond of peace, and presented it to his Saviour as a thank-offering for the victories he had obtained over every foe, thus exhibiting in our own times a resemblance of the apostolic assembly.

(Eusebius of Caesarea, *Life of Constantine* 3.6–7)

The Council of Nicaea was not in fact truly ecumenical (literally 'world-wide' and actually meaning across the Roman empire). The bishop of Rome sent his representatives, otherwise there was just a single bishop from each of Italy, Spain, Gaul, and North Africa. The African bishop was Caecilian of Carthage, the famous Spaniard was Ossius of Cordova who was Constantine's clerical advisor and was named in Constantine's letter to Caecilian quoted earlier. No bishop came from Britain. The overwhelming majority of those present at Nicaea were therefore from the Greek-speaking east. The traditional number of bishops in attendance is 318, but this is a later invention (318 is the number of Abraham's servants in Genesis 14.14). Modern estimates suggest a figure of perhaps 200 to 220. Nevertheless, Nicaea marked one of Constantine's greatest achievements, the most representative Christian gathering since the Last Supper and easily the largest Church council yet held. Eusebius of Caesarea concluded his eyewitness account with the celebration of Constantine's *vicennalia* (20th anniversary), to which the bishops at the council were invited. For a survivor of the Great

Persecution, it was a powerful image to advance past armed soldiers to sit and dine with the emperor.

At the same time, he completed the twentieth year of his reign, for which public festivals were celebrated by the people of the other provinces. But the emperor himself invited and feasted with those ministers of God whom he had reconciled, and thus offered as it were through them a suitable sacrifice to God. Not one of the bishops was missing from the imperial banquet, the circumstances of which were splendid beyond description. Detachments of the bodyguard and other soldiers surrounded the entrance to the palace with drawn swords, and through their midst the men of God proceeded fearlessly into the innermost imperial apartments, where some were the emperor's own companions at table while others reclined on couches arranged on either side. One might have thought that it was an imaginary representation of the kingdom of Christ.

(Eusebius of Caesarea, *Life of Constantine* 3.15)

In the east Constantine continued his public promotion of Christianity. Jerusalem and the Holy Land acquired new prominence during his reign as a focus for pilgrims and a source for sacred relics (see further Chapter 16). Constantine's mother Helena made a ceremonial pilgrimage to the places of Christ's birth and death in 327, and the first great church that Constantine ordered built in the eastern provinces was the Church of the Holy Sepulchre. His instructions to Macarius, bishop of Jerusalem, left no doubt as to the splendour that the site of Christ's passion should receive.

It is for your own Good Sense to make such arrangements and provision of all things needed for the work, that not only the basilica itself may surpass all others whatsoever in beauty but that the details of the building likewise may be of such a kind that they excel the fairest structures in any city of the empire. With respect to the erection and decoration of the walls, be advised that our friend Dracillianus, the deputy of the prefects, and he who is the governor of the province have been entrusted by us with their care. For our pious directions to them are to the effect that craftsmen and labourers and whatever they shall understand from your Good Sense to be needed for the advancement of the work shall forthwith be furnished by their provision. As to the columns and marble, regarding whatever you shall judge upon close inspection of the plan to be especially precious and serviceable, you should be diligent to send information to us in writing so that whatever quantity or type of materials we shall learn from your letter to be needful may be procured from every quarter as required. For it is fitting that the most marvellous place in the world should be worthily decorated.

(Constantine, *Letter to Macarius*, quoted in Eusebius of
Caesarea, *Life of Constantine* 3.31)

Additional churches were built by Constantine and Helena to celebrate Christ's birth at Bethlehem and ascension from the Mount of Olives. But perhaps the clearest indication of the importance that Constantine placed on the Holy Land was his concern for the less well-known site of Mamre. Here Abraham was visited by three divine figures who revealed his wife Sarah's coming pregnancy (Genesis 18.1–10), an episode interpreted by Christians as an early reference to the Trinity. Constantine was informed by his mother-in-law Eutropia that Mamre was polluted by idol worshippers, and ordered the bishops of Palestine to purify the site and erect an appropriate church.

If anyone, after this mandate of ours, shall be guilty of impiety of any kind in this place, he shall be visited with appropriate punishment. The place itself we have directed to be adorned with an unpolluted church, in order that it may become a fitting place for the assembly of holy persons. In the meantime, should any breach of these commands of ours occur, it should be made known to our Clemency immediately by letters from you, so that we may order the person detected to be dealt with in the severest manner as a transgressor of the law. For you are not ignorant that there the Supreme God first appeared to Abraham and conversed with him. Thus it was there that the observance of the divine law first began, there the Saviour Himself with the two angels first vouchsafed to Abraham the manifestation of His presence, there God began to reveal Himself to mankind, there He gave the promise to Abraham concerning his future seed and at once fulfilled that promise, there He foretold that he should be the father of a multitude of nations. For these reasons, it seems to me right that this place should not only be kept pure through your diligence from all defilement but restored to its ancient sanctity, so that nothing hereafter may be done there except the performance of fitting service to Him who is the Almighty God, and our Saviour, and Lord of all.

(Constantine, *Letter to the Palestinian bishops*, quoted in Eusebius of
Caesarea, *Life of Constantine* 3.53)

Alongside Rome and Jerusalem, the third city that received Constantine's particular attention was that which he named after himself. Constantinople, the 'city of Constantine', was built on the site of ancient Byzantion (and is today Istanbul). Dedicated in 330, from the beginning Constantinople had a strongly Christian identity.

> Having resolved to distinguish the city which bore his name with exceptional honour, he embellished it with numerous places of worship, memorials to the martyrs on the largest scale, and other buildings of the most splendid kind, not only within the city itself but in its vicinity. Thus at the same time he rendered honour to the memory of the martyrs and consecrated his city to the martyrs' God. Being filled with divine wisdom, he also determined to purge the city which was to be distinguished by his own name from idolatry of every kind, so that henceforth no statues might be worshipped there in the temples of those falsely reputed to be gods, nor any altars defiled by the pollution of blood, nor sacrifices consumed by fire, nor feasts of demons, nor any of the other ceremonies usually observed by the superstitious.
>
> (Eusebius of Caesarea, *Life of Constantine* 3.48)

Eusebius has slightly exaggerated. There were a few temples in Constantinople, surviving from older Byzantion, and the population was not exclusively Christian. Unlike Rome, however, Constantinople did not have an extensive 'pagan' past that shaped and pervaded the urban landscape. In the course of the fourth century the 'New Rome', as Constantinople became, emerged as the Christian capital for an increasingly Christian empire. It was there that Constantine was buried, in the mausoleum-shrine that he had dedicated to the Holy Apostles.

> He had prepared the place there in the prospect of his own death, anticipating with extraordinary fervour of faith that his body would share in the invocation of the apostles themselves, and that he should thus even after death benefit from the devotions which should be performed to their honour in this place. He accordingly caused twelve coffins to be set up, like sacred pillars in honour and memory of the apostolic company, in the centre of which his own coffin was placed, with those of the apostles ranged six on either side.
>
> (Eusebius of Caesarea, *Life of Constantine* 4.60)

The theological implications of Constantine's mausoleum have troubled some commentators, the layout placing the dead emperor on an equal or greater level than the apostles. Yet the shrine was itself a symbol of the transformation that Constantine had wrought. The Christian Church was now an imperial Church, with wealth and privileges befitting the favoured religion of the empire. Although Christians were still not in the majority when Constantine died in 337, their numbers were growing rapidly and their new-found status was publicly displayed through their magnificent churches and the social prestige of their bishops. This dramatic expansion in turn drove the fundamental changes that redefined Christianity in the fourth century, from the canon of the New Testament and the rise of asceticism to the theological controversies that divided the Church. The reign of Constantine was truly a turning point in the history of both Christianity and the Later Roman empire.

Copyright Acknowledgements

Liber Pontificalis
Translated in R. Davis, *The Book of Pontiffs (Liber Pontificalis): The ancient biographies of the first ninety Roman bishops to* AD *715*, revised edition (Liverpool 2000), by permission of Liverpool University Press

Theodosian Code
Translated in C. Pharr, *The Theodosian Code and Novels and the Sirmondian Constitutions* (Princeton 1952, © 1952 in the name of the author, 1980 renewed in the name of Roy Pharr, executor), by permission of Princeton University Press

Further Reading

T. D. Barnes, *Constantine and Eusebius* (Cambridge, Mass. and London 1981)

T. D. Barnes, *Constantine: Dynasty, Religion and Power in the Later Roman Empire* (Chichester and Malden 2011)

N. H. Baynes, *Constantine the Great and the Christian Church* (London 1929)

H. A. Drake, *Constantine and the Bishops: The Politics of Intolerance* (Baltimore and London 2000)

A. H. M. Jones, *Constantine and the Conversion of Europe* (London 1948)

N. Lenski (ed.), *The Cambridge Companion to the Age of Constantine* (Cambridge 2006)

C. M. Odahl, *Constantine and the Christian Empire* (London and New York 2004)

D. S. Potter, *Constantine the Emperor* (Oxford and New York 2013)

J. Roldanus, *The Church in the Age of Constantine* (London and New York 2006)

P. Stephenson, *Constantine: Unconquered Emperor, Christian Victor* (London 2009)

R. Van Dam, *The Roman Revolution of Constantine* (Cambridge 2007)

5

The Donatist Schism

The Donatist Schism that divided Christian North Africa originated in the Great Persecution and broke out in full in the years immediately following Constantine's conversion. While the controversy had little impact outside the North African region, the issues at stake raised important questions at a crucial stage in Christianity's history. The rise of a Christian emperor opened exciting new opportunities for the Church, but also dramatically increased the significance of internal Church divisions. The Donatist Schism was the first Christian conflict into which a Christian emperor was drawn, and sheds valuable light on the evolution of Christianity and the Christian Roman empire.

It is said that history is written by the victors, and Christian history is no exception. Few writings survive from those now known as the 'Donatists', a label which itself is the invention of their enemies. Even to speak of a 'Donatist Schism' is to endorse the views of the eventual winners, for the 'Donatists' referred to themselves as 'Christians' and at their peak represented the majority of the North African Church. Yet it is the Donatists' opponents who provide the vast bulk of our evidence, notably two African bishops: Optatus of Milevis (author of *De Schismate Donatistarum* or *Against the Donatists*) and Augustine of Hippo.

The catholic Church is made known by simplicity and truth in knowledge, singleness and absolute truth in the sacrament, and unity of minds. A schism, on the other hand, is engendered when the bond of peace is shattered through discordant sentiments, nourished by bitterness, strengthened by rivalry and feuds, so that the impious sons, having deserted their catholic mother, go out and separate themselves, as you have done, and, having been cut off from the root of the mother Church by the blade of bitterness, depart in erratic rebellion. Nor are

> they able to do anything new or anything else, except what they have long since
> learned from their own mother.
>
>   (Optatus, *Against the Donatists* 1.11)

According to Christian convention, a schism is caused by the separation of a smaller group from the larger Church due to a conflict over organization or discipline, not over doctrine. A heresy is a division over doctrinal beliefs. In reality the distinction is not always so clear-cut, but the controversy in North Africa began as an archetypal schism over the disputed election of Caecilian as bishop of the powerful see of Carthage. During the Great Persecution, some clergy unsurprisingly preferred to surrender Bibles or sacred vessels to the authorities rather than face imprisonment or martyrdom. In North Africa the lapsed clerics were known as *traditores* (literally 'handers-over'). The North African Church had a particularly strong tradition of martyr veneration, and the more rigorist African Christians (the future Donatists) rejected such priests and their ceremonies as invalid. Caecilian was a known moderate who opposed rigorist demands, and unfortunately one of the bishops responsible for his election (either in 307/8 or 311/12) was the accused *traditor* Felix of Abthungi. The rigorists denounced Caecilian's consecration as invalid and elected a rival bishop of Carthage, named Majorinus.

> Our subject is a division; and in Africa, as in the other provinces, there was one
> Church, before it was divided by those who ordained Majorinus, whose
> hereditary see you occupy. It must be seen, who remained in the root with the
> whole world, who went out, who occupied another see, who erected altar against
> altar, who performed an ordination in the face of another valid ordination, who
> lies under the sentence of the apostle John, for he says 'they did not belong to us;
> for if they had belonged to us, they would have remained with us' [1 John 2.19].
> Therefore he who has chosen not to remain at one with his brethren has followed
> heretics and, like the Antichrist, has gone out.
>
>   (Optatus, *Against the Donatists* 1.15)

Majorinus died in 313 and was succeeded by Donatus, from whom the Schism takes its name. When Constantine began to pour material benefits into the Church, the rival bishops competed to receive his patronage. Initially, Constantine backed Caecilian. It was to Caecilian that the emperor wrote offering financial aid (see Chapter 4), and Constantine concluded his letter with a promise of support against the bishop's rivals.

> I have learned that certain persons of unsettled mind wish to turn the people away from the most holy and catholic Church by means of shameful corruption. Therefore you should know that when they were present I commanded the proconsul Anulinus and also Patricius, the deputy of the prefects, that they should give proper attention not only to other matters but above all to this, and that they should not allow such an occurrence to be overlooked. Accordingly, if you should see any such persons continuing in this madness, you must without delay go to the aforementioned judges and report the matter to them.
>
> (Constantine, *Letter to Caecilian*, quoted in Eusebius of Caesarea, *Ecclesiastical History* 10.6.4)

Imperial patronage of Christianity had thus immediately drawn the emperor into conflict within the Church and raised the spectre of persecution. Nor were Caecilian's opponents prepared to stand silent. On 15 April 313, the proconsul Anulinus reported to Constantine that he had published the emperor's edicts.

> After a few days certain persons arose, to whom a crowd of people joined themselves, who thought that proceedings should be taken against Caecilian and who presented to my Reverence a sealed packet wrapped in leather and a small document without seal, and earnestly desired that I direct them to the sacred and venerable court of your Worship, which my Insignificance took care to do so that your Majesty might decide on the whole matter. Two documents have been sent, one sealed in a leather envelope with the title 'petition of the catholic Church containing charges against Caecilian, furnished by the party of Majorinus', the other attached unsealed to the same envelope.
>
> (Anulinus, *Letter to Constantine*, quoted in Augustine of Hippo, *Letter* 88)

Optatus preserves what may have been one of the two documents forwarded by Anulinus.

> We petition you, Constantine, best of emperors, since you are of upright stock, as your father did not carry on the persecution in company with the other emperors and Gaul was immune from this outrage, seeing that in Africa there are dissensions between us and other bishops: we petition that your Piety should make haste to have judges given to us from Gaul.
>
> (quoted in Optatus, *Against the Donatists* 1.22)

Interestingly, the authors of the petition did not appeal to Constantine's Christianity but rather to his father Constantius' behaviour in the Great Persecution. At this stage both Caecilian and his opponents were more than willing to accept and indeed request imperial involvement in Church affairs. Constantine's solution was to write to the bishop of Rome.

> A number of messages have been sent to me by Anulinus, the most illustrious proconsul of Africa, in which it is said that Caecilian, bishop of the city of Carthage, has been accused by some of his colleagues in Africa over many matters. It seems to me a very serious concern that in those provinces which divine providence has freely entrusted to my Devotedness, and in which there is a great population, the multitude are found following the wrong course and dividing as it seems in two, while the bishops are at variance. Therefore I have decided that Caecilian himself, with ten of the bishops who appear to accuse him and with ten others whom he may consider necessary for his defence, should sail to Rome. There, in the presence of yourselves and of your colleagues Reticius, Maternus and Marinus, whom I have commanded to hasten to Rome for this purpose, he may receive a hearing in those conditions that you judge to be in accordance with the most holy law.
>
> (Constantine, *Letter to Miltiades of Rome*, quoted in Eusebius of Caesarea, *Ecclesiastical History* 10.5.18–19)

Constantine's concern for North African affairs was in part due to the wealth and resources of the province, and the need to assert his authority as sole emperor in the west following the defeat of Maxentius. Yet his religious motives were equally sincere, the desire to ensure Christian unity and secure divine favour for the empire. Such motives placed Constantine on the side of the moderates like Caecilian who shared his inclusive view of the Church, rather than the more exclusive rigorists. Nevertheless, when Miltiades and his bishops decided in favour of Caecilian in October 313, Constantine permitted Caecilian's opponents to appeal the verdict and accepted their request for a larger council to sit in judgement. The emperor then convened the Council of Arles to meet in southern Gaul in August 314. This marked an important symbolic point in Christian history, the first Church council summoned by an emperor who placed the imperial transport system at the disposal of the bishops in attendance. We have the letter that Constantine sent to bishop Chrestus of Syracuse in Sicily requesting his presence at the council.

> It has come about that the very persons, who ought to hold brotherly and harmonious relations towards each other, are shamefully if not abominably divided among themselves and give occasion for ridicule to those whose minds are strangers to this most holy religion. Therefore it has seemed necessary to me to provide that this dissension, which ought to have ceased by their own voluntary agreement after the judgment that has already been given, should now if at all possible be brought to an end by the presence of many. Thus we have commanded a very large number of bishops from a great many different places to assemble in the city of Arles before the first day of August, and we have thought proper to write to you also. You should secure a public vehicle from the most illustrious Latronian, the governor of Sicily, and you should bring with you two others of the second rank [presbyters], whom you yourself shall choose, together with three servants who may serve you on the way, and present yourself at the aforementioned place before the appointed day. So by your Steadfastness and by the wise unanimity and harmony of the others present, this dispute, which has disgracefully continued until the present time due to certain shameful contentions, after everything has been heard which those who are now at variance with one another have to say and whom we have likewise commanded to be present, may be settled in accordance with the proper faith and that brotherly harmony, even if gradually, may be restored.
>
> (Constantine, *Letter to Chrestus of Syracuse*,
> quoted in Eusebius of Caesarea, *Ecclesiastical History* 10.5.22–23)

The Council of Arles decided once more in favour of Caecilian, yet Donatus' supporters appealed to Constantine again. Two years of confused wrangling followed, until the emperor finally lost patience and resorted to violence in an attempt to crush the Schism. Just like Diocletian in the Great Persecution, Constantine believed that it was his divinely appointed duty to ensure correct religion within his empire. And as the emperor was now Christian, the inner unity of the Church was a matter of imperial concern. So began the first persecution of Christians by a Christian ruler. What is perhaps surprising is not that Constantine resorted to violence, but that he did so reluctantly and for only a short time. In c.321, less than five years after deciding to repress the Donatists, Constantine admitted defeat in a letter addressed to the 'catholic' bishops who supported Caecilian.

> Since our policy was not able to tame that power of ingrained wickedness, deep-seated though it be only in a few minds, and in this depravity they continued to plead on their own behalf so as in no way to allow the object of their criminal delight to be wrested from them, we must take measures, while this whole business concerns but a few, that the mercy of Almighty God towards His people should be temperately applied. For we ought to expect the remedy from Him, to whom all good prayers and deeds are dedicated. But while the heavenly medicine does its work, our policy is to be so far regulated that we practice continual patience, and, whatever their insolence tries or does as a result of their customary intemperance, all this we are to tolerate with the virtue of tranquillity. Let nothing be done to reciprocate an injury; for it is a fool who would usurp the vengeance which we ought to reserve to God.
>
> (Constantine, *Letter to the catholics*, quoted in Optatus, *Against the Donatists*, Appendix 9)

With this decree of toleration, Constantine left the schismatics to the judgement of God. That judgement might be said to have been favourable. Persecuting a sect with such strong beliefs in martyrdom and resistance to oppression was never likely to succeed, and North African support for Donatus steadily increased. In 330 Constantine was forced to follow his own advice when he responded to a petition from the catholic bishops of Numidia.

> Having received the letter from your wise and eminent persons, I have learnt that the heretics or schismatics have, with their wonted shamelessness, thought fit to invade the basilica of that church which I had ordered to be built in the city of Constantina, and that – though frequently admonished, not only by our judges on our orders but by ourselves, to give back that which was not theirs – they refused, while you, however, imitating the patience of the Most High God, have with peaceable mind relinquished to their malice those things that are

yours and are rather requesting another place for yourselves, namely the fiscal land. This petition, according to my customary policy, I have gladly embraced and have immediately given an official letter to the steward, saying that he should transfer our treasury, with all his own rights into the possession of the catholic Church, which I have made a gift with prompt generosity and have ordered to be handed over to you forthwith.

(Constantine, *Letter to the Numidian bishops*, quoted in Optatus,
Against the Donatists, Appendix 10)

Reading behind the positive rhetoric, Constantine had built a church for the catholic community in the Numidian city of Cirta (Constantina). When the church was completed, however, the local Donatists simply moved in and resisted every attempt to expel them. All that the emperor could do was promise to build the catholics another church. It was a vivid statement of the Donatists' strength within North Africa, and while Constantine's involvement set important precedents for later Christian emperors his efforts to secure unity had failed. After Constantine's death, imperial intervention in the Schism decreased but the divisions remained. The authority Donatus wielded is reflected in the bitter words of his foe Optatus.

In the people's mouths, indeed, he was rarely called bishop, but Donatus of Carthage. And he fully deserved to be named and reproached as the prince of Tyre, that is of Carthage, because he was first of bishops, as though he himself were more than the rest; and since he wished to have no human traits, he lifted up his heart, not like the heart of a human being, but like the heart of God, as he craved to be something more than other humans. God's speech to him follows on, 'You have said, I am God'. Thus, although he did not use this expression, he either did or suffered all that fulfils the sense of this expression. He raised up his heart, so that he judged no human comparable with himself, and he seemed higher to himself because of his inflated thoughts, since whatever is above humanity is virtually God. Then, whereas bishops ought to serve God, he exacted so much for himself from his bishops that they all revered him with no less fear than God; that is to say, since he thought himself God, and since humans should swear by God alone, he suffered humans to swear by himself in the same way as by God. If anyone had made this error, he ought to have prevented it; as he did not prevent him, he thought himself God. Moreover, whereas, before his proud behaviour, all who believed in Christ used to be called Christians, he had the audacity to divide the people with God, so that those who followed him were no longer called Christians but Donatists; and if any ever came to him from any province of Africa, he did not ask them anything, according to the usual human custom, about the rains, the state of peace, or the produce of the year, but these were his words to every individual who came: 'How does my party stand among you?'.

(Optatus, *Against the Donatists* 3.3)

By the end of the fourth century the stage was set for renewed conflict. The issues at stake had evolved, particularly regarding clerical authority and the nature of Christian sacraments, and the catholic position was reinforced by the emergence of Augustine of Hippo as a leading spokesman. While the Donatists remained isolated in North Africa, their catholic rivals fostered ties with the wider Church and empire. In 404 a catholic Council of Carthage formally requested direct imperial support.

As we have fulfilled our episcopal and peace-seeking duty towards them, and they, who could make no reply to the truth, have turned to contemptible acts of violence such as setting ambushes for numerous bishops and clergy (not to speak of laity) and the seizure or attempted seizure of various churches, it is for the Imperial Clemency to counsel as to how the catholic Church, which has borne them in Christ from her sacred womb and nourished them with firmness of faith, should be fortified by their foresight, lest audacious persons get the upper hand in a religious era, by terrorizing a defenceless population since they cannot lead them astray and so corrupt them.

(Council of Carthage (404), synodal letter)

For Augustine, this appeal and the imperial condemnation of Donatism that followed required considerable soul-searching. Augustine had previously opposed religious coercion whatever the cause. The conflict with the Donatists led him to change his mind, and in so doing to formulate one of the earliest Christian justifications for the repression of those in error and their forced conversion to the true faith. These arguments were laid down in a letter that Augustine sent to Vincentius of Cartennae, a former friend who was now a Donatist bishop.

You are of the opinion that no one should be compelled to follow righteousness; and yet you read that the householder said to his servants, 'Whomsoever you shall find, compel them to come in' [Luke 14.23]. You also read how he who was at first Saul, and afterwards Paul, was compelled, by the great violence with which Christ coerced him, to know and to embrace the truth; for you cannot but think that the light which your eyes enjoy is more precious to men than money or any other possession. This light, lost suddenly by him when he was cast to the ground by the heavenly voice, he did not recover until he became a member of the Holy Church. You are also of the opinion that no coercion is to be used with any man in order for his deliverance from the fatal consequences of error; and yet you see that, in examples which cannot be disputed, this is done by God, who loves us with more real regard for our profit than any other can; and you hear Christ saying, 'No man can come to me except the Father draw him' [John 6.44], which is done in the hearts of all those who through fear of the wrath of God betake themselves to Him.

(Augustine of Hippo, *Letter* 93.5)

Augustine then continues:

Originally, my opinion was that no one should be coerced into the unity of Christ and that we must act only by words, fight only by arguments, and prevail by force of reason, lest we should have those whom we knew as avowed heretics feigning themselves to be catholics. But this opinion of mine was overcome not by the words of those who controverted it, but by the conclusive instances to which they could point. For, in the first place, there was set over against my opinion my own town, which, although it was once wholly on the side of Donatus, was brought over to the catholic unity by fear of the imperial edicts, but which we now see filled with such detestation of your ruinous perversity that it would scarcely be believed that it had ever been involved in your error. There were so many others which were mentioned to me by name, that, from facts themselves, I was made to own that to this matter the word of Scripture might be understood as applying: 'Give opportunity to a wise man, and he will be yet wiser' [Proverbs 9.9]. For how many were already, as we assuredly know, willing to be catholics, being moved by the indisputable plainness of truth, but daily putting off their avowal of this through fear of offending their own party! How many were bound, not by truth – for you never pretended to that as yours – but by the heavy chains of inveterate custom, so that in them was fulfilled the divine saying: 'A servant (who is hardened) will not be corrected by words; for though he understand, he will not answer' [Proverbs 29.19]! How many supposed the sect of Donatus to be the true Church, merely because ease had made them too listless, or conceited, or sluggish to take pains to examine catholic truth! How many would have entered earlier had not the calumnies of slanderers, who declared that we offered something other than we do upon the altar of God, shut them out! How many, believing that it mattered not to which party a Christian might belong, remained in the schism of Donatus only because they had been born in it, and no one was compelling them to forsake it and pass over into the catholic Church!

(Augustine of Hippo, *Letter* 93.17)

An attempt was made to resolve the dispute through debate, although no one had much interest in negotiation. In June 411 over 250 bishops from each side attended the Conference of Carthage, presided over by the imperial official Flavius Marcellinus. The proceedings of the Conference survive, and are more notable for squabbles between local rivals than for any significant discussion. Almost all North African sees had two bishops, one catholic and one Donatist, competing for authority.

The clerk recited: 'Severian, bishop of Ceramussa, I approved the mandate and signed it at Carthage before the distinguished tribune and notary Marcellinus'. When that had been read, Severian said 'The diocese is all catholic'. Habetdeum, the deacon of bishop Primian [Donatist bishop of Carthage] said 'We have the venerable Adeodatus there'. Severian, bishop of the catholic church, said 'Show him'. Adeodatus, bishop, said 'Ceramussa near Milevis is part of my people'. Severian, bishop of the catholic church, said 'The whole church there is catholic from the beginning. There were never Donatists there'. Adeodatus, bishop, said 'It is part of my people. It was his violence that drove my clergy and priests away'. Severian, bishop of the catholic church, said 'He is lying, as God is my witness'.

(*Acts* of the Conference of Carthage 1.133–34)

The organization and imperial involvement behind the 411 Conference was primarily the work of the catholics, and Marcellinus duly found in their favour. A violent persecution followed which severely weakened the Donatists, but in 429 the Vandal invasion of North Africa began. The Vandals were 'Arian' Christians (see Chapter 6), regarded as heretics by catholics and Donatists alike, and the common enemy may have helped draw the two parties closer together. Our main source for this period, Victor of Vita's *History of the Vandal Persecution*, was written from a catholic viewpoint and makes no reference to the Donatists. Yet the Schism appears to have endured. The eastern emperor Justinian reconquered North Africa in 534, and in 535 an imperial edict addressed to the Praetorian Prefect of Africa condemned the Donatists alongside Arians and Jews.

> Your Sublimity must take care that no Arians, Donatists or Jews or others who are known not to adhere to the orthodox religion share in any manner in ecclesiastical rites, but that impious persons are entirely excluded from sacred things and temples and no permission whatever shall be granted them to ordain bishops or clergymen, or to baptize any persons, making them adherents of their error, because such sects have been condemned not only by our but also by former laws and are followed only by impious and polluted men.
>
> (Justinian, *Novel* 37)

The exact strength of any surviving Donatist presence in Justinian's reign cannot be determined. But the Schism that began in the time of Constantine was finally ended only in the eighth century after Christian North Africa had fallen to Islam.

Copyright Acknowledgements

Further Reading

P. Brown, *Religion and Society in the Age of Saint Augustine* (London 1972)
P. Brown, *Augustine of Hippo*, revised edition (London 2000)
W. H. C. Frend, *The Donatist Church: A Movement of Protest in Roman North Africa*, 2nd edition (Oxford 1971)
S. L. Greenslade, *Schism in the Early Church*, 2nd edition (London 1964)

J. J. O'Donnell, *Augustine, Sinner and Saint: A New Biography* (London 2005)

J. B. Rives, *Religion and Authority in Roman Carthage from Augustus to Constantine* (Oxford 1995)

B. D. Shaw, *Sacred Violence: African Christians and Sectarian Hatred in the Age of Augustine* (Cambridge 2011)

M. A. Tilley, *The Bible in Christian North Africa: The Donatist World* (Minneapolis 1997)

G. G. Willis, *Saint Augustine and the Donatist Controversy* (London 1950)

6

The Doctrine of the Trinity

The fourth century witnessed the transformation of Christianity into the dominant faith of the Later Roman empire. It also witnessed the first great doctrinal controversies to divide the imperial Church. There had been theological debates within Christianity from the beginning, notably over Christ's divinity and the Christian conception of God. But imperial patronage from Constantine onwards sharply increased the stakes involved in such conflicts and their impact on the life of the empire. The fourth-century Trinitarian debates are traditionally and inaccurately known as the 'Arian Controversy', as they began with a dispute between the presbyter Arius and his bishop Alexander of Alexandria. How could the Son be God and yet distinct from God the Father? How could monotheistic Christians believe in One God and yet also believe in a Trinity? In the simplest terms, how could God be three in one? These questions may appear paradoxical yet they lie at the heart of the Christian message, and the conflicts they aroused redefined the nature of Christian belief for centuries to come.

In c.321, the Alexandrian presbyter Arius clashed with his bishop Alexander over how to define the divinity of the Son and His relationship with the Father.

Our faith from our forefathers, which we have learned also from you, Blessed Pope, is this: We acknowledge One God, alone unbegotten, alone eternal, alone without beginning, alone true, alone having immortality, alone wise, alone good, alone sovereign; judge, governor, and administrator of all, unalterable and unchangeable, just and good, God of Law and Prophets and New Testament; who begot an only-begotten Son before eternal times, through whom He has made both the ages and the universe; and begot Him, not in semblance, but in truth; and that He made Him subsist at His own will, unalterable and unchangeable; the perfect creature of God, but not as one of the creatures; offspring, but not as one of things begotten; not as Valentinus pronounced that the offspring of the Father was an emanation; nor as Manichaeus taught that the offspring was a portion consubstantial (*homoousios*) to the Father; or as Sabellius, dividing the Monad, speaks of a Son-Father; nor as Hieracas, of one torch from another, or as a lamp divided into two; nor that He who was before, was afterwards generated or new-created into a Son, as you too yourself, Blessed Pope, in the midst of the church and in session has often condemned; but, as we say, at the will of God, created before times and before ages, and gaining life and being and His glories from the Father, who gave real existence to those together with Him.

> (Arius, *Letter to Alexander*, quoted in Athanasius of Alexandria,
> *De Synodis* 16)

Given Arius' heretical reputation, we need to recognize the sincere beliefs that inspired his controversial teachings. Above all, Arius defended the unique divinity of God the Father. Contrary to some accusations he did not deny that the Son was also God, but he clearly subordinated the Son's divinity from that of the Father. For Arius, those who exalted the Son to the same Godhead as the Father compromised their individual identities within the Trinity, an error that he attributed to the third-century heretics Mani (the founder of Manichaeism) and Sabellius (who described the Trinity as one God with three faces or modes). Arius was not alone in his concerns, particularly in his opposition to Sabellian Modalism. But in his separation of Father and Son, Arius had gone too far and threatened to undermine the Son's divinity entirely. If the Son was so inferior to the Father, could He be our Saviour? This was the reaction of Alexander of Alexandria.

Who ever heard such assertions before? Or who that hears them now is not astonished and does not stop his ears lest they should be defiled with such language? Who that has heard the words of John, 'In the beginning was the Word' [John 1.1], will not denounce the saying of these men, that 'there was a time when He was not'? Or who that has heard in the Gospel, 'the only-begotten Son', and 'by Him were all things made', will not detest their declaration that He is 'one of the things that were made'? For how can He be one of those things which were made by Himself? Or how can He be the only-begotten, when, according to them, He is counted as one among the rest, since He is Himself a creature and a work? And how can He be 'made of things that were not', when the Father said, 'My heart has uttered a good Word' [Psalm 45.1], and 'Out of the womb I have begotten you before the morning star' [Psalm 110.3]? Or again, how is He 'unlike in essence to the Father', seeing that He is 'His perfect image' [Colossians 1.15] and 'The brightness of His glory' [Hebrews 1.3], and says 'He that has seen Me has seen the Father' [John 14.9]? And if the Son is the Word and Wisdom of God, how was there 'a time when He was not'? It is the same as if they should say that God was once without Word and without Wisdom. And how is He 'subject to change and variation', who says, by Himself, 'I am in the Father, and the Father in Me' [John 14.10], and 'I and the Father are One' [John 10.30], and by the prophet, 'Behold Me, for I am, and I change not' [Malachi 3.6]? For although one may refer this expression to the Father, yet it may now be more aptly spoken of the Word, because though He has been made man, He has not changed; but as the Apostle has said, 'Jesus Christ is the same yesterday, today, and forever' [Hebrews 13.8].

(Alexander of Alexandria, *Encyclical Letter*, quoted in Socrates, *Ecclesiastical History* 1.6, c.324)

When Constantine conquered the east in 324 and united the empire under his rule, the conflict between Arius and Alexander had spread to involve almost the entire eastern Church. Constantine initially hoped that the issue could be resolved peacefully.

I understand that the origin of the present controversy is this. When you, Alexander, demanded of the presbyters what opinion they each maintained respecting a certain passage in the divine Law – or rather, I should say, when you asked them regarding some futile point of dispute – then you, Arius, inconsiderately insisted on an opinion which ought never to have been conceived at all, or if conceived, should have been buried in profound silence. Thus it was that a dissension arose between you, fellowship was withdrawn, and the holy people, rent into diverse parties, no longer preserved the harmony of the common body. Accordingly, let each of you now exhibit an equal degree of forbearance, and receive the advice which your fellow-servant justly gives to you. What is this advice? It was wrong in the first instance to ask such questions as these, or to reply to them when asked. For those points of discussion, which are required by the authority of no law but rather are suggested by the contentious spirit fostered by idle leisure, even though they may be intended merely as an intellectual exercise, ought certainly to be confined to our own thoughts and not hastily produced in popular assemblies nor unadvisedly committed to the hearing of the laity. For how very rare are those people able either accurately to comprehend or adequately to explain subjects so sublime and so exceedingly difficult?

(Constantine, *Letter to Alexander and Arius*, quoted in Eusebius of Caesarea, *Life of Constantine* 2.69)

The emperor's letter did not actually reach Alexander and Arius, and Constantine soon discovered that the questions at stake were far more significant than he had realized. He therefore summoned the Council of Nicaea in June–July 325. In the presence of over 200 bishops, Arius was exiled and a creed was composed which for the first time sought to represent the agreed orthodox faith of the Church.

We believe in one God, Father Almighty, Maker of all things, seen and unseen; and in one Lord Jesus Christ the Son of God, begotten as only begotten of the Father, that is of the essence (*ousia*) of the Father, God of God, Light of Light, true God of true God, begotten not made, consubstantial (*homoousios*) with the Father, through whom all things came into existence, both things in heaven and things on earth; who for us men and for our salvation came down and was incarnate and became man, suffered and rose again the third day, ascended into the heavens, and is coming to judge the living and the dead; and in the Holy Spirit. But those who say 'there was a time when He did not exist', and 'before being begotten He did not exist', and that 'He came into being from non-existence', or who allege that the Son of God is from another *hypostasis* or *ousia*, or is alterable or changeable, these the catholic and apostolic Church condemns.

(The original Nicene Creed, 325)

Nicaea condemned the most extreme ideas associated with Arius, such as that the Son was created from nothing or subject to change. The Son is not only God but true God and is begotten of the essence (*ousia*) of the Father. Yet the original Nicene Creed raised almost as many problems as it resolved. The Holy Spirit, included as an afterthought at Nicaea, became a major subject of debate from the 350s onwards. The Greek terms *ousia* and *hypostasis* were used as synonyms in the Nicene anathemas but were later redefined to describe the Trinity. Most contentious of all was Nicaea's use of the term 'consubstantial' (*homoousios*) for the relationship between Father and Son. *Homoousios* was not a scriptural term and its meaning was highly ambiguous. Eusebius of Caesarea, who had supported Arius before the council, felt the need to write to his congregation in order to justify his acceptance of the controversial creed.

This declaration of faith being propounded by them, we did not neglect to investigate the sense in which they used the expressions 'of the essence of the Father' and 'consubstantial with the Father'. Accordingly, questions and answers were put forth and the meaning of these terms was clearly defined. It was generally admitted that the phrase 'of the essence' affirmed that the Son is indeed of the Father but does not subsist as if a part of Him. To this interpretation of the sacred doctrine, which declares that the Son is of the Father but is not a part of His essence, it seemed right for us to assent. Therefore we ourselves accepted this explanation, and nor did we decline even the term 'consubstantial', having regard for peace and fearing to deviate from the correct meaning. On the same grounds we also admitted the expression 'begotten, not made', since they said that 'made' is a term applicable in common to all the creatures which were made by the Son, to whom the Son has no likeness. Consequently, He is not a work like those which came to be through Him but is of an essence far excelling any work, an essence which the Divine Oracles teach was generated from the Father by such a mode of generation as cannot be explained or even conceived by any originated nature. Thus also when the declaration that the Son is 'consubstantial' with the Father was discussed, it was agreed that this must not be understood in a corporeal sense or in any way analogous to mortal creatures, for there is no division of essence or severance or any change in the Father's essence and power (since all such things are alien to the unoriginated nature of the Father). That He is consubstantial with the Father then simply implies that the Son of God has no resemblance to created things, but is in every respect like the Father only who begot Him.

(Eusebius of Caesarea, *Letter to his See*, quoted in Socrates,
Ecclesiastical History 1.8)

Eusebius spoke for much of the eastern Church in his distrust of the term *homoousios*, which he accepted only as safeguarding the basic unity of Father and Son. The danger with such language was that it seemed to imply that Father and Son were one entity, and so threatened to fall into the Sabellian Modalism that Arius had feared and deny the individual identities of the Trinity. Until Constantine's death in 337, no one directly challenged Nicaea. But the Nicene

Creed was largely ignored and the theological debates continued. The leading figure to emerge in these years was Athanasius, who in 328 succeeded Alexander as bishop of Alexandria. Deeply controversial in his own lifetime, Athanasius would eventually emerge as the 'champion of orthodoxy' against the 'Arian heresy'. In 335 he was condemned at the Council of Tyre on charges of violence, although according to Athanasius:

> All the proceedings against me, and the fabricated stories about the breaking of the chalice and the murder of Arsenius, were for the sole purpose of introducing impiety into the Church and of preventing them [the Arians] being condemned as heretics.
>
> (Athanasius of Alexandria, *Apologia contra Arianos* 85)

It was Athanasius who constructed the vision of an 'Arian Controversy'. He divided the fourth-century Church into two polarised factions: the 'orthodox' (whom he represented) and the 'Arians' (everyone he opposed). Athanasius laid down that vision at length in his three *Orationes contra Arianos* (*Orations against the Arians*) written c.339–346.

> When the blessed Alexander cast out Arius, those who remained with Alexander remained Christians; but those who went out with Arius abandoned the Saviour's Name to us who were with Alexander, and they were henceforth called Arians. Behold then, after the death of Alexander, those who are in communion with his successor Athanasius, and with whom the same Athanasius communicates, are instances of the same rule; neither do any of them bear his name, nor is he named from them, but all again and customarily are called Christians. For though we have a succession of teachers and become their disciples, yet, because we are taught by them the teachings of Christ, we are and are called Christians and nothing else. But those who follow the heretics, though they have countless successors, yet in every respect they bear the name of the founder of their heresy. While Arius is dead, and many of his followers have succeeded him, nevertheless those who hold the doctrines of that man, as being known from Arius, are called Arians.
>
> (Athanasius of Alexandria, *Orationes contra Arianos* I.3)

In the polarised vision of Athanasius, all those who opposed him shared the original teachings of Arius and so were not Christians but 'Arians'. Athanasius' polemical argument has exerted a powerful influence on all subsequent interpretations of the fourth-century debates, but this owes more to Athanasius' later fame than historical accuracy. Arius himself was of no real significance after Nicaea and there were no later 'Arians' who followed his teachings. Nor was there any agreement on what doctrines might be described as 'orthodox'. Instead, the middle decades of the fourth century saw a wide spectrum of theological positions emerge, each offering a different interpretation of the Son's divinity and His place within the Trinity.

The Dedication Council of Antioch met in 341 to consecrate the Golden Church begun by Constantine and completed under his son Constantius II (337–361). Some ninety eastern bishops attended, representing the chief cities of Asia Minor, Syria and Palestine. The council addressed a letter to bishop Julius of Rome, in which the bishops insisted (probably in response to Athanasius' polemic) that:

> We have not been followers of Arius, for how could we, who are bishops, follow a presbyter?
>
> (*Letter to Julius*, 341, quoted in Athanasius of Alexandria, *De Synodis* 22)

The eastern bishops then issued a new doctrinal statement, the Dedication Creed.

> We believe, conformably to the evangelical and apostolic tradition, in One God, the Father Almighty, the Framer, and Maker, and Provider of the Universe, from whom are all things. And in One Lord Jesus Christ, His Son, only-begotten God, by whom are all things, who was begotten before all ages from the Father, God from God, whole from whole, sole from sole, perfect from perfect, King from King, Lord from Lord, Living Word, Living Wisdom, true Light, Way, Truth, Resurrection, Shepherd, Door, both unalterable and unchangeable; exact Image of the Essence, Will, Power and Glory of the Godhead of the Father; the first born of every creature, who was in the beginning with God, God the Word, as it is written in the Gospel, 'and the Word was God' [John 1.1]; by whom all things were made, and in whom all things consist; who in the last days descended from above, and was born of a Virgin according to the Scriptures, and was made man, mediator between God and man, and Apostle of our faith, and Prince of life, as He says, 'I came down from heaven, not to do Mine own will, but the

will of Him that sent Me' [John 6.38]; who suffered for us and rose again on the third day, and ascended into heaven, and sat down on the right hand of the Father, and is coming again with glory and power, to judge living and dead. And in the Holy Spirit, who is given to those who believe for comfort and sanctification and perfection, as also our Lord Jesus Christ enjoined His disciples, saying, 'Go ye, teach all nations, baptizing them in the name of the Father, and the Son, and the Holy Spirit' [Matthew 28.19]; namely of a Father who is truly Father, and a Son who is truly Son, and of the Holy Spirit who is truly Holy Spirit, the names not being given without meaning or effect, but denoting accurately the peculiar subsistence (*hypostasis*), rank, and glory of each that is named, so that they are three in subsistence, and in agreement one.

(The Dedication Creed, 341, quoted in Athanasius of Alexandria,
De Synodis 23)

This Dedication Creed was certainly not 'Arian' but nor by later standards was it 'orthodox'. While the Son's divinity was exalted, the key Nicene expressions 'consubstantial' and 'from the essence of the Father' were deliberately omitted. Great emphasis was placed on the distinct identities of the Trinity, in opposition to the potential Sabellian implications of Nicaea which had been fuelled by Athanasius' contemporary Marcellus of Ancyra. Yet the Trinitarian doctrine still had to be reconciled with Christian monotheism, and the Son remained subordinate to the Father. Like the Nicene Creed, the Dedication Creed thus failed to resolve the ongoing debates. Indeed, the Council of 341 was only the beginning. Over the next two decades a veritable flood of councils and creedal statements divided the Church in both east and west as the alternative theological solutions gradually took shape.

One striking feature of the doctrinal works of the 330s and 340s is their near total silence regarding Nicaea. The majority of eastern bishops regarded the Nicene Creed with suspicion and preferred to consign it to oblivion. The man who restored Nicaea to the forefront of debate was once again Athanasius. In the *De Decretis Nicaenae Synodi* (*On the Council of Nicaea*), written in the early 350s, Athanasius upheld the Nicene Creed as the only defence of 'orthodoxy' against the 'Arian heresy'.

Since the generation of the Son from the Father is other than that which pertains to the nature of human beings and He is not only like (*homoios*) but also inseparable from the essence (*ousia*) of the Father and He and the Father are one, as He Himself said [John 10.30], and the Word is always in the Father and the Father in the Word – as is the radiance in relation to the light, for this is what the phrase means – the council understanding all this aptly wrote 'consubstantial' (*homoousios*). They did this in order to overturn the perversity of the hypocrites and to show that the Word is other than the things which come to be. For they immediately added, 'But those who say that the Son of God is out of nothing, or created, or alterable, or a thing made, or from another essence (*ousia*), these the holy and catholic Church anathematizes'. By saying this, they showed clearly that 'from the essence' and 'consubstantial' are destructive of the catchwords of the impiety, that He is a creature and a thing made and a generated being and changeable and that He was not before he was begotten. The one who thinks such things is contradicting the council. But the one who does not hold the doctrines of Arius necessarily holds and intends the doctrines of the council.

(Athanasius of Alexandria, *De Decretis Nicaenae Synodi* 20)

Athanasius' long-term influence was immense, but at this stage his supporters were very much in a minority. At the opposite end of the theological spectrum were the so-called 'Neo-Arians' or 'Anomoians', who maintained that the Son was entirely unlike (*anomoios*) in essence to the Father. Their founders Aetius and Eunomius also began to teach in the 350s, and emphasized a clear logical separation between the Father who alone is ingenerate (without beginning) and the begotten Son.

If 'ingenerate' and 'God' have exactly the same meaning, then the Ingenerate has begotten the Ingenerate. But if 'ingenerate' has one meaning and 'God' has another meaning, then it is not impossible to say that God has begotten God, since one of them receives His existence from ingenerate essence. However, if that which is before God is nothing, as is true, then 'God' and 'ingenerate' do have the same meaning, since the offspring cannot be ingenerate. Therefore the offspring does not allow himself to be mentioned together with his God and Father. May the true God who is Himself ingenerate, and who for that reason is alone addressed as the only true God by the one whom He sent, Jesus Christ, who truly came into existence before the ages and who is truly a generate being, preserve you men and women strong and safe from impiety, in Christ Jesus our Saviour, through whom be all glory to God the Father, now and forever and for all ages. Amen.

(Aetius, *Syntagmation*, quoted in Epiphanius of Salamis, *Panarion* 76.12)

The 'Anomoians' strongly defended Christian monotheism but threatened to deny the divinity of Christ entirely. Partly in reaction against this extreme viewpoint, the bishop Basil of Ancyra summoned a council in 358. Basil and his colleagues stood between Athanasius and the Dedication Creed, wishing to defend the unity of Father and Son without accepting the contentious term *homoousios*. Their position came to be known as 'Homoiousian' (from *homoiousios*, 'of like essence'), although Basil preferred the expression *homoios kat' ousian* ('like in essence') to define the similarity yet separation between Father and Son.

It is impossible to conceive that when He came from a state that was natural to Him to one that was not natural, that is from God to becoming Son of Man, He became like those to whom that state is natural (that is, those who are men by nature) in the state that is not natural to Him, while in the state that is natural to Him He is not like His natural Father, He who was begotten God from God. Therefore it is plain that those who refuse to say that the Son is like the Father in essence also refuse to say that He is Son, but a creature only. Nor do they say that the Father is Father, but only Creator. However, the 'likeness' does not bring the Son into a relationship of identity with the Father but into one of similarity in essence and of ineffable legitimacy, as coming from Him without passion. To repeat, just as when He was born in the likeness of men and in the likeness of sinful flesh, He was not brought into a relationship of identity with man but into one of similarity with the essence of the flesh, so also to speak of the Son as like in essence to the Father who begot Him will not bring His essence into a relationship of identity with the Father but into one of similarity.

(Basil of Ancyra, *Encyclical Letter*, quoted in Epiphanius of Salamis, *Panarion* 73.9)

All of these differing arguments circulated during the reign of Constantius II. The most influential doctrine of the mid-fourth century, however, occupied the middle-ground of the theological spectrum. Seeking an end to the debates, Constantius summoned twin councils to meet simultaneously in Ariminum (west) and Seleucia (east) in late 359. The western bishops expressed support for Nicaea and the eastern bishops for the Dedication Creed, but under imperial pressure both groups eventually accepted a conservative statement that reduced the Son's relationship with the Father to the simple expression 'like' (*homoios*). This 'Homoian' creed was formalized at a special Council of Constantinople in January 360.

We believe in one God, the Father, Almighty, from whom are all things. And in the only-begotten Son of God, who was begotten from God before all ages and before all beginning, through whom all things came into existence, visible and invisible, begotten only-begotten, alone from the Father alone, God from God, like (*homoios*) the Father who begot Him according to the Scriptures, whose generation no one knows save alone the Father who begot Him. We know that this only-begotten Son of God, the Father sending Him, came from heaven as it is written for the destruction of sin and death, and was born from the Holy Spirit, from the Virgin Mary as regards the flesh as it is written, and consorted with the disciples, and having fulfilled all the economy according to the Father's will was crucified and died, and was buried and descended to the lower world (at whom hell itself quailed); who also rose again from the dead on the third day, and sojourned with the disciples, and when forty days were fulfilled was taken up to heaven, and sits on the Father's right hand, purposing to come on the last day of the resurrection in the Father's glory so as to render to each according to his deeds. And in the Holy Spirit, whom the only-begotten Son of God Himself, Christ our Lord and God, promised to send as a Paraclete to the race of men, as it is written the Spirit of truth, whom He sent to them when He had ascended to heaven. But as for the term *ousia*, which was adopted simply by the fathers but being unknown to the people occasioned offence because the Scriptures themselves do not contain it, it has pleased us that it should be abolished and that no mention at all should be made of it henceforth, since indeed the divine Scriptures nowhere have made mention of the *ousia* of Father and Son. Nor indeed should the term *hypostasis* be used of Father and Son and Holy Spirit. But we say the Son is like (*homoios*) the Father, as the divine Scriptures say and teach. But let all the heresies which have either been condemned previously or have come about more recently and are in opposition to this creed be anathema.

(Creed of Constantinople, 360, quoted in Athanasius of Alexandria,
De Synodis 30)

Looking back on the adoption of this creed, Jerome was moved to write:

At that moment the term *ousia* was abolished, the Nicene Faith stood condemned by acclamation. The whole world groaned, and was astonished to find itself Arian.

(Jerome, *Against the Luciferians* 19)

The 'Homoian' creed was not actually 'Arian', and under Constantius and later Valens (eastern emperor 364–378) represented the orthodox faith of the imperial Church. But later generations regarded the creed as heretical, which proved a major source of conflict over the next two centuries. For it was during the reigns of Constantius and Valens that the Goths and other Germanic peoples increasingly adopted Christianity, and so came to be condemned as 'Arian' by Roman Christians (see further Chapter 17). The three men who played the leading role in refuting the 'Homoians' and securing the triumph of what became orthodoxy were the Cappadocian Fathers – Basil of Cappadocian Caesarea, his younger brother Gregory of Nyssa, and their friend Gregory of Nazianzus. It was Basil who finally solved the dilemma of how to express both the unity of the Trinity and their individual identities. He did so by redefining the terms *ousia* and *hypostasis*, which had been used as synonyms at Nicaea and condemned outright by the 'Homoians'.

The distinction between *ousia* and *hypostasis* is the same as that between the general and the particular; as, for instance, between the animal and the particular man. Wherefore, in the case of the Godhead, we confess one *ousia* so as not to give a variant definition of existence, but we confess a particular *hypostasis*, in order that our conception of Father, Son and Holy Spirit may be without confusion and clear. If we have no distinct perception of the separate characteristics, namely fatherhood, sonship, and sanctification, but form our conception of God from the general idea of existence, we cannot possibly give a sound account of our faith. We must therefore confess the faith by adding the particular to the common. The Godhead is common; the fatherhood particular. We must therefore combine the two and say, 'I believe in God the Father'. The like course must be pursued in the confession of the Son; we must combine the particular with the common and say, 'I believe in God the Son'. So in the case of the Holy Spirit we must make our utterance conform to the appellation and say, 'I believe also in the divine Holy Spirit'. Hence it results that there is a satisfactory preservation of the unity by the confession of the one Godhead, while in the distinction of the individual properties regarded in each there is the confession of the peculiar properties of the Persons. On the other hand those who identify *ousia* and *hypostasis* are compelled to confess only three Persons (*prosopa*), and in their hesitation to speak of three *hypostases* are convicted of failure to avoid the error of Sabellius.

(Basil of Cappadocian Caesarea, *Letter* 236.6, to Amphilochius of Iconium)

The Cappadocian Fathers built on the earlier arguments of Athanasius to refine the Nicene Creed as the symbol of orthodox Christianity. Their Trinitarian vision might be summarised as 'three *hypostases* in one *ousia*', three individual identities in one divine essence. This vision gathered growing support in the 360s and 370s, but the triumph of 'Nicene orthodoxy' also depended on events outside the theological sphere. In 378 the 'Homoian' emperor Valens was killed in battle with the Goths at Adrianople. His successor as eastern emperor was Theodosius I (379–395), a Spaniard by birth and a supporter of Nicaea. Almost immediately upon his accession, Theodosius passed an edict expressing his judgement in no uncertain terms.

> It is Our will that all the peoples who are ruled by the administration of Our Clemency shall practice that religion which the divine Peter the apostle transmitted to the Romans, as the religion which he introduced makes clear even unto this day. It is evident that this is the religion that is followed by the Pontiff Damasus [of Rome] and by Peter, bishop of Alexandria [Athanasius' successor], a man of apostolic sanctity. That is, according to the apostolic discipline and the evangelic doctrine, we shall believe in the single Deity of the Father, the Son and the Holy Spirit, under the concept of equal majesty and of the holy Trinity. We command that those persons who follow this rule shall embrace the name of catholic Christians. The rest, however, whom We adjudge demented and insane, shall sustain the infamy of heretical dogmas, their meeting places shall not receive the name of churches, and they shall be smitten first by divine vengeance and secondly by the retribution of Our own initiative, which We shall assume in accordance with the divine judgement.
>
> (*Theodosian Code* 16.1.2, AD 380)

Theodosius followed his edict by summoning a new council to meet in Constantinople early the next year. Attended by some 150 bishops, the Council of 381 is remembered in Christian tradition as the second ecumenical council, for it was here that a revised version of the Nicene Creed was proclaimed as the orthodox faith of the Church.

> We believe in one God, Father, Almighty, maker of heaven and earth and of all things visible and invisible. And in one Lord Jesus Christ, the only-begotten Son of God, who was begotten from the Father before all ages, light from light, true God

from true God, begotten not made, consubstantial with the Father, through whom all things came into being, who for us men and for our salvation came down from heaven, was incarnate from the Holy Spirit and the Virgin Mary and became man, was crucified for us under Pontius Pilate, suffered and was buried, rose on the third day in accordance with the Scriptures and ascended into heaven, is seated at the right hand of the Father, and is coming again with glory to judge the living and the dead, of whose kingdom there will be no end. And in the Holy Spirit, the lord and life-giver, who proceeds from the Father, who together with the Father and the Son is worshipped and glorified, who spoke through the prophets. And in one holy catholic and apostolic Church. We confess one baptism for the remission of sins. We await the resurrection of the dead, and the life of the age to come. Amen.

(Niceno-Constantinopolitan Creed, 381)

This creed, technically known as the Niceno-Constantinopolitan Creed, is the 'Nicene Creed' that is read every Sunday in many modern churches. At an official level, the Council of Constantinople in 381 marked the end of the fourth-century Trinitarian debates. Alongside the formula 'three *hypostases* in one *ousia*', the creed safeguarded the mystery of the Trinity: three Persons in one Godhead. The reality, of course, was more complex. Gregory of Nyssa described the arguments that could be heard on the Constantinople streets in the early 380s.

The whole city is full of it, the squares, the market places, the crossroads, the alleyways; old-clothes men, money changers, food sellers, they are all busy arguing. If you desire someone to change a piece of silver, he philosophizes about the Begotten and the Unbegotten. If you ask the price of a loaf of bread, you are told by way of reply that the Father is greater and the Son is subordinate. If you enquire whether the bath is ready, the answer is that the Son was made out of nothing.

(Gregory of Nyssa, *De Deitate Filii et Spiritus Sancti*)

Gregory's words offer a valuable reminder of the importance of the theological controversies to the fourth-century Later Roman empire. However arcane the issues at stake may seem to many of us today, they were issues that mattered not only to Late Roman bishops and intellectuals but to the ordinary men and women going about their daily lives in shops and on city streets. Nor did those controversies end in 381 with the Council of Constantinople. The 'Homoian'

Christianity of the Germanic invaders led to renewed disputes over 'Arianism' in the fifth-century west. And in the east the Trinitarian debates led directly into the still more wide-ranging doctrinal questions raised by the divinity and humanity of the incarnate Christ.

Copyright Acknowledgements

Further Reading

L. Ayres, *Nicaea and its Legacy: An Approach to Fourth-Century Trinitarian Theology* (Oxford 2004)

M. R. Barnes and D. H. Williams (eds), *Arianism after Arius: Essays in the Development of the Fourth Century Trinitarian Conflicts* (Edinburgh 1993)

T. D. Barnes, *Athanasius and Constantius: Theology and Politics in the Constantinian Empire* (Cambridge, Mass. and London 1993)

J. Behr, *The Nicene Faith*, The Formation of Christian Theology, Volume 2 (New York 2004)

R. C. Gregg (ed.), *Arianism: Historical and Theological Reassessments* (Philadelphia 1985)

R. C. Gregg and D. E. Groh, *Early Arianism – A View of Salvation* (Philadelphia 1981)

D. M. Gwynn, *Athanasius of Alexandria: Bishop, Theologian, Ascetic, Father* (Oxford 2012)

R. P. C. Hanson, *The Search for the Christian Doctrine of God: The Arian Controversy 318–381* (Edinburgh 1988)

J. N. D. Kelly, *Early Christian Creeds*, 3rd edition (London 1972)

T. A. Kopecek, *A History of Neo-Arianism*, 2 volumes (Massachusetts 1979)

J. T. Lienhard, *Contra Marcellum: Marcellus of Ancyra and Fourth-Century Theology* (Washington, D.C. 1999)

W. G. Rusch (ed.), *The Trinitarian Controversy* (Philadelphia 1980)

M. Wiles, *Archetypal Heresy: Arianism through the Centuries* (Oxford 1996)

R. D. Williams, *Arius: Heresy and Tradition*, 2nd Impression (London 2001)

F. M. Young, *From Nicaea to Chalcedon: A Guide to the Literature and its Background* (Philadelphia 1983)

7

Scripture and Liturgy

> Our Father in heaven,
>   hallowed be your name.
> Your kingdom come.
> Your will be done,
>   on earth as it is in heaven.
> Give us this day our daily bread.
> And forgive us our debts,
>   as we also have forgiven our debtors.
> And do not bring us to the time of trial.
>   (Matthew 6.9–13)

The fourth and fifth centuries AD were the years of transition in which Christianity took the shape we recognize in the modern world. Nowhere is this more apparent than in the crucial sphere of Scripture and Liturgy, from the Biblical canon and the order of a church service to the ritual of baptism and the annual calendar dominated by Easter and Christmas. The precise details of these defining characteristics of Christianity still vary to this day between different denominations. But it was within the Later Roman empire that their patterns took shape, as the diversity of the earliest Christian communities gave way to the greater structure and uniformity of the imperial Church.

The formation of the Christian scriptural canon was a gradual and at times controversial process. The authority of the four Gospels of Matthew, Mark, Luke and John had been established in the second century, as had the collection of Pauline letters. Debate continued, however, regarding the letters attributed to the original apostles and Revelation. When Eusebius of Caesarea wrote his *Ecclesiastical History* around the beginning of the fourth century, he felt it necessary to record his judgement on the accepted and disputed books of the New Testament.

First must be placed the holy quartet of the Gospels, followed by the Acts of the Apostles. After this must be reckoned Paul's epistles, and after them the epistle called 1 John and likewise 1 Peter. To these may be added, if it really seems proper, the Revelation of John, concerning which we shall give the different opinions at the proper time. These are classed as the accepted writings. Among the disputed writings, which are nevertheless familiar to many, are the epistles known as James, Jude, and 2 Peter, and those called 2 and 3 John, whether they are the work of the evangelist or of another person with the same name. Among the rejected writings must be placed the Acts of Paul, the Shepherd [of Hermas], and the Revelation of Peter; and in addition the Epistle of Barnabas and the Teachings of the Apostles, together with the Revelation of John if this seems proper, for as I said before, some reject it but others include it among the accepted writings. Moreover, some have found a place for the Gospel according to the Hebrews, with which those Hebrews who have accepted Christ are especially delighted. These may all be reckoned among the disputed writings, but I have felt compelled to give a catalogue of these also, distinguishing those writings which according to the tradition of the Church are true, genuine, and accepted from those others which are not canonical but disputed and yet are familiar to most ecclesiastical writers. We must not confuse these with the writings cited by heretics under the names of the apostles, including for instance the Gospels of Peter, Thomas, Matthias, and several others besides these, and the Acts of Andrew, John, and other apostles. No one belonging to the succession of ecclesiastical writers has ever seen fit to refer to any of these in his writings.

(Eusebius of Caesarea, *Ecclesiastical History* 3.25.1–6)

Eusebius identified a solid core of recognized authoritative texts. Yet a number of writings eventually included within the New Testament remained under dispute, reflecting the variety of Christian interpretations at the time of Constantine's conversion. As Christian numbers expanded, Constantine sought to encourage reading of the Scriptures. He therefore wrote to Eusebius as a renowned Biblical expert, asking the bishop to provide copies of the Scriptures for the new city of Constantinople.

It has happened, through the favourable providence of God our Saviour, that great numbers have united themselves to the most holy Church in the city which is called by my name. Thus it seems highly fitting, since the city is rapidly advancing in prosperity in all other respects, that the number of churches should also be increased. You must therefore receive with all readiness my decision

> regarding this matter. I have thought it proper to instruct your Prudence to
> order fifty copies of the sacred Scriptures, to be written on prepared parchment
> in a legible manner and in a convenient and portable form by professional
> calligraphists thoroughly practiced in their art, the provision and use of which
> texts you know to be most needful for instruction in church.
>
> (Constantine, *Letter to Eusebius*, quoted in Eusebius of
> Caesarea, *Life of Constantine* 4.36)

Constantine's letter does not identify precisely what writings are meant when
he refers to the divine Scriptures. Indeed, there is no evidence that the first
Christian emperor attempted to define the scriptural canon more closely, even at
the Council of Nicaea which might have provided a natural setting. Debate
therefore continued for another generation. In 367, Athanasius of Alexandria
wrote a *Festal Letter* to the churches of Egypt for the annual celebration of Easter.
This famous letter contains the oldest extant list of New Testament books that
duplicates the New Testament canon in the modern Bible, alongside the Christian
Old Testament and a repeated warning against those works which Christians
should not regard as authoritative.

> As I begin to mention these things, in order to commend my audacity, I will
> employ the example of Luke the evangelist and say myself: Inasmuch as certain
> people have attempted to set in order for themselves the so-called apocryphal
> books and to mix these with the divinely inspired Scripture, about which we are
> convinced it is just as those who were eyewitnesses from the beginning and
> assistants of the Word handed down to our ancestors, it seemed good to me,
> because I have been urged by genuine brothers and sisters and instructed from
> the beginning, to set forth in order the books that are canonized, transmitted,
> and believed to be divine, so that those who have been deceived might condemn
> the persons who led them astray, and those who have remained pure might
> rejoice to be reminded.
>
> There are, then, belonging to the Old Testament in number a total of twenty-
> two, for, as I have heard, it has been handed down that this is the number of the
> letters in the Hebrew alphabet. In order and by name they are as follows: first,
> Genesis; then Exodus; then Leviticus; and after this, Numbers; and finally
> Deuteronomy. After these is Joshua, the son of Nun; and Judges; and after this,
> Ruth; and again, next four books of Kings, the first and second of these being
> reckoned as one book, and the third and fourth likewise being one. After these

are First and Second Chronicles, likewise reckoned as one book; then First and Second Esdras, likewise as one. After these is the book of Psalms; and then Proverbs; then Ecclesiastes and the Song of Songs. After these is Job; and finally the Prophets, the twelve being reckoned as one book; then Isaiah; Jeremiah and with it, Baruch; Lamentations and the Letter; and after it, Ezekiel and Daniel. To this point are the books of the Old Testament.

Again, one should not hesitate to name the books of the New Testament. For these are the four Gospels, Matthew, Mark, Luke, and John; then after these, Acts of the Apostles and seven letters, called catholic, by the apostles, namely: one by James; two by Peter; then three by John; and after these, one by Jude. After these there are fourteen letters by Paul, written in this order: first to the Romans; then two to the Corinthians; and after these, to the Galatians; and next to the Ephesians; then to the Philippians and to the Colossians; and after these, two to the Thessalonians; and that to the Hebrews; and additionally, two to Timothy, one to Titus, and finally that to Philemon. And besides, the Revelation of John.

These are the springs of salvation, so that someone who thirsts may be satisfied by the words they contain. In these books alone the teaching of piety is proclaimed. Let no one add to or subtract from them. Concerning them the Lord put the Sadducees to shame when he said, 'You err because you do not know the Scriptures or their meaning' [Matthew 22.29, Mark 12.24], and he reproved the Jews, 'Search the Scriptures, for it is they that testify to me' [John 5.39]. But for the sake of greater accuracy, I add this, writing from necessity. There are other books, in addition to the preceding, which have not been canonized, but have been appointed by the ancestors to be read to those who newly join us and want to be instructed in the word of piety: the Wisdom of Solomon, the Wisdom of Sirach, Esther, Judith, Tobit, the book called Teaching of the Apostles, and the Shepherd [of Hermas]. Nevertheless, beloved, the former books are canonized; the latter are (only) read; and there is no mention of the apocryphal books. Rather (the category of apocrypha), is an invention of heretics, who write these books whenever they want and then generously add time to them, so that, by publishing them as if they were ancient, they might have a pretext for deceiving the simple folk.

(Athanasius of Alexandria, *Festal Letter* 39.16–21)

The fact that Athanasius felt the need to circulate this letter in 367 suggests that controversies over the canon were an ongoing concern. Nevertheless, by the closing decades of the fourth century the approved texts of the Old and New Testaments appear to have become almost universally accepted. The most important scriptural developments during these years focused instead on the translation of the Biblical texts. The conversion of the Germanic peoples led to the creation of a Gothic Bible by the missionary Ulfila (see Chapter 17). But the most influential translation of all was the work of Jerome, who in 382 was asked by bishop Damasus of Rome to prepare a new Latin text of the Bible. The existing Latin translations varied widely and were often of poor quality, although revising them was not a popular task as Jerome knew well.

> You urge me to make a new work out of an old one, and, as it were, to sit in judgment on the copies of the Scriptures which are now scattered throughout the whole world; and, inasmuch as they differ from one another, you would have me decide which of them agree with the Greek original. The labour is one of love, but at the same time both perilous and presumptuous; for in judging others I must myself be judged by all; and how can I dare to change the language of the world in its hoary old age and carry it back to the early days of its infancy? Is there a man, learned or unlearned, who will not, when he takes the volume into his hands, and perceives that what he reads does not suit his settled tastes, break out immediately into violent language, and call me a forger and a profane person for having the audacity to add anything to the ancient books, or to make any changes or corrections therein? Now there are two consoling reflections which enable me to bear the odium – in the first place, the command is given by you who are the supreme bishop; and secondly, even on the showing of those who revile us, readings at variance with the early copies cannot be right. For if we are to pin our faith to the Latin texts, it is for our opponents to tell us which; for there are almost as many forms of texts as there are copies. If, on the other hand, we are to glean the truth from a comparison of many, why not go back to the original Greek and correct the mistakes introduced by inaccurate translators, and the blundering alterations of confident but ignorant critics, and, further, all that has been inserted or changed by copyists more asleep than awake?
>
> (Jerome, *Preface to the Four Gospels*, AD 383)

Whatever his doubts, Jerome devoted himself to translating the Greek New Testament and the Hebrew Old Testament until his death in 420. His labours formed the basis of what became the Vulgate Bible, which for over a thousand years stood as the definitive Latin Biblical text and was read more widely than any other work in medieval European history.

No less important for Christian identity than the definition of the canon of Scripture was the development of the church liturgy. Our evidence for the services held in the earliest churches is very fragmentary and focused around the celebration of the eucharist (Greek: 'thanksgiving'). Practices varied widely across different Christian communities, but gradually a liturgical service structure emerged which included scriptural readings, preached sermons and the communion ceremony itself. During the Late Roman period, particular liturgical formulas became widespread and have remained influential down to the present day. The Greek Orthodox Church eventually adopted what is known as the Liturgy of St John Chrysostom. The formula has evolved over time and its association with John Chrysostom (bishop of Constantinople 398–404) is disputed, but essential elements of the Liturgy are firmly rooted in the fourth century.

Priest: The grace of our Lord Jesus Christ, and the love of the God and Father, and the fellowship of the Holy Spirit be with you all.

People: And with your spirit.

Priest: Let us lift up our hearts.

People: We have them with the Lord.

Priest: Let us give thanks to the Lord.

People: It is fitting and right to worship the Father, the Son, and the Holy Spirit, the consubstantial and undivided Trinity.

Priest: It is fitting and right to hymn you, to bless you, to praise you, to give you thanks, to worship you in all places of your dominion. For you are God, ineffable, inconceivable, invisible, incomprehensible, existing always and in the same way, you and your only-begotten Son and your Holy Spirit. You brought us out of non-existence into existence; and when we had fallen, you raised us up again, and did not cease to do everything until you had brought us up to heaven, and granted us the kingdom that is to come. For all these things we give thanks to you and to your only-begotten Son and to your Holy Spirit, for all that we know and do not know, your seen and unseen benefits that have come upon us. We give you thanks also for this ministry; vouchsafe to receive it from our hands, even though thousands of archangels and ten thousands of angels stand before you, cherubim and seraphim, with six wings and many eyes, flying on high, singing the triumphal hymn, proclaiming, crying, and saying:

People: Holy, holy, holy, Lord of Sabaoth; heaven and earth are full of your glory. Hosanna in the highest. Blessed is he who comes in the name of the Lord. Hosanna in the highest.

Priest: With these powers, Master, lover of man, we also cry and say: holy are you and all-holy, and your only-begotten Son, and your Holy Spirit; holy are you and all-holy and magnificent is your glory; for you so loved the world that you gave your only-begotten Son that all who believe in Him may not perish, but have eternal life. When He had come and fulfilled all the dispensation for us, on the night in which He handed Himself over, He took bread in His holy and undefiled and blameless hands, gave thanks, blessed, broke, and gave it to His holy disciples and apostles saying, 'Take, eat; this is my body, which is broken for you for forgiveness of sins'.

People: Amen.

Priest: Likewise the cup also after supper, saying 'Drink from this, all of you; this is my blood of the new covenant, which is shed for you and for many for the forgiveness of sins'.

People: Amen.

(Liturgy of St John Chrysostom)

Just as the Liturgy of St John Chrysostom used in Constantinople became across the centuries the dominant formula of the Greek east, so in the west the Roman Rite came to supersede the variety of local liturgical traditions that existed in early Latin Christianity. Again this formula evolved over time, but parallels can be found in the writings of Ambrose of Milan (bishop 374–397) and Innocent I of Rome (401–417).

Priest: The Lord be with you.

People: And with your spirit.

Priest: Up with your hearts.

People: We have them with the Lord.

Priest: Let us give thanks to the Lord our God.

People: It is fitting and right.

Priest: It is truly fitting and right, our duty and our salvation, that we should always and everywhere give you thanks, O Lord, holy Father, almighty eternal God, through Christ our Lord; through whom angels praise your majesty, dominions adore, powers fear, the heavens and the heavenly hosts and the blessed seraphim, joining together in exultant celebration. We pray you, bid our voices also to be admitted with theirs, beseeching you, confessing, and saying:

People: Holy, holy, holy. Lord God of Sabaoth. Heaven and earth are full of your glory. Hosanna in the highest. Blessed is he who comes in the name of the Lord. Hosanna in the highest.

Priest: We therefore pray and beseech you, most merciful Father, through your Son Jesus Christ our Lord, to accept and bless these gifts, these offerings, these holy and unblemished sacrifices; above all, those which we offer to you for your holy catholic Church; vouchsafe to grant it peace, protection, unity, and guidance throughout the world, together with your servant N. our Pope, and N. our bishop, and all orthodox upholders of the catholic and apostolic faith. Remember, Lord, your servants, men and women, and all who stand around, whose faith and devotion are known to you, for whom we offer to you, or who offer to you this sacrifice of praise for themselves and for all their own, for the redemption of their souls, for the hope of their salvation and safety, and pay their vows to you, the living, true, and eternal God. In fellowship with and venerating above all the memory of the glorious ever-Virgin Mary, mother of God and our Lord Jesus Christ, and also of your blessed apostles and martyrs Peter, Paul, Andrew, James, John, Thomas, Philip, Bartholomew, Matthew, Simon and Thaddaeus, Linus, Cletus, Clement, Sixtus, Cornelius, Cyprian, Laurence, Chrysogonus, John and Paul, Cosmas and Damian, and all your saints; by their merits and prayers grant us to be defended in all things by the help of your protection; through Christ our Lord.

Therefore, Lord, we pray you graciously to accept this offering made by us your servants, and also by your whole family; and to order our days in peace; and to command that we are snatched from eternal damnation and numbered among the flock of your elect; through Christ our Lord. Vouchsafe, we beseech you, O God, to make this offering wholly blessed, approved, ratified, reasonable, and acceptable; that it may become to us the body and blood of your dearly beloved Son Jesus Christ our Lord; who, on the day before He suffered, took bread in His holy and reverend hands, lifted up His eyes to heaven to you, O God, His almighty Father, gave thanks to you, blessed, broke, and gave it to His disciples, saying 'Take and eat from this, all of you; for this is my body'. Likewise after supper, taking also this glorious cup in His holy and reverend hands, again He gave thanks to you, blessed, and gave it to His disciples, saying 'Take and drink from it, all of you; for this is the cup of my blood, of the new and eternal covenant, the mystery of faith, which will be shed for you and for many for forgiveness of sins. As often as you do this, you will do it for my remembrance'.

(The Roman Rite)

The church service also provided the setting for clergy to address their flocks and offer theological and moral teaching. With Christian congregations rapidly expanding, the Later Roman period was a golden age for preaching. John Chrysostom, the greatest preacher of all, earned the title *chrysostomos* ('golden-mouth') for the power of his delivery. As bishop of Constantinople, he memorably condemned the wealthy who preferred silver chamber pots to aiding the poor.

In point of senselessness, tell me, wherein do those who make silver jars, pitchers, and scent bottles differ from the man who owned a golden plane tree? And wherein do those women differ (ashamed indeed I am, but it is necessary to speak it) who make chamber utensils of silver? It is you who should be ashamed, that are the makers of these things. When Christ is starving, do you so revel in luxury? Yea rather, so play the fool! What punishment shall these not suffer? And do you still ask, when the Devil has thus made you ridiculous, why there are robbers? Why murderers? Why such evils? For even the mere possession of silver dishes indeed is not in keeping with a soul devoted to wisdom, but is altogether a piece of luxury; but making unclean vessels also of silver, is this then luxury? Nay, I will not call it luxury, but senselessness; nay, nor yet this, but madness; nay rather, worse even than madness. I know that many persons make jokes at me for this; but I heed them not, only let some good result from it. In truth, to be wealthy does make people senseless and mad. Did their power reach to such an excess, they would have the earth too of gold, and walls of gold, perchance the heaven too, and the air of gold. What a madness is this, what an iniquity, what a burning fever! Another, made after the image of God, is perishing of cold; and you do furnish yourself with such things as these? O the senseless pride! What more would a madman have done? Do you pay such honour to your excrements, as to receive them in silver?

(John Chrysostom, *Homily on Colossians* 2.16–19)

Another recurring theme of Chrysostom's sermons was his attack upon those who preferred the theatre and circus games to attending church.

Why do I talk about the theatre? Often if we meet a woman in the marketplace, we are disturbed. But you sit in your upper seat, where there is such an invitation to outrageous behaviour, and see a woman, a prostitute, entering bareheaded and with a complete lack of shame, dressed in golden garments, flirting coquettishly and singing harlots' songs with seductive tunes, and uttering disgraceful words. She behaves so shamelessly that if you watch her and give consideration, you will bow your head in shame. Do you dare to say you suffer no human reaction? Is your body made of stone? Or iron? I shall not refrain from saying the same things again. Surely you are not a better philosopher than those great and noble men, who were cast down merely by such a sight? Have you not heard what Solomon says: 'If someone walks onto a fire of coals, will he not burn his feet? If someone lights a fire in his lap, will he not burn his clothing? It is just the same for the man who goes to a woman that doesn't belong to him' [Proverbs 6.27–29]. For even if you did not have intimate relations with the prostitute, in your lust you coupled with her and you committed the sin in your mind. And it was not only at that time, but also when the theatre has closed, and the woman has gone away, her image remains in your soul, along with her words, her figure, her looks, her movement, her rhythm, and her distinctive and meretricious tunes; and having suffered countless wounds you go home. Is it not this that leads to the disruption of households? Is it not this that leads to the destruction of temperance, and the break-up of marriages? Is it not this that leads to wars and battles, and odious behaviour lacking any reason? For when, saturated with that woman, you return home as her captive, your wife appears more disagreeable, your children more burdensome, and your servants troublesome, and your house superfluous.

(John Chrysostom, *Against the Games and Theatres*)

Church services were thus an occasion for scriptural exegesis and moral exhortation. The development of the liturgy in turn made music and hymn-singing an important part of worship, and it was again during the fourth century that such practices became firmly established. Augustine of Hippo recorded the introduction of hymn-singing from the east into western churches while he was living in Milan in 386.

Greatly did I weep when I heard your hymns and canticles, deeply moved by the sweet-singing voices of your Church. The voices flowed into my ears and the truth was poured into my heart, so that my feelings of piety overflowed and my tears ran down, but they were tears of gladness. The Church of Milan had only recently begun to employ this form of consolation and exhortation, the brethren singing together with great earnestness of voice and heart. For it was only a year, or not much more, since Justina, the mother of the boy emperor Valentinian [Valentinian II (375–392)], had persecuted your servant Ambrose in the interests of the heresy into which she had been seduced by the Arians. The faithful people kept guard in the church, prepared to die with their bishop, your servant. My mother, your handmaid, was there and took a chief part in that period of vigilance, living a life of prayer. Although I was still not yet fired by the warmth of your Spirit, nevertheless I was stirred by the alarm and excitement of the city. It was at this time, following the manner of the eastern churches, that the singing of hymns and psalms was instituted, so that the people would not waste away in the tedium of their watch. This custom, retained down to the present, is now imitated by many and indeed almost all of your congregations throughout the world.

(Augustine of Hippo, *Confessions* 9.6–7)

A number of the hymns composed in the Later Roman period have remained in use in modern churches. The Christmas carol 'Of the Father's Love Begotten' is based upon the work of the Latin Christian poet Prudentius (348–c.413).

Of the Father's love begotten
ere the worlds began to be,
he is Alpha and Omega,
he the source, the ending he,
of the things that are, that have been,
and that future years shall see,
evermore and evermore.

O that birth for ever blessed,
when the Virgin, full of grace,
by the Holy Ghost conceiving,
bare the Saviour of our race,
and the babe, the world's Redeemer,
first revealed his sacred face,
evermore and evermore.

O ye heights of heaven, adore him;
angel hosts, his praises sing;
powers, dominions, bow before him,
and extol our God and King:
let no tongue on earth be silent,
every voice in concert ring,
evermore and evermore.

('Of the Father's Love Begotten', from Prudentius, *Liber Cathemerinon* 9)

The most famous Greek hymn in honour of the Virgin Mary, the Akathistos Hymn to the *Theotokos*, was probably composed in the sixth century and in tradition became associated with the defence of Constantinople against the Persians and Avars in 626.

Unto you, O *Theotokos*, invincible Champion, your City, in thanksgiving ascribes the victory for the deliverance from sufferings. And having your might unassailable, free us from all dangers, so that we may cry unto you:

Rejoice, O Bride Ever-Virgin.

The Archangel was sent from Heaven to cry 'Rejoice!' to the *Theotokos*. And beholding you, O Lord, taking bodily form, he stood in awe, and with his bodiless voice he cried aloud to her such things as these:

Rejoice, you through whom joy shall shine forth.
Rejoice, you whom the curse will vanish.
Rejoice, the Restoration of fallen Adam.
Rejoice, the Redemption of the tears of Eve.
Rejoice, O Height beyond human logic.
Rejoice, O depth invisible even to the eyes of Angels.
Rejoice, for you are the King's throne.
Rejoice, you bear Him, Who bears the universe.
Rejoice, O Star revealing the Sun.
Rejoice, O Womb of divine Incarnation.
Rejoice, you through whom creation is renewed.
Rejoice, you through whom the Creator is born a Babe.
Rejoice, O Bride Ever-Virgin.

(Akathistos Hymn)

The church service was the gathering place of the Christian community, in which the congregation came together in worship. To be a full member of that community, entitled to receive the bread and wine of the eucharist, required the initiation of the believer through the ritual of baptism.

John the baptizer appeared in the wilderness, proclaiming a baptism of repentance for the forgiveness of sins. And people from the whole Judean countryside and all the people of Jerusalem were going out to him and were baptized by him in the river Jordan, confessing their sins. Now John was clothed with camel's hair, with a leather belt around his waist, and he ate locusts and wild honey. He proclaimed, 'The one who is more powerful than I is coming after me; I am not worthy to stoop down and untie the thong of his sandals. I have baptized you with water; but he will baptize you with the Holy Spirit'. In those days Jesus came from Nazareth of Galilee and was baptized by John in the Jordan. And just as he was coming up out of the water, he saw the heavens torn apart and the Spirit descending like a dove on him. And a voice came from heaven, 'You are my Son, the Beloved; with you I am well pleased'.

(Mark 1.4–11)

In the early church, baptism marked both full membership in the body of Christ and the one remission of sins. There was ongoing debate over when a Christian should receive baptism, whether as an infant in a world where child mortality was high or as an adult able to understand the commitment to a Christian life. The North African Tertullian, writing around the year 200, condemned infant baptism in language which suggests that this practice was already widespread.

According to the circumstances and disposition and even age of each individual, the delay of baptism is preferable; especially, moreover, in the case of little children. For why is it necessary, if there really is no need, that the sponsors likewise should be thrust into danger who may themselves by reason of mortality fail to fulfil their promises or may be disappointed by the development of an evil disposition in those whom they represented? The Lord does indeed say, 'Forbid them not to come to me' [Matthew 19.14]. Let them come, then, while they are growing up; let them come while they are learning, while they are learning what they are coming to. Let them become Christians when they have become able to know Christ. Why does the innocent period of life hasten to the remission of sins? More caution would be exercised in worldly matters, should one who is not trusted with earthly substance be trusted with divine? Let them know how to ask for salvation, so that you may at least seem to have given to one who asks.

(Tertullian, *On Baptism* 18)

During the Late Roman period the rising flood of converts to Christianity raised new problems for the Church. Many Christians, like the emperor Constantine, preferred to defer their baptism until close to their deaths to gain the utmost benefit from the remission of their sins. Others sought immediate initiation into the Church, for motives which varied widely. In the first three centuries, while Christians were an illegal and at times persecuted minority, there was little cause to doubt the commitment of those who professed themselves believers. But in the fourth century, imperial patronage of the Church made conversion attractive for more worldly reasons. In order to ensure that converts understood the commitment involved in accepting baptism, the fourth-century Church placed strong emphasis on the catechumenate in which candidates for baptism received instruction in the Christian faith and preparation for the ritual itself. The most influential surviving texts for the education of catechumens are the *Catechetical Lectures* attributed to Cyril of Jerusalem (bishop c.350–387). In the *Procatechesis* (Prologue) to his lectures, Cyril cautioned those who sought baptism on false pretences.

We, the ministers of Christ, have admitted everyone, and occupying as it were the place of door-keepers, we have left the door open. Possibly you have entered with your soul bemired with sins, and with a will defiled. You entered, and were allowed; your name was inscribed. Tell me, do you behold this venerable constitution of the Church? Do you view her order and discipline, the reading of Scriptures, the presence of the ordained, the course of instruction? Be abashed at the place, and be taught by what you see. Go out opportunely now, and enter most opportunely tomorrow. If the fashion of your soul is avarice, put on another fashion and come in. Put off your former fashion, cloak it not up. Put off, I pray you, fornication and uncleanness, and put on the brightest robe of chastity. This charge I give you, before Jesus the Bridegroom of souls, come in and see their fashions. A long notice is allowed you; you have forty days for repentance. You have full opportunity both to put off and wash, and to put on and enter. If you persist in an evil purpose, then the speaker is blameless but you must not look for grace, for the water will receive you but the Spirit will not accept you. If anyone is conscious of his wound, let him take the salve; if any has fallen, let him arise. Let there be no Simon [Magus] among you, no hypocrisy, no idle curiosity about the matter. Possibly too you have come on another pretext. It is possible that a man is wishing to pay court to a woman, and came hither on that account. The remark applies in like manner to women also in their turn. A slave also perhaps wishes to please his master, and a friend his friend. I accept this bait for the hook and welcome you, though you came with an evil purpose, yet as one to be saved by a good hope. Perhaps you knew not whither you were coming, nor in what kind of net you are taken. You have come within the Church's nets: be taken alive and flee not. Jesus is angling for you, not in order to kill but by killing to make you alive, for you must die and rise again.

(Cyril of Jerusalem, *Procatechesis* 4–5)

The *Catechetical Lectures* were delivered at Lent, culminating in the baptism ceremony that took place at Easter. After the *Procatechesis*, Cyril gave a further eighteen lectures to the catechumens, followed by five mystagogical lectures in Easter week in which baptism is depicted as an imitation of the life of Christ.

Now that you have been 'baptized into Christ' and have 'put on Christ' [Galatians 3.27], you have become conformed to the Son of God. For God 'destined us for adoption as His children' [Ephesians 1.5], so He has made us like to the 'glorious body of Christ' [Philippians 3.21]. Having therefore become 'partakers of Christ' [Hebrews 3.14], you are properly called Christs or anointed ones, and of you God said, 'Touch not my anointed ones' [Psalm 105.15]. Now you have been made anointed ones by receiving the sign of the Holy Spirit; and all things have been wrought in you by imitation because you are images of Christ. He bathed in the river Jordan, and having invested the waters with the fragrance of His Godhead, He came up from them and the Holy Spirit in the fullness of His being lighted on Him, like resting upon like. And to you in the same manner, after you had come up from the pool of the sacred streams, you were anointed in a manner corresponding with Christ's anointing. This is the Holy Spirit, of whom the blessed Isaiah spoke when he prophesied in the person of the Lord, 'The Spirit of the Lord is upon me, because He has anointed me; He has sent me to preach glad tidings to the poor' [Isaiah 61.1].

(Cyril of Jerusalem, *Mystagogical Lectures* 3.1)

In his *Catechetical Lectures*, Cyril of Jerusalem addressed himself to adults. Over the course of the Later Roman period, however, infant baptism became established as the normal practice of the Church. In the west, this development was shaped particularly by the teachings of Augustine of Hippo, who insisted upon the doctrine of original sin and therefore the need for all humanity, even otherwise guiltless infants, to receive divine grace. Augustine's arguments have been criticized by some modern commentators, but they exerted enormous influence upon medieval western Christianity.

What can be plainer than the many weighty testimonies of the divine declarations, which afford to us the clearest proof possible that without union with Christ there is no man who can attain to eternal life and salvation; and that no man can unjustly be damned – that is, separated from that life and salvation – by the judgment of God? The inevitable conclusion from these truths is this, that, as nothing else is effected when infants are baptized except that they are incorporated into the Church, in other words, that they are united with the body and members of Christ, unless this benefit has been bestowed upon them, they are manifestly in danger of damnation. Damned, however, they could not be if they really had no sin. Now, since their tender age could not possibly have contracted sin in its own life, it remains for us, even if we are as yet unable to understand, at least to believe that infants inherit original sin.

And therefore, if there is an ambiguity in the Apostle's words when he says, 'By one man sin entered into the world, and death by sin; and so it passed upon all men' [Romans 5.12]; and if it is possible for them to be drawn aside and applied to some other sense, then is there anything ambiguous in this statement: 'Unless a man be born again of water and of the Spirit, he cannot enter into the kingdom of God' [John 3.5]? Is this, again, ambiguous: 'You shall call His name Jesus, for He shall save His people from their sins' [Matthew 1.21]? Is there any doubt of what this means: 'The healthy need not a physician, but they that are sick' [Matthew 9.12]? – that is, Jesus is not needed by those who have no sin, but by those who are to be saved from sin. Is there anything, again, ambiguous in this: 'Unless men eat the flesh of the Son of man', that is, become partakers of His body, 'they shall not have life' [from John 6.53]? By these and similar statements, which I now pass over – absolutely clear in the light of God, and absolutely certain by His authority – does not truth proclaim without ambiguity, that unbaptized infants not only cannot enter into the kingdom of God but cannot have everlasting life, unless in the body of Christ, in order that they may be incorporated into which they are washed in the sacrament of baptism? Does not truth, without any doubt, testify that for no other reason are they carried by pious hands to Jesus (that is, to Christ, the Saviour and Physician), than that they may be healed of the plague of their sin by the medicine of His sacraments?

(Augustine of Hippo, *On Merit and the Forgiveness of Sins,*
and the Baptism of Infants 3.7–8)

The transformation of Christian worship in the fourth and fifth centuries extended far beyond the confines of the church service and the baptismal ritual. As Christianity became a dominant influence on all aspects of Late Roman society, so the very rhythms of the calendar were reshaped according to Christian values. Sunday as the holy day of rest was already enshrined in the legislation of Constantine (see Chapter 4). The focal point of the Christian year was the festival of Easter, at which baptisms were performed and the life and death of Christ were celebrated. The correct dating of Easter was a recurring subject of controversy in the early Church, and at the great Council of Nicaea in 325 this was regarded as an issue no less crucial than the doctrine of the Trinity. In the letter that Constantine circulated after the council, the emperor proclaimed the importance of the feast, the need for unity, and the error of dating Easter according to the Jewish reckoning of the Passover.

In a case of such importance and respecting such a religious festival, a discordant judgment must be wrong. Our Saviour left us one feast in commemoration of the day of our deliverance, I mean the day of His most holy passion, and He has willed that His catholic Church should be one. Its members may be scattered in many and diverse places, yet they are cherished by the one pervasive spirit, that is by the will of God. But let your Holiness' good sense reflect how grievous and scandalous it is that on the same days some should be engaged in fasting and others in festive enjoyment; and again, that after the days of Easter some should be attending banquets and amusements while others are fulfilling the appointed fasts. It is, therefore, as I assume you all see clearly, plainly the will of divine providence that this practice should receive fitting correction and be reduced to one uniform rule. Since it was thus necessary for this matter to be rectified so that we might have nothing in common with that nation of parricides who slew their Lord, and since an arrangement consistent with propriety is already observed by all the churches of the western, southern, and northern parts of the world, and by some of the eastern also, for these reasons all are unanimous on this present occasion in thinking it worthy of adoption. And I myself have undertaken that this decision should meet with the approval of your Good Sense, in the hope that your Prudence will gladly embrace that practice which is observed at once in the city of Rome, in Italy and all Africa, in Egypt, in the Spains, the Gauls, the Britains, the Libyas, in the whole of Greece, and in the dioceses of Asia, Pontus, and Cilicia with entire harmony of will. And you will consider not only that the number of churches is far greater in the regions I have enumerated than in any other, but also that it is most fitting that all should hold in common that which sound reason appears to demand, and to avoid any participation in the perjured conduct of the Jews.

(Constantine, *Letter to the churches*, quoted in Eusebius of Caesarea, *Life of Constantine* 3.18–19)

Differences over the dating of Easter still remained (and have remained to the present day), but the festival's pre-eminence in the Christian calendar was never challenged. Gregory of Nazianzus captured perfectly just what the death and resurrection of Christ meant for the Late Roman Christian.

> Yesterday I was crucified with Christ; today I am glorified with Him. Yesterday I died with Him; today I am brought to life with Him. Yesterday I was buried with Him; today I rise with Him.
>
> (Gregory of Nazianzus, *Oration* 1.4)

Easter's pre-eminence may have been unchallenged, but the Later Roman period did see the emergence of new festivals throughout the Christian year. Many commemorated the apostles and martyrs, or notable episodes in the lives of Christ and the Virgin Mary. For the subsequent history of both Christianity and the western world, the most significant of these new festivals was without question Christmas. No evidence from before the fourth century suggests that Christ's birth was celebrated on 25 December. In the early Church, the traditional date was 6 January, which became the feast of Epiphany. The winter solstice was 25 December, and in the third century was hailed as the birthday of the Unconquered Sun, Sol Invictus. The first explicit reference to a Christian significance for that date occurs in an illustrated calendar from Rome known as the *Codex-Calendar of 354*. This calendar has two entries under 25 December:

> *N(atalis) Invicti* (the birthday of the Unconquered Sun)
> *Natus Christus in Bethleem Judeae* (Christ was born in Bethlehem of Judaea)

The commemoration of Christ's birth on 25 December thus appears to have originated in the west, in part to provide a Christian counterpart to the birthday of the Sun. Christmas also drew on elements of the popular celebration of the Saturnalia (recorded under 17 December in the *Codex-Calendar of 354*). In the course of the fourth century, the new festival then spread to the east, where it faced resistance from those who preferred the traditional date of 6 January. John Chrysostom, preaching in Antioch in 386, reports that Christmas had only reached the city within the last ten years. Indeed, John felt it necessary to rally support for the festival in a homily he gave in honour of Philogonius, an earlier bishop of Antioch, on 20 December.

> A feast is approaching which is the most solemn and awe-inspiring of all feasts. If one were to call it the metropolis of all feasts, one wouldn't be wrong. What is it? The birth of Christ according to the flesh. In this feast namely Epiphany, holy Easter, Ascension and Pentecost have their beginning and their purpose. For if Christ hadn't been born according to the flesh, He wouldn't have been baptized, which is Epiphany. He wouldn't have been crucified, which is Easter. He wouldn't have sent the Spirit, which is Pentecost. So from this event, as from some spring, different rivers flow – these feasts of ours are born. But not only on this account would it be right to give precedence to this day, but also because what happened on it is much more awe-inspiring than all other days. I say this because the fact that Christ died after becoming human was the consequence of that: even if He didn't commit sin, still He assumed a mortal body. And that too was an amazing fact: that, although God, He was willing to become human and to condescend to take so much on Himself that not even the imagination can embrace. It's this that's most awe-inspiring, and completely perplexing.
>
> (John Chrysostom, *Concerning Blessed Philogonius*)

By the end of the Late Roman period, Christmas was firmly established in the Christian calendar in east and west alike. There was one further Late Roman development, however, that has exerted no less an influence upon subsequent history. In the sixth century, yet another controversy arose over calculating the date of Easter. A monk by the name of Dionysius Exiguus prepared a new table of Easter dates in 525, and in doing so came to a far-reaching conclusion. The existing Easter tables numbered the passing years from the reign of Diocletian, remembered as the instigator of the Great Persecution. Dionysius preferred to calculate the years from the Incarnation of Christ. As he explained to the contemporary bishop Petronius:

> We, rather than beginning from the 248th year of that tyrant, have refused to tie to our cycles the memory of that impious persecutor; but we have chosen instead to designate the periods of the years from the Incarnation of our Lord Jesus Christ: in so far as the beginning of our hope would be more obvious to us, and

> the cause of human salvation, that is, the passion of our Redeemer, might shine
> more clearly.
>
> (Dionysius Exiguus, *Letter to Petronius* 20)

Dionysius' formula proved an unqualified success, and was eventually adopted across the western world. Although his 'year of the Incarnation' was slightly cumbersome, and so later generations followed Bede and preferred *anno domini*: 'in the year of the Lord'.

Copyright Acknowledgements

Further Reading

K. Aland, *Did the Early Church Baptize Infants?* (London 1963)
P. F. Bradshaw, *Early Christian Worship: A Basic Introduction to Ideas and Practice* (London 1996)
T. K. Carroll, *Preaching the Word* (Wilmington, Delaware 1984)
G. Dix, *The Shape of the Liturgy* (London 1945)
J. W. Drijvers, *Cyril of Jerusalem: Bishop and City* (Leiden 2004)
M. Dujarier, *A History of the Catechumenate: The First Six Centuries* (New York 1979)

D. Dunn-Wilson, *A Mirror for the Church: Preaching in the First Five Centuries* (Grand Rapids and Cambridge 2005)

E. Foley, *Foundations of Christian Music: The Music of Pre-Constantinian Christianity* (Bramcote 1992)

R. C. D. Jasper and G. J. Cuming, *Prayers of the Eucharist: Early and Reformed*, 3rd revised edition (Collegeville, Minn. 1990)

J. Jeremias, *Infant Baptism in the First Four Centuries*, translated by D. Cairns (London 1960)

W. Mayer and P. Allen, *John Chrysostom* (London and New York 2000)

L. M. McDonald, *The Formation of the Christian Biblical Canon*, revised edition (Peabody 1995)

B. M. Metzger, *The Canon of the New Testament: its Origin, Development, and Significance* (Oxford 1987)

A. A. Mosshammer, *The Easter computus and the Origins of the Christian era* (Oxford 2008)

D. E. Smith, *From Symposium to Eucharist: the Banquet in the Early Christian World* (Minneapolis 2003)

E. Werner, *The Sacred Bridge: The Interdependence of Liturgy and Music in Synagogue and Church during the First Millennium*, 2 volumes (New York 1959–1984)

E. C. Whitaker, *Documents of the Baptismal Liturgy*, 2nd edition (London 1970)

D. F. Wright, *What Has Infant Baptism Done to Baptism? An Enquiry at the End of Christendom* (Milton Keynes 2005)

8

The Ecclesiastical Hierarchy

The first Christian communities were guided by the apostles who had known the living Christ. With the passing of the apostles, and then of the generation whom the apostles had taught, the early Christians faced a crisis of leadership. The Second Coming had not arrived. Who would now guide the congregations, teach the new converts, and impose discipline on those in error? The books of the New Testament refer to *episkopoi* ('overseers', bishops), *presbuteroi* ('elders', presbyters) and *diakonoi* ('servants', deacons). But there is no sense of an established clerical hierarchy with clearly defined titles and functions. Only gradually did the organized clergy of later centuries emerge, with the crucial formative period once again in the years on either side of Constantine's conversion.

Within the New Testament, the most explicit statement of what was expected of an *episkopos* occurs in 1 Timothy, one of the three Pastoral Epistles (1–2 Timothy and Titus). Although attributed to Paul, these three letters were written several decades after Paul's death, probably in the early or mid-second century. The author of 1 Timothy exalted the bishop more as a moral exemplar than as a spiritual leader.

Whoever aspires to the office of bishop (*episkopos*) desires a noble task. Now a bishop must be above reproach, married only once, temperate, sensible, respectable, hospitable, an apt teacher, not a drunkard, not violent but gentle, not quarrelsome, and not a lover of money. He must manage his own household well, keeping his children submissive and respectful in every way – for if someone does not know how to manage his own household, how can he take care of God's church? He must not be a recent convert, or he may be puffed up with conceit and fall into the condemnation of the Devil. Moreover, he must be well thought of by outsiders, so that he may not fall into disgrace and the snare of the Devil.

(1 Timothy 3.1–7)

When the Pastoral Epistles were composed, the status of the bishop was still open to debate. Approximately contemporary to the author of 1 Timothy was Ignatius of Antioch, who was martyred in Rome under the emperor Trajan in c.115. In a series of letters written as he travelled to meet his fate, Ignatius composed the earliest extant defence of what would become known as the monarchical episcopate, a single bishop at the head of each individual Christian community. The bishop must still set an example of Christian conduct, as in 1 Timothy. For Ignatius, however, the bishop was also responsible for spiritual, pastoral and liturgical leadership. Presbyters and deacons were clearly defined as subordinate clergy, and only through the bishop could his community share in the wider Church of Christ.

Follow, all of you, the bishop, as Jesus Christ does the Father; and follow the presbytery as you would the apostles. Moreover, reverence the deacons as the commandment of God. Let no man do anything pertaining to the Church without the bishop. Let that be considered a valid eucharist which is [administered] either by the bishop or by one to whom he has entrusted it. Wherever the bishop appears, there let the people be, even as wherever Christ Jesus is, there is the catholic Church. It is not lawful without the bishop either to baptize or to celebrate a love-feast. But whatsoever he approves, that also is well-pleasing to God, so that everything that is done may be secure and valid.

(Ignatius, *Letter to the Smyrnaeans* 8.1–2)

We must not assume that Ignatius necessarily represented the views of all or even the majority of the Christians of his time. The first Christian communities varied widely, and that original diversity only gave way slowly to the later principle of 'one community, one bishop'. Nevertheless, in the course of the second and third centuries the monarchical bishop gradually became the dominant institution of the early Church. Episcopal leadership helped Christianity to maintain a common faith and a common moral life, and to survive the periodic outbreaks of persecution. Cyprian of Carthage (bishop 249–258), celebrated the bishop's role in preserving the Church's unity.

This unity we ought firmly to hold and maintain, especially those of us who are bishops presiding in the Church, that we may also prove the episcopate itself to be one and undivided. Let no one deceive the brotherhood by falsehood; let no one corrupt the truth of the faith by a faithless treachery. The episcopate is one; it is a whole in which each bishop enjoys full possession. The Church likewise is one, though she is spread abroad and multiplies with the increase of her progeny: even as the sun has many rays, yet one light; and the tree has many branches, yet one strength seated in the deep-lodged root; and as when many streams flow down from one source, though a multiplicity of waters seems to be diffused from the bountifulness of the overflowing abundance, yet unity is still preserved in the source itself. Separate a ray of the sun from its orb, and its unity forbids this division of light; break a branch from the tree, once broken it can bud no more; cut off the stream from its fountain, and that which is cut off dries up. Thus the Church, flooded with the light of the Lord, sheds forth her rays through the whole world, yet it is one light which is spread upon all places, nor is the unity of the body separated.

(Cyprian of Carthage, *On the Unity of the catholic Church* 5)

By the end of the third century, the clerical hierarchy was well established. A single bishop headed the Christian community in each city, served in turn by presbyters and then deacons. Bishops communicated with each other by letters and, when matters arose that one bishop could not handle alone, gathered in councils for debate. The bishops themselves were public figures and were targeted for special persecution under Valerian in 257–260, when Cyprian died, and during Diocletian's Great Persecution. A hierarchy also emerged within the episcopate, and despite the tensions between the Church and the empire that hierarchy increasingly mirrored the structure of Roman provincial government. In each province the chief bishop was the metropolitan, the bishop of the provincial capital. He presided over local disputes and oversaw episcopal appointments in his province. The greatest bishops presided over the most important cities: Antioch, Alexandria, and of course Rome.

The reality was not as clear-cut as this simplified overview might suggest. Local communities still held to their own peculiar customs and the authority of individual bishops was often contested. But when Constantine offered his support to Christianity from 312 onwards the essential pattern of ecclesiastical power was already established. Imperial patronage in turn reinforced the emerging hierarchy. At the Council of Nicaea in 325, a series of canons laid down the rights of metropolitan bishops, confirmed the prestige of the greatest sees, and reasserted the hierarchy of bishops, presbyters and deacons.

(4) It is by all means proper that a bishop should be appointed by all the bishops in the province; but should this be difficult, either on account of urgent necessity or because of distance, three at least should meet together, with those who are absent also giving their approval and their consent in writing, and then the ordination should take place. But in every province the ratification of what is done should be left to the metropolitan.

(6) Let the ancient customs in Egypt, Libya and Pentapolis prevail, that the bishop of Alexandria has authority over all these places. For this is also customary for the bishop of Rome. Likewise in Antioch and the other provinces, let the churches retain their privileges. And this is to be universally understood, that if anyone be made a bishop without the consent of the metropolitan, the great Synod has declared that such a man ought not to be a bishop. If, however, two or three bishops shall from love of contradiction oppose the common choice of the rest, it being a reasonable one and in accordance with the ecclesiastical canons, then let the choice of the majority prevail.

(7) Since custom and ancient tradition have prevailed that the bishop of Aelia [Jerusalem] should be honoured, let him have his proper honour, saving its due dignity to the metropolis [Caesarea].

(18) It has come to the knowledge of the holy Synod that, in certain districts and cities, the deacons administer the eucharist to the presbyters, whereas neither canon nor custom permits that they who have no authority to offer should give the Body of Christ to those who do offer. And this also has been made known, that some of the deacons now receive the eucharist even before the bishops. Let all such practices be utterly done away, and let the deacons remain within their proper bounds, knowing that they are the ministers of the bishop and inferior to the presbyters. Let them receive the eucharist according to their order, after the presbyters, and let either the bishop or the presbyter administer it to them. Furthermore, let not the deacons sit among the presbyters, for that is contrary to canon and due order. And if, after this decree, anyone shall refuse to obey, let him be deposed from the diaconate.

(Canons of the Council of Nicaea)

The Nicene canons bear witness both to the diversity that still existed within early fourth-century Christianity and to the efforts of the new imperial Church to impose uniformity. Those efforts were never entirely successful, and the issues raised at Nicaea continued to be debated at later councils. The hierarchy within the clergy, from deacon to presbyter to bishop, was now almost universally accepted. But the authority of the metropolitans and particularly of the pre-eminent sees was more controversial. Canon 7 at Nicaea acknowledged the status of the bishop of Aelia, as Jerusalem was then known. But the metropolitan of that province was the bishop of Palestinian Caesarea, who in 325 was the historian Eusebius. The rivalry between Jerusalem and Caesarea was only resolved in 451 when the Council of Chalcedon recognized Jerusalem's superiority. Constantinople's foundation five years after the Council of Nicaea posed a still greater challenge. In 381 the Council of Constantinople affirmed the status of the bishop of the new imperial city:

The bishop of Constantinople shall have the primacy of honour after the bishop of Rome, because Constantinople is new Rome.

(Council of Constantinople, canon 3)

This claim led to conflict alike with Rome and with Constantinople's eastern rivals Alexandria and Antioch. Over the following century, however, the bishops of these four cities together with Jerusalem acquired authority as the five patriarchs of the late-antique Church, later termed the Pentarchy.

Ecclesiastical politics was merely one of the many roles that a bishop had to play. Within his church, he was a preacher and teacher, responsible for the celebration of the liturgy, the imposition of penance, and the charitable care of his congregation. As a prominent social leader, he was also now a central figure in civic administration and an important source of wealth and patronage. The bishop represented the local community in the great councils and before imperial officials, and potentially even before the emperor. These increasing responsibilities led to new debates over how episcopal leadership should be held and exercised. The concern for moral leadership already emphasized in 1 Timothy remained strong as bishops and lesser clergy struggled with the need to reconcile their spiritual and worldly duties.

Famous bishops were held up as ideals for emulation. In 380, Gregory of Nazianzus offered an oration in honour of Athanasius of Alexandria, who had died in 373:

The duties of his office he discharged in the same spirit as that in which he had been preferred to it ... He was sublime in action, lowly in mind; inaccessible in virtue, most accessible in intercourse; gentle, free from anger, sympathetic, sweet in words, sweeter in disposition; angelic in appearance, more angelic in mind; calm in rebuke, persuasive in praise, without spoiling the good effect of either by excess, but rebuking with the tenderness of a father, praising with the dignity of a ruler, his tenderness was not dissipated, nor his severity sour; for the one was reasonable, the other prudent, and both truly wise; his disposition sufficed for the training of his spiritual children, with very little need of words, his words with very little need of the rod, and his moderate use of the rod with still less for the knife.

(Gregory of Nazianzus, *Oration* 21.9, On the Great Athanasius)

A number of Church leaders also composed treatises reflecting upon their duties for the inspiration of themselves and others. John Chrysostom, the future bishop of Constantinople, wrote his work *On the Priesthood* while himself a priest in Antioch in the 380s. He warned his fellow clergy against the 'wild beasts', the vices that threatened their virtue.

Do you ask what those wild beasts are? They are wrath, despondency, envy, strife, slanders, accusations, falsehood, hypocrisy, intrigues, anger against those who have done no harm, pleasure at the indecorous acts of fellow ministers, sorrow at their prosperity, love of praise, desire of honour (which indeed most of all drives the human soul headlong to perdition), doctrines devised to please, servile flatteries, ignoble fawning, contempt of the poor, paying court to the rich, senseless and mischievous honours, favours attended with danger both to those who offer and those who accept them, sordid fear suited only to the basest of slaves, the abolition of plain speaking, a great affectation of humility but banishment of truth, the suppression of convictions and reproofs or rather the excessive use of them against the poor, while against those who are invested with power no one dare open his lips.

(John Chrysostom, *On the Priesthood* 3.9)

The duty of the priest was to protect his congregation, just as a shepherd watches over his flock. To guide sheep, however, is an easier task than to guide wayward humanity:

The shepherds with great authority compel the sheep to receive the remedy when they do not willingly submit to it. For it is easy to bind them when cautery or cutting is required, and to keep them inside the fold for a long time, whenever it is expedient, and to bring them one kind of food instead of another, and to cut them off from their supplies of water, and all other things which the shepherds may decide to be conducive to their health they perform with great ease. But in the case of human infirmities, it is not easy in the first place for a man to discern them, for no man 'knows the things of a man, save the spirit of man which is in him' [1 Corinthians 2.11]. How then can anyone apply the remedy for the disease of which he does not know the character, often indeed being unable to understand it even should he happen to sicken with it himself? And even when it becomes manifest, it causes him yet more trouble: for it is not possible to doctor all men with the same authority with which the shepherd treats his sheep. For in this case also it is necessary to bind and to restrain from food, and to use cautery or the knife: but the reception of the treatment depends on the will of the patient, not of him who applies the remedy.

(John Chrysostom, *On the Priesthood* 2.2–3)

Chrysostom's older contemporary Ambrose of Milan (bishop 374–397) offered similar advice to a Latin-speaking audience. In *On the Duties of the Clergy*, written in 388/9, Ambrose too emphasized the morality required of those who hold priestly office and the need for harmony among priests as well as between the priest and the congregation:

One should strive to win preferment, especially in the Church, only by good actions and with a right aim; so that there may be no proud conceit, no idle carelessness, no shameful disposition of mind, no unseemly ambition. A plain simplicity of mind is enough for everything, and commends itself quite sufficiently. When in office, again, it is not right to be harsh and severe, yet nor may one be too easy; lest on the one hand we should seem to be exercising a despotic power, and on the other to be by no means filling the office we had taken up.

Never protect a wicked man, nor allow the sacred things to be given over to an unworthy one; on the other hand, do not harass and press hard on a man whose fault is not clearly proved. Injustice quickly gives offence in every case, but especially in the Church, where equity ought to exist, where like treatment should be given to all, so that a powerful person may not claim the more, nor a rich man appropriate the more. For whether we be poor or rich, we are one in

> Christ. Let him that lives a holier life claim nothing more thereby for himself; for
> he ought rather to be the more humble for it.
>
> (Ambrose of Milan, *On the Duties of the Clergy* 2.24.119–120 and 124)

This tension between the reality of clerical power and the spiritual and moral standards expected of those who hold divine office has remained throughout the Church's history. The fourth century was a crucial formative age, as Christianity first came to terms with its new status as the dominant religion of the Roman world. Gregory of Nazianzus and Athanasius, John Chrysostom and Ambrose were remembered as 'fathers of the Church', men whose lives and writings offered models to guide the clergy of subsequent generations. Yet those models were constantly reinterpreted as circumstances changed, for each new generation faced its own challenges and priests too had to move with the times.

By the late fourth century, the bishop was an established figure within the elite of an increasingly Christian Roman empire. But in the fifth century the empire in the west collapsed. For the clergy, the breakdown of imperial authority made them vulnerable but the rise of the Germanic kingdoms opened new opportunities to redefine their roles. One example was the career of Sidonius Apollinaris, bishop of Clermont-Ferrand in Gaul from 470 or 472 until 489. A leading aristocrat and the son-in-law of former emperor Avitus (455–456), Sidonius in the 470s found himself living under Visigothic rule. His vision of the ideal bishop for these changing times was laid down in an oration that Sidonius delivered in Bourges to justify his nomination of his friend Simplicius as the bishop of that city:

> I testify that in the man whom I have chosen as suited for your needs I have
> considered neither money nor influence; I have weighed to the last scruple every
> circumstance affecting his own person; the times in which we live, the respective
> needs of city and province, and I decide that the man most fitted for this office is
> he whose career I shall now briefly relate. He is Simplicius, on whom a blessing
> already rests. Hitherto a member of your order, but henceforth of ours, if God
> approve him through your voices, he answers by conduct and profession, so well
> satisfying the claims of both, that the State will find in him one to admire and the
> Church one to love. If birth is still to command respect, as the Evangelist teaches
> (for St. Luke, beginning his eulogy of St. John, considers it of the highest moment
> that he sprang from a line of priestly tradition, and exalts the importance of his
> family before celebrating the nobility of his life), I will recall the fact that his

relatives have presided alike over the Church and the tribunal. His family has been distinguished in either career by many bishops and prefects; it had become almost their hereditary privilege to administer the divine and human laws.

Turning to his age, we find that he has at once the vigour of youth and the caution of maturity; comparing his talents with his acquirements, we see nature and learning rivalling each other. If we ask whether he is given to hospitality, we find him generous to a fault, lavishing his substance on all men small and great, whether they are clerics, laymen, or strangers, and entertaining those most of all who are least likely to return his kindness. When an embassy had to be undertaken, more than once he has represented his city, before barbaric kings in furs or Roman emperors in purple.

He is a man constant in adversity, loyal in danger, unassuming in prosperity; of simple tastes in dress, affable in conversation, never putting himself forward among his friends, but in discussion easily the first. A friendship of which he knows the worth he will pursue with ardour, hold with constancy, and never abandon; on the other hand, a declared hostility he pursues with honourable frankness, not believing in it till the last moment, and laying it down at the earliest. Extremely accessible just because he seeks nothing for himself, he desired not so much to assume the priesthood as to prove himself worthy to hold it.

(Sidonius Apollinaris, *Letter* 7.9.15–22 (abridged))

Sidonius' ideal bishop still required the qualities expected of clergy in previous centuries. He was a moral exemplar and teacher, who guided his congregation in both behaviour and doctrine. But the changing world of the fifth century also required bishops to meet new standards. Sidonius hailed his friend Simplicius for the nobility of his birth and the respect he received from the State no less than from the Church. Increasing wealth and social status made hospitality and charity ever more important episcopal duties, and a bishop had to be comfortable before Germanic kings as well as Roman emperors. It was this balance of spiritual and secular obligations that shaped the many roles that bishops played in the medieval age.

The collapse of western imperial power had still further implications for the bishop of the greatest city in the west: Rome. During the early Christian centuries, the Roman church was exalted due to the city's status as the heart of the empire and Rome's association with the leading apostles Peter and Paul. But the term *papas* ('father', Pope) was not yet used in a special sense to designate the bishop of Rome, and the Roman church possessed only a shadow of the prestige of the medieval 'Papal Monarchy'.

According to Christ's words to Peter, quoted in Matthew's Gospel:

> You are Peter, and on this rock I will build my church, and the gates of Hades will not prevail against it. I will give you the keys of the kingdom of heaven, and whatever you bind on earth will be bound in heaven, and whatever you loose on earth will be loosed in heaven.
>
> (Matthew 16.18–19)

The first bishop of Rome to invoke this verse to reinforce his authority as Peter's heir was Stephen (bishop 254–257). However, Stephen's assertion of primacy was rejected by his contemporary Cyprian of Carthage, who insisted upon the equality of all bishops in his work *On the Unity of the catholic Church* quoted earlier. Tension over Rome's standing within the Church increased as Christianity expanded following Constantine's conversion. The bishop of Rome was universally recognized as possessing special status, as was confirmed in 325 by the sixth canon of the Council of Nicaea. But any Roman claim to leadership over the wider Church was highly controversial. During the Trinitarian doctrinal debates a number of eastern bishops in exile appealed to Rome for aid, notably Athanasius of Alexandria. The right of Rome's bishop to hear such appeals was affirmed by the Western Council of Serdica in 343:

> If any bishop has had judgement passed upon him in any case, and considers himself to have good reason for judgement being given afresh upon it, if you agree, let us honour the memory of the most holy apostle Peter; let there be written letters to the Roman bishop either by those who tried the case or by the bishops who live in the neighbouring province. If he decide that judgement be given afresh, let it be given afresh, and let him appoint judges. If, however, he is of the opinion that the case is such that what was done should not be reviewed, then the decision shall hold.
>
> (Western Council of Serdica, canon 3c)

The bishops who approved this canon represented the Latin-speaking churches of the west, and only a handful of eastern bishops were present (including Athanasius). The majority of Greek-speaking Christians did not recognize Rome's right to hear appeals. While the eastern Christians openly attributed to Rome a primacy of honour, this did not extend to any acknowledgement of practical jurisdiction. And even in the west, Roman authority in the late fourth century was challenged by the holders of other powerful sees such as Ambrose of Milan.

Ambrose's contemporary as Roman bishop was Damasus (366–384). Described by his enemies as the *auriscalpius matronarum* ('the ladies' ear-tickler'), Damasus' most significant legacy was his patronage of Jerome's Vulgate Bible translation. But his career also highlighted the new social prominence of the bishop within the city of Rome. His entry in the sixth-century *Liber Pontificalis* (*Book of Pontiffs*), a collection of biographies of the early Roman bishops, records his achievements:

> He built two basilicas: one to St Laurence close to the Theatre and the other on the Via Ardeatina where he is buried. At the Catacombs, the place where lay the bodies of the apostles St Peter and St Paul, he [dedicated and] adorned with verses the actual tablet at the place where the holy bodies lay. He searched for and discovered many bodies of holy martyrs, and also proclaimed their [acts] in verses. He issued a decree about the church. He was maliciously accused on a charge of adultery, [but] when a synod was held he was cleared by 44 bishops.
>
> (*Liber Pontificalis* 39.2–3)

By Damasus' episcopate the Roman bishop was unquestionably a prominent figure in both the imperial Church and elite society. In the ironic words of the fourth-century senator Vettius Agorius Praetextatus:

> Make me bishop of Rome, and I will become a Christian at once.
>
> (quoted in Jerome, *Against John of Jerusalem* 8)

Yet it was only in the fifth and sixth centuries that the Roman church began to lay solid foundations for the rise of the medieval papacy. Much of the credit for this achievement rests with two men, each of whom received the title 'the great' from later generations: Leo (bishop 440–461) and Gregory (bishop 590–604).

Leo was one of the few late-antique bishops of Rome to play a central role in the eastern doctrinal controversies, and his *Tome* was upheld as a statement of orthodoxy at the Council of Chalcedon in 451 (see Chapter 19). He was also a great preacher, who placed renewed emphasis on Rome's status as the city of Peter and Paul:

Besides that reverence which today's festival [June 29, the Feast of Peter and Paul] has gained from all the world, it is to be honoured with special and peculiar exultation in our city, that there may be a predominance of gladness on the day of their martyrdom in the place where the chief of the apostles met their glorious end. For these are the men through whom the light of Christ's gospel shone on you, O Rome, and through whom you, who were the teacher of error, were made the disciple of Truth. These are the holy fathers and true shepherds, who gave you claims to be numbered among the heavenly kingdoms, and built you under much better and happier auspices than they by whose zeal the first foundations of your walls were laid, and of whom the one that gave you your name [Romulus] defiled you with his brother's blood. These are they who promoted you to such glory, that being made a holy nation, a chosen people, a priestly and royal state, and the head of the world through the blessed Peter's holy See you did attain a wider sway by the worship of God than by earthly government.

(Leo the Great, *Sermon* 82.1)

In the vacuum of authority created by the decline of imperial power in the west, it was Leo who took responsibility for the defence of Rome.

For the sake of the Roman name he undertook an embassy and travelled to the king of the Huns, Attila by name, and he delivered the whole of Italy from the peril of the enemy.

(*Liber Pontificalis* 47.7)

After Leo's death, the disappearance of the last western emperor in 476 further strengthened the Roman bishops as the spiritual successors to the empire. By the 590s, Gregory not only led the Roman church but had taken over many of the roles once played by the Roman emperors. He was responsible for the grain supply that fed Rome, and defended the city from imperial and Germanic pressure. Gregory also exerted significant influence throughout the western Church, most famously through the missionary conversion of Britain (see Chapter 17).

The career of Gregory the Great witnessed a high-water mark in the early history of the Roman see, and laid the foundations for later Popes. Despite their emerging claims to superior authority, however, the bishops of Rome were still expected to fulfil the same roles as other members of the episcopate. Gregory placed great weight upon his responsibilities as the moral and spiritual guide of his community. For Gregory, as for his predecessors, the bishop was to be an example to others, dignified but humble, contemplative but social, able to deal well with people from all walks of life. He laid down that vision in a work that was to be read at the courts of Charlemagne and Alfred the Great, the *Regula pasturalis* or *Pastoral Rule*:

> We must especially examine how someone should come to hold supreme authority; and then, holding such authority, how they should live; and then, living well, how they should teach; and then, teaching correctly, with how great consideration every day they must consider their own infirmity. For otherwise humility may flee when authority is assumed, or the way of life may be at variance with taking on authority, or teaching may be wanting from the way of life, or presumption may unduly exalt the teaching. Therefore let fear temper desire; and afterwards, authority being assumed by those who did not seek it, let their way of life commend them. Then it is necessary that the good which is displayed in the life of the pastor should also be multiplied by their words. Finally, regarding whatever works we may achieve, consideration of our own infirmity should subdue us lest the swelling of pride extinguish even these before the eyes of hidden judgment.
>
> (Gregory the Great, *Pastoral Rule*, Prologue)

Copyright Acknowledgements

Further Reading

A. Brent, *Ignatius of Antioch: A Martyr Bishop and the Origin of Episcopacy* (London 2007)

P. Brown, *Poverty and Leadership in the Later Roman Empire* (Hanover, N.H. and London 2002)

H. Chadwick, *The Role of the Christian Bishop in Ancient Society* (Berkeley 1980)

E. Duffy, *Saints and Sinners: A History of the Popes*, 2nd edition (New Haven and London 2002)

P. Norton, *Episcopal Elections 250–600: Hierarchy and Popular Will in Late Antiquity* (Oxford 2007)

C. Rapp, *Holy Bishops in Late Antiquity: The Nature of Christian Leadership in an Age of Transition* (Berkeley, Los Angeles and London 2005)

J. Richards, *The Popes and the Papacy in the Early Middle Ages, 476–752* (London 1979)

K. Schatz, *Papal Primacy: From its Origins to the Present* (Collegeville, Minn. 1996)

A. Sterk, *Renouncing the World yet Leading the Church: the Monk-Bishop in Late Antiquity* (Cambridge, Mass. and London 2004)

W. Telfer, *The Office of a Bishop* (London 1962)

H. von Campenhausen, *Ecclesiastical Authority and Spiritual Power in the Church of the first three centuries*, translated by J. A. Baker (London 1969)

9

Emperor and Bishop

When Jesus was teaching in Jerusalem, some Jews approached him and asked whether it was lawful to pay taxes to the emperor. Jesus requested the denarius coin with which the taxes were paid.

> He said to them, 'Whose head is this, and whose title?' They answered, 'The emperor's'. Then he said to them, 'Give therefore to the emperor the things that are the emperor's, and to God the things that are God's'.
>
> (Matthew 22.20–21)

The early Christians had a tense relationship with the power of the Roman state. It was a Roman governor who sent Jesus to his death, although the Gospels place the chief blame on the Jewish leaders rather than Pontius Pilate. In the following two centuries outright imperial persecution was rare, with the deaths of Peter and Paul under Nero the most obvious exception. But Christianity remained illegal. One test used to expose Christians was their rejection of the imperial cult, the veneration of emperors as divine. Pliny the Younger, as governor of Pontus-Bithynia on the Black Sea, reported such an investigation to the emperor Trajan in c.112:

> I thought it right to dismiss those who said that they neither were nor ever had been Christians, when they had recited after me a formula of invocation to the gods and had made offerings of wine and incense to your statue, which I had ordered to be brought into court for this purpose together with the images of the

gods, and furthermore had reviled the name of Christ. None of these things, so it is said, those who are really Christians can be made to do.

(Pliny the Younger, *Letter* 10.96, to Trajan)

For Christians who were also loyal to the Roman empire, the imperial cult encapsulated the tension between their spiritual and secular allegiance. Around AD 200, the North African Tertullian wrote an *Apology* in defence of Christianity. He spoke for many when he protested that, although Christians would not honour the emperor as divine, still they prayed for the empire and for the emperor whom God had chosen to rule:

Why should I dwell any longer on the reverence and piety of Christians for the emperor? We must respect him as called to his office by our Lord. On valid grounds I might say that Caesar is more ours than yours, for our God has appointed him. Therefore he is mine, and I do more for his welfare, not merely because I ask it of Him who alone can give it, or because I ask it as one who deserves to receive, but also because by placing the majesty of Caesar below God, I commend him the more to the favour of the Deity to whom alone I subordinate him. But I do subordinate him to one I regard as more glorious than himself. Never will I call the emperor God.

(Tertullian, *Apology* 33.1–3)

Christianity's relationship with the Roman state reached its nadir during the empire-wide persecutions of the third century, culminating in the Great Persecution of Diocletian. Following the conversion of Constantine, however, even those who had witnessed imperial violence first hand could look upon the empire as a vehicle of divine providence. In 335 Eusebius of Caesarea delivered an oration commemorating the consecration of Constantine's Church of the Holy Sepulchre in Jerusalem. Far from denouncing Rome as the source of all persecution, Eusebius hailed the coming of Christ in the time of Augustus, the first Roman emperor.

As the knowledge of one God and one manner of religion, the saving doctrine of Christ, was made known to all mankind, so at the same time the entire dominion of the Roman empire was entrusted to a single sovereign and profound peace reigned throughout the world. Thus at the same moment, by the appointment of the same divine will, two beneficial shoots sprang up together for mankind: the Roman empire and the teaching of Christ.

(Eusebius of Caesarea, *De Sepulchro Christi* 16.5)

The man through whom God brought that providential plan to fruition was Constantine. Eusebius' experiences during the Great Persecution magnified his joyful response to the rise of a Christian emperor. In the closing words of his *Life of Constantine*, Eusebius contrasted the fates of the persecutors with the blessings God granted to His chosen ruler:

The Supreme God has made it manifest how great a difference He perceives between those whose privilege it is to worship Him and His Christ and those who have chosen the opposite. The calamitous ends in every instance of those who provoked His enmity by daring to assail His Church revealed the punishment for their hostility to God, just as the death of Constantine conveyed to all men the rewards of the love of God. He alone and pre-eminent among the Roman emperors worshipped God; he alone boldly proclaimed to all the doctrine of Christ; he alone as none before him had ever done honoured His Church; he alone abolished utterly the error of polytheism and exposed idolatry in every form. And so he alone both during his life and after his death was accounted worthy of such honours as none can say have ever been achieved by any other, whether Greek or barbarian or even among the ancient Romans themselves, for none have ever been recorded worthy of comparison with him.

(Eusebius of Caesarea, *Life of Constantine* 4.74–5)

As we saw in earlier chapters, Constantine himself fully shared this belief in divine providence and that God had chosen him to rule the empire. According to Eusebius, the emperor once remarked to bishops whom he was entertaining to dinner:

You are bishops of those within the Church; I am also perhaps a bishop appointed by God over those outside.

(quoted in Eusebius of Caesarea, *Life of Constantine* 4.24)

Constantine's words have sometimes been interpreted as a statement of 'Caesaropapism', the doctrine that a ruler chosen by God acquired the authority to dictate on religious matters. It is true that from Constantine onwards an emperor like a bishop could claim to act as God's representative. However, 'Caesaropapism' is an anachronistic concept that reflects the modern separation between Church and State. Such a separation did not exist in Constantine's time. The emperor was by definition a religious as well as political figure, and Constantine made no claim to dictate to the Church. In his letter to the Council of Arles in 314, after the Donatists had appealed to him against their condemnation by that council, the emperor wrote:

> They demand my judgement, when I myself await the judgement of Christ. For I tell you, as is the truth, that the judgement of the priests should be regarded as if God Himself were in the judge's seat. For these have no power either to think or to judge except as they are instructed by Christ's teaching.
>
> (Constantine, *Letter to the catholic bishops*, quoted in Optatus, *Against the Donatists*, Appendix 5)

The vast majority of Constantine's Christian contemporaries shared Eusebius' joy at their release from persecution and welcomed the emperor's patronage. Yet some began to question the cost of imperial involvement in their religion. Donatus of Carthage, from whom the Donatist Schism received its name, clashed with Constantine and then with Constantine's youngest son Constans (emperor 337–350). It was Donatus who first protested:

> What has the Church to do with the emperor?
>
> (Donatus of Carthage, quoted in Optatus, *Against the Donatists* 3.3)

Similar sentiments were expressed at greater length by Ossius of Cordova to Constantine's second son Constantius II (emperor 337–361). During the 350s, Constantius sought to unify the Church in support of doctrines that Ossius regarded as 'Arian'. Ossius urged the emperor to leave Church affairs to the bishops:

Cease these proceedings, I beseech you, and remember that you are a mortal man. Be afraid of the day of judgement, and keep yourself pure thereunto. Intrude not yourself into ecclesiastical matters, neither give commands to us concerning them; but learn them from us. God has put into your hands the kingdom; to us He has entrusted the affairs of His Church; and as he who would steal the empire from you would resist the ordinance of God, so likewise fear on your part lest by taking upon yourself the government of the Church, you become guilty of a great offence. It is written, 'Give to the emperor the things that are the emperor's, and to God the things that are God's' [Matthew 22.21]. Neither therefore is it permitted to us to exercise an earthly rule, nor have you, Sire, any authority to burn incense.

(Ossius, *Letter to Constantius*, quoted in Athanasius of Alexandria,
Historia Arianorum 44)

During the reigns of Constantine and his sons, the voices calling for the Church's separation from secular interference were very much in the minority. Even Donatus and Ossius were more than willing to accept imperial patronage when emperors acted in their favour. Yet further tension was inevitable, for Constantine's conversion had transformed Church–State relations. Who had the authority to settle disputes between Christian emperors and Christian bishops? Would imperial or clerical power prevail? These questions came to a head when Theodosius I (emperor 379–395) clashed with one of the leading bishops of the age, Ambrose of Milan.

Theodosius and Ambrose initially came into conflict in c.388 after a riot in the town of Callicinum on the Euphrates river destroyed a Jewish synagogue. The emperor ordered the local bishop to rebuild the synagogue, but reversed his decision on Ambrose's insistence that a Christian ruler should never aid the Jews. Then in 390 the general Butheric was lynched in Thessalonica after imprisoning a charioteer. Furious, Theodosius ordered in the army and 7,000 men, women and children were massacred. Ambrose compared Theodosius' crime to that of David in the Old Testament and called upon Theodosius to repent:

Are you ashamed, emperor, to do what was done by David, the king and prophet and according to the flesh, forefather of the family of Christ? David was told that a rich man, who had numerous flocks, on the arrival of a guest seized the only sheep of a poor man and killed it, and he recognized that in this he was himself being accused because this was what he had done and he said: 'I have sinned against the Lord' [2 Samuel 12.13]. Don't therefore take it ill, emperor, if you are told: 'you have done what the prophet told king David that he had done'. For if you listen to this attentively, and say: 'I have sinned against the Lord', if you repeat that royal and prophetic saying: 'O come, let us worship and fall down before Him, and let us weep before the Lord our Maker' [Psalm 95.6], you too will be told: 'Because you have repented, the Lord will forgive your sin and you shall not die' [2 Samuel 12.13].

(Ambrose of Milan, *Letter* 51.7, to Theodosius)

Later in the same letter, Ambrose declared that he would not permit Theodosius to receive the eucharist:

I dare not offer the sacrifice, if you intend to be there. Or is what is not allowed when the blood of one innocent victim has been shed, allowed when the blood has been shed of many? I do not think so.

(Ambrose of Milan, *Letter* 51.13, to Theodosius)

In effect, Ambrose therefore became the first bishop to excommunicate a Christian ruler. He continued to deny Theodosius communion until the emperor performed a public act of penance, which he did after eight months on Christmas Day 390. The clash of these two powerful personalities foreshadowed the conflicts of later centuries, but Ambrose and Theodosius were reconciled in a relationship of mutual respect. When Theodosius died in 395, Ambrose recalled the emperor's penance in the funeral oration that he delivered in Theodosius' honour:

Freed, therefore, from the uncertainty of the contest, Theodosius of revered memory now enjoys eternal light and lasting peace, and in return for the deeds he performed in this body he rejoices in the fruits of divine recompense. It was therefore because Theodosius of revered memory loved the Lord his God he has earned the fellowship of the saints. And I too – to close my address with some sort of peroration – have loved a merciful man, humble in power, endowed with a pure heart and a gentle disposition, a man such as the Lord is wont to love, saying 'In whom shall I find consolation if not in the humble and meek' [Isaiah 66.2]. I have loved a man who valued a critic more than a flatterer. He threw to the ground all the royal attire he was wearing; he wept publicly in church over his sin which had stolen upon him through the deceit of others; with groans and tears he prayed for forgiveness. What private citizens blush to do the emperor did not blush to do, to perform public penance; and afterwards not a day passed on which he did not grieve for that fault of his.

(Ambrose of Milan, *On the Death of Theodosius I* 32–34)

Theodosius I was the last man to rule over a unified Roman empire. Upon his death the empire was divided between his two sons, a division that remained until the final western emperor was deposed in 476. During the dark days of the fifth century new interpretations of the relationship of Church and State emerged. Eusebius of Caesarea had written at a time of Christian triumph and celebrated the Roman empire as itself part of God's providential plan. Augustine of Hippo composed his masterwork the *City of God* against the background of the Sack of Rome by Alaric and the Goths in 410. The empire was less central to Augustine's vision of divine providence, and he insisted that good emperors received their true reward not in this world but in the next.

We call rulers happy if they rule justly; if they are not inflated with pride amid the praises of those who pay them sublime honours and the obsequiousness of those who salute them with excessive humility, but rather remember that they are men; if they use their power in the service of His majesty by promoting the greatest possible expansion of His worship; if they fear, love, and worship God; if more than their own kingdom, they love that kingdom in which they are not afraid to share rule; if they are slow to punish but ready to pardon; if they apply punishment as necessary to govern and defend the state, and not to gratify their own enmity; if they grant pardon, not so that iniquity may go unpunished but with the hope that the transgressor may amend their ways; if they compensate whatever severity they must decree with the gentleness of mercy and the liberality of benevolence; if they restrain their luxury all the more because they might have been unrestrained; if they prefer control over their depraved desires to control over any number of subject peoples; and if they do all these things not through ardent desire for empty glory but through love of eternal blessedness, and they do not neglect to offer to the true God, who is their God, the sacrifices of humility, contrition, and prayer for their sins. Such Christian emperors we call happy; happy in hope during the present time, and to be happy in reality hereafter.

(Augustine of Hippo, *City of God* 5.24)

Augustine then compared the fate of Constantine to those of his Christian successors.

God in His goodness did not wish those who believe that He is to be worshipped with a view to eternal life to think that no one could attain to the highest positions and to dominion in this world unless they were a worshipper of demons, conceiving that these spirits have great power in this sphere. For this reason He gave to the emperor Constantine, who was not a worshipper of demons but of the true God Himself, such a fullness of worldly gifts as no one would even have dared to hope for. To him God even granted the honour of founding a city, a companion to the Roman empire and the daughter, as it were, of Rome itself, but without any temple or image of demons. Constantine reigned for a long period as sole emperor, and unaided held and defended the whole Roman world. In directing and carrying out his wars he was greatly victorious; in overthrowing usurpers he was highly successful; and he died of sickness and old age after a long life and left his sons to succeed him in the empire. And yet, so that no emperor should become a Christian in order to receive the happiness of Constantine (when everyone should become a Christian for the sake of eternal life), God took away Jovian far sooner than Julian and permitted that Gratian should be slain by a usurper's sword.

(Augustine of Hippo, *City of God* 5.25)

A Christian emperor must rule with justice, humility and mercy, and love and honour God. Yet they should not expect earthly rewards for their piety. Constantine may have been exalted due to God's plan, but the orthodox Jovian (363–364) ruled for just eight months, less even than the pagan Julian 'the Apostate' (361–363). Augustine's belief in the blessed life to come offered reassurance to the faithful in the rapidly changing world of the fifth century. And his vision of the ideal ruler offered a model for Germanic kings no less than for Roman emperors, and so provided an interpretation of Christian history that could survive the end of the Roman empire in the west.

The empire's fall also reinforced western arguments for the superiority of spiritual authority over secular power. The Spaniard Ossius of Cordova had already expressed this separation between emperor and bishop. In the late fifth century a far stronger statement was made by Gelasius (bishop of Rome 492–496) in a letter to the eastern emperor Anastasius in 494:

> There are two powers, august Emperor, by which this world is ruled from the beginning: the consecrated authority of the bishops, and the royal power. In these matters the priests bear the heavier burden as they will render account, even for rulers of men, at the divine judgment. Besides, most gracious son, you are aware that, although you are the ruler of the human race, nevertheless you devoutly bow your head before those who are leaders in things divine and look to them for the means of your salvation.
>
> (Gelasius of Rome, *Letter* 12, to Anastasius)

Gelasius' doctrine of the 'two powers' exerted a powerful influence in the west, where the bishops of Rome took over many of the roles of the departed emperors. In the east, the empire survived. The emperor Justinian (527–565) offered a more equal interpretation of the relationship between Church and State:

> The priesthood and the empire are the two greatest gifts which God, in His infinite clemency, has bestowed upon mortals. The former has reference to divine matters, the latter presides over and directs human affairs, and both, proceeding from the same principle, adorn the life of mankind. Nothing therefore should be such a source of care to the emperors as the honour of the priests who constantly pray to God for their salvation. For if the priesthood is everywhere free from blame, and the empire full of confidence in God is administered equitably and judiciously, general good will result and whatever is beneficial will be bestowed upon the human race.
>
> (Justinian, *Novel* 6, Preface)

The eastern Roman or Byzantine empire would endure for almost a thousand years, the cooperation between emperor and bishop an essential element in its long survival. In the west new debates would arise, with the empire of Charlemagne and the medieval papacy.

Copyright Acknowledgements

Further Reading

T. D. Barnes, *Athanasius and Constantius: Theology and Politics in the Constantinian Empire* (Cambridge, Mass. and London 1993)

H. A. Drake, *Constantine and the Bishops: The Politics of Intolerance* (Baltimore and London 2000)

S. L. Greenslade, *Church and State from Constantine to Theodosius* (London 1954)

R. A. Markus, *Saeculum: History and Society in the Theology of St Augustine* (Cambridge 1970)

N. McLynn, *Ambrose of Milan: Church and Court in a Christian Capital* (Berkeley and Los Angeles 1994)

F. Millar, *The Emperor in the Roman World (31 BC – AD 337)* (London 1997)

O. O'Donovan and J. L. O'Donovan (eds), *From Irenaeus to Grotius: A Sourcebook in Christian Political Thought* (Grand Rapids and Cambridge 1999)

C. Rapp, *Holy Bishops in Late Antiquity: The Nature of Christian Leadership in an Age of Transition* (Berkeley, Los Angeles and London 2005)

K. M. Setton, *Christian Attitudes towards the Emperor in the Fourth Century* (New York 1941)

10

Asceticism and Monasticism

The ideal of *askesis*, pursuing a life of austerity and self-discipline in the quest for spiritual growth, has a very long history in human culture. The western conception of asceticism has strong Christian associations, but Christian ascetic values emerged against a background of Graeco-Roman philosophy and Jewish teachings. Those values are already visible in the Gospel accounts of John the Baptist and Jesus, and remained prominent among early Christians. In the fourth century, there was a dramatic transformation in the status and influence of asceticism within Christianity. With the end of persecution, the ascetic lifestyle provided a new expression of faith to take the place of martyrdom. Simultaneously, Christianity's growth following Constantine's conversion led some men and women to seek a deeper religious experience through their ascetic commitment, whether as individual hermits or in communal monasteries.

Antony was by descent an Egyptian. His parents were of good family and possessed considerable wealth, and as they were Christians he was reared in the same faith. In infancy he was brought up with his parents, knowing nothing apart from them and his home. When he was older and had become a boy, he could not endure to learn to read and write or to associate with other boys. All that he yearned to do, as has been written of Jacob, was to live as a plain man at home. He used to attend the Lord's house with his parents, and neither was he idle as a child nor did he become contemptuous when he was older, but was both obedient to his father and mother and attentive to what was read, keeping in his heart what was profitable in what he heard. Though as a child he was brought up in moderate wealth, he did not trouble his parents for varied or luxurious food and nor was this a source of pleasure to him, but he was content simply with what he found and did not seek anything further.

After the death of his father and mother he was left alone with one young sister. He was about eighteen or twenty years of age, and on him the care both of home and sister rested. Six months had not passed after the deaths of his parents when, as he went according to custom to the Lord's house, he thought to himself and reflected as he walked how the apostles had left everything they had and followed the Saviour, and how those in Acts sold their possessions and brought the proceeds and laid them at the apostles' feet for distribution to the needy. What great hope was laid up for these people in heaven! Pondering over these things, he entered the church. It happened that the Gospel was being read, and he heard the Lord saying to the rich man, 'If you wish to be perfect, go, sell everything you possess and give it to the poor and you will have treasure in heaven; then come, follow me' [Matthew 19.21].

(Athanasius of Alexandria, *Life of Antony* 1–2)

The most renowned ascetic of the fourth century was the Egyptian monk Antony (c.251–356), who would become the model for the anchoretic or eremitic monasticism of the solitary hermit. Antony's biography was written shortly after his death and is attributed to bishop Athanasius of Alexandria. The *Life* is not always entirely reliable (the survival of letters in Antony's name questions the claim that he could not read or write), but allows us to sketch the major events of Antony's career. When he left the church having heard the Gospel reading, Antony heeded the Saviour's call. Committing his sister to the care of faithful virgins, he sold his property and gave the money to the poor and devoted himself to asceticism. Antony was obviously not the first. There was a house of virgins in his village and he was able to seek guidance from a hermit who lived nearby. But Antony was not content to remain so close to civilization. Over the decades he moved ever further into the deep desert, resisting the Devil's temptations and seeking to avoid the crowds who followed him.

When he saw himself beset by many, and not able to withdraw as he wished, he feared that the miracles which the Lord wrought through him might either make him proud or cause others to think more of him than they should. He therefore considered carefully and departed to go into the upper Thebaid where he was unknown. Having received loaves of bread from the brethren, he sat down by the bank of the river and looked for a boat to pass, so that by embarking he might travel up the river with them. While he was considering these things, a voice came to him from above, saying 'Antony, where are you going and why?'. He was not disturbed, for he had become accustomed to be called often in this way, and after listening he answered that 'Since the crowds do not permit me to be at peace, I wish to go into the upper Thebaid on account of the many annoyances that come upon me here and especially because they demand of me things beyond my power'. But the voice said to him, 'Even if you go into the Thebaid, or even if you should go down to the pastures as you have in mind, you will have to endure more and indeed double the amount of toil. If you truly wish to be alone, depart now into the inner desert'. When Antony said, 'Who will show me the way, for I know it not?', immediately the voice pointed out to him Saracens about to go in that direction. Antony approached them and asked that he might go with them into the desert. And they, as though they had been commanded by divine providence, received him willingly. After journeying with them for three days and three nights, he came to a very lofty mountain. At the foot of the mountain ran a clear spring, whose waters were sweet and very cold, while beyond there was a plain and a few untended palm trees. Antony, as if moved by God, loved the place, for this was the place which the voice who spoke with him by the banks of the river had pointed out. Having received loaves of bread from his fellow travellers, he remained alone on the mountain, no one else living with him.

(Athanasius of Alexandria, *Life of Antony* 49–50)

On this Inner Mountain (Mount Colzim), some 160 kilometres south-east of modern Cairo, Antony settled until his death forty years later. Aside from brief visits to other hermits, he made only one major journey, to Alexandria in 338 to denounce the 'Arians'. He continued to teach the disciples and philosophers who came to him, and at his death in 356 his reported age was over one hundred. His fame spread widely, while the *Life of Antony* was swiftly translated into Latin and exerted great influence in the west. In Athanasius' words, Antony made 'the desert a city'.

From then on, there were monasteries in the mountains and the desert was made a city by monks, who came forth from their own people and enrolled themselves for the citizenship in the heavens.

(Athanasius of Alexandria, *Life of Antony* 14)

If Antony established the model for the solitary eremitic hermit, his younger contemporary Pachomius (292–346) offered a different, more communal ideal for the ascetic life. Conscripted into the army, Pachomius converted after being impressed by the charity of Christians who brought the recruits food and drink. Attracted to an ascetic lifestyle, like Antony he looked to a local hermit for guidance. Unlike Antony, Pachomius' calling was to found a collective monastery, which he did at the deserted village of Tabennesi in c.320. As he attracted more followers, Pachomius evolved a communal structure based on mutual support. The Bohairic *Life of Pachomius* offers an early glimpse of how his monastery was organized.

[Pachomius] appointed some from among the capable brothers as his assistants to take care of their souls' salvation. He appointed one at the head of the first house, that of the lesser stewards, with a second to help him in preparing the tables and in cooking. He appointed another brother also, with his second – men who were faithful on every score – to look after the food and the care of the sick brothers. If anyone wanted to abstain from what was served at table or from what was served to the sick, there was no one to prevent him from doing so. And at the doorway he appointed other brothers whose 'speech was seasoned with salt' [Colossians 4.6] to receive visitors according to each one's rank. They also instructed those who came to become monks, for their salvation, until he clothed them in the monk's habit. Similarly, he appointed other faithful brothers noted for their piety to transact sales and make purchases. In each house the brothers in service were replaced every three weeks, and a new class was appointed. They performed 'in fear and trembling' [Philippians 2.12] the task assigned them by the housemaster. He appointed still others with a housemaster and a second to work at the shops and at the mat-making and to be ready for every obedience. He likewise established three instructions a week: one on Saturdays and two on the holy Sunday.

(Bohairic *Life of Pachomius* 26)

The idea of ascetics living together in a communal setting was not itself new. But Pachomius introduced a higher level of organization and founded a series of monasteries (including a women's convent) united in a single network. By Pachomius' death in 346 his movement had spread through much of southern Egypt, and by the end of the fourth century the Pachomian communities have been estimated at some 7,000 members. The *Rules* which governed the Pachomian monks were not fully refined until after Pachomius' death, and were translated into Latin by Jerome. There were over 140 rules covering every aspect of monastic life, from food and clothing to the treatment of the sick and the requirement that all must learn to read.

(1) When someone uninstructed comes to the assembly of the saints, the porter shall introduce him according to his rank from the door of the monastery and give him a seat in the gathering of the brothers. He shall not be allowed to change his place or rank of sitting until the *oikiakos*, that is his own housemaster, transfers him to the place he should have.

(2) He shall sit with all modesty and meekness, tucking under his buttocks the lower edge of the goat skin that hangs over his shoulder down his side, and carefully girding up his garment – that is, the linen tunic without sleeves called *lebitonarium* – in such a way that it covers his knees.

(31) Each master shall teach, in his own house, how they must eat with manners and meekness. If anyone speaks or laughs while eating, he shall do penance and be rebuked there at once, and he shall stand until another of the brothers who are eating gets up.

(42) Let no one who is not sick enter the infirmary. The one who falls sick shall be led by the master to the refectory for the sick. And if he needs a mantle or a tunic or anything else by way of covering or food, let the master himself get these from the ministers and give them to the sick brother.

(89) No one shall enter the cell of his neighbour without first knocking.

(114) No one shall eat anything in his cell.

(140) There shall be no one whatever in the monastery who does not learn to read and does not memorize something of the Scriptures, at least the New Testament and the Psalter.

(The *Rules* of Pachomius)

Christian asceticism was by no means limited to Egypt and, while Antony and Pachomius offered influential models, ascetic practices took many different forms. Another leading eastern figure was Basil of Cappadocian Caesarea (330–379), whose *Asketikon* became known in the west under the misleading title *The Rules of St Basil*. A collection of responses to ascetic questions rather than a formal monastic rule, Basil's *Asketikon* emphasized the importance of manual labour and communal prayer over excessive fasting and austerity.

What need is there to say how great an evil is idleness, since the Apostle declares plainly 'He who does not work, let him not eat' [2 Thessalonians 3.10]? So then, since daily food is necessary for each person, so work is also necessary, in accordance with one's capacity. It was not for nothing that Solomon wrote in praise 'She did not eat the bread of idleness' [Proverbs 31.27]. And again the

Apostle speaks of himself, 'And we did not eat anyone's bread without paying, but worked in toil and hardship, night and day' [2 Thessalonians 3.8], though he had the right, since he was proclaiming the Gospel, 'To live from the Gospel' [1 Corinthians 9.14]. Moreover, the Lord Himself associates slothfulness with evil living, saying 'You evil and slothful servant' [Matthew 25.26]. And the wise Solomon not only praises the worker in the words just recalled, but also rebukes one who is slothful by comparing him with the smallest of creatures, saying 'Go to the ant, sluggard' [Proverbs 6.6]. So we should fear lest this is brought against us in the day of judgement, when He who gave us the capacity for work requires from us work commensurate with our capacity. For, He says, 'To whom they entrusted much, of him they will require the more' [Luke 12.48].

Now when some beg off work on a pretext of the prayers and the psalmody, you must know that for all the other tasks there is a particular time for each, as Ecclesiastes says 'There is a season for everything' [Ecclesiastes 3.1]. But for prayer and psalmody, as with many other things, every time is suitable; so that if it is possible, or rather if it contributes to the upbuilding of the faith, we praise God with the tongue, as it is written 'In psalms and hymns and spiritual songs' [Colossians 3.16], while we employ our hands at work, but if not, then in the heart. In this way we fulfil prayer even in the midst of work, giving thanks to Him who gave both strength of hand to work and cleverness of mind to acquire the skill and also bestowed the material with which to work, both in the tools we use and in what is requisite for the crafts we practice, whatever they happen to be. And we pray that the works of our hands may be directed to the goal of being well pleasing to God.

(Basil of Cappadocian Caesarea, *Asketikon*, Longer Responses 37.2)

Elsewhere in the east more extreme practices were known. The most famous example, in his own lifetime as well as today, was Symeon Stylites the Elder (c.395–459). A Syrian shepherd who entered a monastery, Symeon sought a more personal expression of his ascetic commitment and in 412 became the first stylite or 'pillar-saint'.

He made a pillar [*stylos*] four cubits high and stood on it for seven years, and his fame spread everywhere. After this the crowds built for him two enclosures from unmortared stone and they put up a door to the inner enclosure. They made for him a pillar thirty cubits high, and he stood on it for fifteen years during which time he performed many healings.

(Antonius, *Life of Symeon Stylites* 12)

Symeon's final pillar was 40 cubits (c.60 feet) high, with a six-foot-square platform. By the time of his death he had lived on pillars of varying heights for 47 years, and the extent of his fame is reflected in the magnificent ruins that still survive from the great complex that grew up around his column, known in Arabic as Qal'at Sim'ān ('the Fortress of Symeon'). Other stylite monks appeared across Syria and Asia Minor, although the custom never became established in the west.

Not everyone welcomed the rise of the Christian ascetic. For the orator Libanius, writing in defence of traditional temples, the monks represented Christian fanaticism and violence.

> You [emperor Theodosius I] have not ordered the temples to be shut up, nor forbidden entrance to them; nor have you banished from the temples and altars either fire or incense or the offerings of other perfumes. Yet this black-robed tribe, who eat more than elephants and through the quantities of drink they consume exhaust those who accompany their drinking with chanting, but who hide their excesses through their pale artificial countenances – these men, O Emperor, even while your law is in force, run to attack the temples with sticks and stones and iron, and even, without these, with hands and feet.
>
> (Libanius, *Pro Templis*, Oration 30.8, c.386)

Christians likewise worried that the ascetic movement might be taken too far. Some condemned the more extreme acts of asceticism as expressions of vainglory rather than piety, while others feared that exalting monks and virgins would create divisions and reduce 'ordinary' Christians to second-class citizens of the Church. One of the most controversial figures was Eustathius of Sebaste, whose ascetic ideals influenced Basil of Cappadocian Caesarea. Eustathius' promotion of strict asceticism led to accusations that he degraded marriage and despised those who preferred a normal Christian life. He was condemned in the mid-fourth century (the exact date is uncertain) at the Council of Gangra in modern Turkey, and the canons passed by that council attest to the tensions that such issues had aroused.

> (1) If anyone condemns marriage, abominating and blaming a woman who is a believer and devout and who sleeps with her own husband, as if she could not enter the Kingdom of God, let him be anathema.

(2) If anyone condemns him who eats flesh, which is without blood and has not been offered to idols nor strangled, and is faithful and devout, as though the man were without hope of salvation because of his eating, let him be anathema.

(9) If anyone remains virgin or observes continence, abstaining from marriage because he abhors it and not on account of the beauty and holiness of virginity itself, let him be anathema.

(12) If anyone under pretence of asceticism wears the philosopher's cloak and, as if this gave him righteousness, despises those who with piety wear ordinary coats and use other common and customary dress, let him be anathema.

(15) If anyone forsakes his own children and does not nurture them, nor so far as lies in him rear them in proper piety, but neglects them under pretence of asceticism, let him be anathema.

These things we write, not to cut off those in the Church of God who wish to lead an ascetic life according to the Scriptures, but those who undertake the profession of asceticism in a spirit of pride exalting themselves above those who live more simply and introducing novelties contrary to the Scriptures and the ecclesiastical canons.

(Canons of the Council of Gangra)

The growing prominence of monks and virgins created tensions not only with the wider laity but with the episcopal hierarchy. The spiritual charisma of ascetic figures such as Antony or Symeon was a potential challenge to the authority of the bishops over the Christian community. Yet asceticism was never necessarily incompatible with an ecclesiastical career, and over time increasing numbers of monks took clerical office. Athanasius of Alexandria actively recruited monks as bishops, occasionally rather against their will. His *Letter to Dracontius*, a reluctant recruit who had fled his assigned see, became a classic statement of the monk-bishop ideal.

Make haste then, beloved, do not hesitate any longer nor suffer those who would prevent you; but remember Him who has given, and come to us who love you and who give you advice from the Scriptures, in order that you may both be installed by us and, as you minister in the churches, make remembrance of us. For you are not the only one to have been elected from among the monks, nor the only one to have presided over a monastery or to have been beloved by monks. For you know that Serapion was a monk, and presided over such a number of monks; you are not unaware of the number of monks to whom

Apollos was father; you know Agathon, and are not ignorant of Ariston. You remember Ammonius, who went abroad with Serapion. Perhaps you have also heard of Mouitos in the upper Thebaid, and can learn about Paul at Latopolis, and many others. And yet these, when elected, did not gainsay; but taking Elisha as an example, knowing the story of Elijah, and having learnt all about the disciples and apostles, they grappled with the charge; they did not despise the ministry and were not more severe towards themselves, but rather looked for the reward of their labour, advancing themselves and guiding others onwards. How many have they turned away from the idols? How many have ceased from their familiarity with demons because of their warning? How many servants have they brought to the Lord, so as to cause those who saw such wonders to marvel at the sight? Or is it no great marvel to make a pupil live as a virgin, and a young man to live in continence, and an idolater to come to know Christ?

(Athanasius of Alexandria, *Letter to Dracontius* 7)

The Christian ascetic revolution of the fourth century began in the east, but the movement swiftly spread westward. A number of western ascetics were inspired by visits to the monks of Egypt and Syria or by works like the *Life of Antony*. One such figure was Jerome, who wrote of his experiences in the Syrian desert in his exhortation to the virgin Eustochium.

How often, when I was living in the desert, in the vast solitude parched by the burning sun which gives the hermits a savage dwelling place, did I imagine myself among the pleasures of Rome! I used to sit alone because I was filled with bitterness. Sackcloth disfigured my unshapely limbs and my skin from long neglect had become as black as an Ethiopian's; tears and groans were my daily portion, and if drowsiness chanced to overcome my struggles against it, my bare bones which hardly held together clashed against the ground. Of my food and drink I say nothing; for even in sickness, the solitaries have nothing but cold water and to eat one's food cooked is looked upon as self-indulgence. Now, although in my fear of hell I had consigned myself to this prison, where I had no companions but scorpions and wild beasts, I often found myself among bevies of girls. My face was pale and my frame chilled with fasting, yet my mind was burning with desire and the fires of lust kept bubbling up before me when my flesh was as good as dead.

Helpless, I cast myself at the feet of Jesus. I watered them with my tears, I wiped them with my hair, and then I subdued my rebellious body with weeks of abstinence. I do not blush to avow my abject misery. Rather I lament that I am not now what once I was. I remember how I often cried aloud all night until the break of day and did not stop beating my breast until tranquillity returned at the Lord's chiding. I used to dread my very cell as though it knew my thoughts and, stern and angry with myself, I used to make my way alone into the desert. Wherever I saw hollow valleys, craggy mountains, steep cliffs, there I made my oratory, there the house of correction for my unhappy flesh. There also – the Lord Himself is my witness – when I had shed copious tears and strained my eyes toward heaven, I sometimes felt myself among angelic hosts and for joy and gladness sang, 'For the scent of your good ointments we will run after you' [Song of Solomon 1.3].

(Jerome, *Letter* 22.7)

Jerome extolled the virtues of personal asceticism, particularly to the women of his circle (see further Chapter 14). Other western travellers to the east admired the communal monasticism of Pachomius and Basil of Cappadocian Caesarea. John Cassian lived for more than a decade with the Egyptian monks, and in the 420s wrote his *Institutes* to promote collective asceticism in southern Gaul.

I shall try so far as I can, with the help of God, faithfully to explain only their institutions and the rules of their monasteries, and especially the origin and causes of the principal faults, of which they reckon eight, and the remedies for them according to their traditions – since my purpose is to say a few words not about God's miracles, but about the way to improve our character and the attainment of the perfect life in accordance with that which we received from our elders. In this too I will try to satisfy your directions, so that, if I happen to find that anything has been either withdrawn or added in those countries not in accordance with the example of the elders established by ancient custom, but according to the fancy of anyone who has founded a monastery, I will faithfully add it or omit it, in accordance with the rule which I have seen followed in the monasteries anciently founded throughout Egypt and Palestine. For I do not believe that a new establishment in the west, in the parts of Gaul, could find anything more reasonable or more perfect than are those customs in the observance of which the monasteries that have been founded by holy and spiritually minded fathers since the rise of apostolic preaching endure even to our own times. I shall, however, venture to exercise this discretion in my work – that where I find anything in the rule of the Egyptians which, either because of the severity of the climate, or owing to some difficulty or diversity of habits, is impossible in these countries, or hard and difficult, I shall to some extent balance it by the customs of the monasteries which are found throughout Pontus and Mesopotamia; because, if due regard be paid to what things are possible, there is the same perfection in the observance although the power may be unequal.

(John Cassian, *Institutes*, Preface)

A century after Cassian, the most famous of all early western monastic rules was compiled. Benedict of Nursia (c.480–c.550), an Italian monk, drew on the works of Pachomius, Basil of Cappadocian Caesarea and Augustine as well as Cassian. The *Rule of St Benedict* exerted enormous influence on the history of western monasticism and remains a source of inspiration to this day.

Now, brethren, that we have asked the Lord who it is that shall dwell in His tabernacle, we have heard the conditions for dwelling there; and if we fulfil the duties of tenants, we shall be heirs of the kingdom of heaven. Our hearts and our bodies must, therefore, be ready to do battle under the biddings of holy obedience; and let us ask the Lord that He supply by the help of His grace what is impossible to us by nature. And if, flying from the pains of hell, we desire to reach life everlasting, then, while there is yet time, and we are still in the flesh, and are able during the present life to fulfil all these things, we must make haste to do now what will profit us forever.

We are, therefore, about to found a school of the Lord's service, in which we hope to introduce nothing harsh or burdensome. But even if, to correct vices or to preserve charity, sound reason dictates anything that turns out somewhat stringent, do not at once fly in dismay from the way of salvation, the beginning of which cannot but be narrow. But as we advance in the religious life and faith, we shall run the way of God's commandments with expanded hearts and unspeakable sweetness of love; so that never departing from His guidance and persevering in the monastery in His doctrine till death, we may by patience share in the sufferings of Christ, and be found worthy to be co-heirs with Him of His kingdom.

(The *Rule of St Benedict*, Prologue)

Christian asceticism took many forms. Some individuals sought the solitude of the desert or the isolation of the stylite's pillar. Others preferred the collective harmony and discipline of the communal monastery. Many Christians who could not commit themselves to a fully monastic lifestyle adopted ascetic practices in their homes or for certain periods of time. All looked to asceticism to help them achieve a closer spiritual bond with God. And while ascetics are often said to 'renounce' the world, they never in truth stood apart. Pilgrims reached Antony on his mountain and Symeon on his pillar, while the monasteries of Pachomius and Benedict played an integral role in their wider communities. For 'ordinary' Christians, the ascetics offered inspiration and guidance, a source of hope and practical aid. The rise of the ascetic movement was one of Late Antiquity's greatest legacies to the subsequent history of Christianity and the western world.

Copyright Acknowledgements

Further Reading

D. Brakke, *Athanasius and the Politics of Asceticism* (Oxford 1995)
P. Brown, *The Body and Society: Men, Women and Sexual Renunciation in Early Christianity* (New York 1988)
D. Caner, *Wandering, Begging Monks: Spiritual Authority and the Promotion of Monasticism* (Berkeley, Los Angeles and London 2002)
D. J. Chitty, *The Desert a City: An Introduction to the Study of Egyptian and Palestinian Monasticism under the Christian Empire* (Oxford 1966)

E. A. Clark, *Reading Renunciation: Asceticism and Scripture in Early Christianity* (Princeton 1999)

M. Dunn, *The Emergence of Monasticism: From the Desert Fathers to the Early Middle Ages* (Oxford 2000)

S. Elm, *Virgins of God: The Making of Asceticism in Late Antiquity* (Oxford and New York 1994)

W. Harmless, *Desert Christians: An Introduction to the Literature of Early Monasticism* (New York and Oxford 2004)

C. Leyser, *Authority and Asceticism from Augustine to Gregory the Great* (Oxford 2000)

P. Rousseau, *Ascetics, Authority, and the Church in the Age of Jerome and Cassian* (Oxford 1978)

P. Rousseau, *Pachomius: The Making of a Community in Fourth-Century Egypt* (Berkeley, Los Angeles and London 1985)

T. Shaw, *The Burden of the Flesh: Fasting and Sexuality in Early Christianity* (Minneapolis 1998)

V. L. Wimbush and R. Valantasis (eds), *Asceticism* (New York and Oxford 1995)

11

Christianization

When Constantine converted to Christianity in 312, Christians made up approximately 10–15 per cent of the Roman empire's 60 million inhabitants. A century later, Christianity was the dominant religion of the empire. The Church had become an institution of great power and wealth, and Christian values had spread to all walks of life. Yet this 'Christianization' of the Later Roman empire was neither straightforward nor an exclusively one-way process. The relationship between Christianity and traditional Graeco-Roman religion took many different forms, from outright conflict to toleration and mutual interaction, and Christianity's rise to pre-eminence changed not only the empire but Christianity itself.

The traditional cults and religious practices of the ancient Greeks and Romans are usually and rather inaccurately known as 'paganism'. No one in the ancient world ever identified their own religion as 'pagan'. The term was coined by Christians as a catch-all to describe anyone whose beliefs were neither Christian nor Jewish. *Paganos* originally meant either 'rural dweller' (in contrast to the early urban Christians) or 'civilian' (as opposed to a soldier for Christ). 'Paganism' was therefore not a clearly defined religion in the same sense as Christianity or Islam, and included everything from the veneration of household deities and natural forces to worship of the Olympian gods and goddesses such as Zeus (in Latin Jupiter) and Athena (Minerva). There was no 'pagan' Bible, little or no professional clergy, and no rigid separation between right and wrong beliefs. The sheer diversity of 'paganism' in comparison to the relatively black and white ideals of Christianity further complicated the crucial years of transition that followed Constantine's conversion.

The vast majority of Constantine's subjects were not Christian, and the Great Persecution had just demonstrated the inability of a Roman emperor to impose religion upon the empire. Nevertheless, at least according to the emperor's biographer Eusebius of Caesarea, Constantine attempted to suppress traditional cult practices.

The emperor first sent governors to the various provinces, mostly men who were devoted to the saving faith, and if any preferred paganism he forbade them to offer sacrifice. This ruling applied also to those who surpassed the provincial governors in rank and dignity, and even to those who occupied the highest offices and held the authority of prefects. If they were Christians, they were free to act consistently with their faith. If not, then the law required them to abstain from idolatrous sacrifices. Soon after this, two laws were issued simultaneously. One restricted the abominations of idolatry which in time past had been practiced in every city and country district, so that no one should erect cult images, or practice divination or other false arts, or offer sacrifice in any way. The second commanded the building of places of worship and the expansion in length and breadth of the churches of God, as though it were expected that, with the madness of polytheism wholly removed, nearly everyone would henceforth attach themselves to the service of God.

(Eusebius of Caesarea, *Life of Constantine* 2.44–45)

Constantine's efforts to promote Christianity are hardly in doubt. But despite Eusebius' rhetoric, positive discrimination in favour of Christians did not necessarily also require the persecution of 'pagans'. No surviving law of Constantine matches Eusebius' claim of a universal ban on idolatry and sacrifice, and in his own words Constantine expressed a rather different view. While openly pro-Christian and denouncing 'pagan' error, Constantine rejected the use of sanctions and instead followed a policy of contemptuous toleration.

Let no one use what they have received by inner conviction to the detriment of another. Rather, let everyone as far as possible apply what they have seen and understood to the benefit of their neighbour, and if that is impossible then let them relinquish the attempt. It is one thing voluntarily to undertake the contest for immortality, it is quite another to compel others to do so from fear of punishment. These are my words, and I have enlarged on these topics more than my ordinary clemency required because I do not wish to dissemble or be false to the true faith, especially since I understand that some people are saying that the rites of the temples and the power of darkness have been entirely removed.

> I would indeed have earnestly recommended such removal to all mankind, were it not that the rebellious spirit of those wicked errors still remains obstinately fixed in the minds of some to the detriment of the common good.
>
> (Constantine, *Letter to the eastern provincials*, quoted in Eusebius of Caesarea, *Life of Constantine* 2.60)

It is still possible that Constantine did legislate against traditional religious practices. The earliest existing law condemning sacrifice was passed in 341 by Constantine's sons and invoked the will of their father.

> Superstition shall cease; the madness of sacrifices shall be abolished. For if any man in violation of the law of the sainted emperor, Our father, and in violation of this command of Our Clemency, should dare to perform sacrifices, he shall suffer the infliction of a suitable punishment and the effect of an immediate sentence.
>
> (*Theodosian Code* 16.10.2)

Under the first Christian emperors, some measures were therefore taken to restrict the religious freedoms of those who followed traditional Graeco-Roman religion. This was balanced, however, by respect for the bulk of the population who shared those traditional beliefs. In any case, the passing of a law was no guarantee that the law could be enforced, and there is little evidence for direct Christian–'pagan' conflict under Constantine or his sons. Constantius II, Constantine's final surviving son, died in 361. His successor was Constantine's nephew Julian, commonly known as Julian 'the Apostate' (361–363). The last 'pagan' to rule the Roman empire, Julian concealed his beliefs during Constantius' reign but expressed them openly when he took power, as he proclaimed in a letter to his old tutor Maximus.

> I worship the gods openly, and the whole mass of the troops who are returning with me worship the gods. I sacrifice oxen in public. I have offered to the gods many hecatombs as thank-offerings. The gods command me to restore their worship in its utmost purity, and I obey them, yes, and with a good will. For they promise great rewards for my labours, if only I am not remiss.
>
> (Julian, *Letter* 8.415C–D, to Maximus of Ephesus, written November 361)

Julian's self-appointed aim was the 'restoration' of traditional religion. Yet his own beliefs were far from traditional. Raised as a Christian, Julian was influenced by the Neoplatonic philosophy of Maximus and developed a highly idiosyncratic vision of 'paganism' which combined intellectual spirituality with large-scale animal sacrifice. Once he became emperor, he promoted the creation of a 'Pagan Church' directly modelled on Christianity, with a hierarchy of priests and support for charity.

> Though just conduct in accordance with the laws of the state will of course be the concern of the governors of cities, you in your turn will properly take care to exhort men not to transgress the laws of the gods, since those are sacred. Moreover, inasmuch as the life of a priest ought to be more holy than the political life, you must guide and instruct men to adopt it. The better sort will naturally follow your guidance. Indeed, I pray that all men may, but at any rate I hope that those who are naturally good and upright will do so; for they will recognize that your teachings are particularly adapted to them. You must above all exercise philanthropy, for from it result many other blessings, and moreover that choicest and greatest blessing of all, the good will of the gods. For just as those who are in agreement with their masters about their friendships and ambitions and loves are more kindly treated than their fellow slaves, so we must suppose that God, who naturally loves human beings, has more kindness for those men who love their fellows.
>
> (Julian, *Letter to a Priest* 288C–289B)

In his attempt to restore the pre-eminence of the ancient gods over Christianity, Julian thus drew on the Church for inspiration and gave 'paganism' a more defined structure and clerical leadership. He largely avoided open persecution of Christians, not least to avoid the creation of new martyrs, and preferred to undermine the Church by more subtle means. But even for many who believed in the traditional gods, Julian seemed alien. His intellectualism and his love of blood sacrifice set him apart, and his attempted 'restoration' was doomed to fail. In 362 Julian was based in Antioch while he prepared for an attack upon the Persian empire to the east. During his stay he visited the shrine of Apollo at nearby Daphne. Julian himself describes his dismay at what he found.

> I imagined in my own mind the sort of procession it would be, like a man seeing visions in a dream, with beasts for sacrifice, libations, choruses in honour of the

god, incense, and the youths of your city there surrounding the shrine, their souls adorned with all holiness and themselves attired in white and splendid garments. But when I entered the shrine I found there no incense, not so much as a cake, not a single beast for sacrifice. For a moment I was amazed and thought that I was still outside the shrine and that you were waiting the signal from me, doing me that honour because I am supreme pontiff. But when I began to inquire what sacrifice the city intended to offer to celebrate the annual festival in honour of the god, the priest answered 'I have brought with me from my own house a goose as an offering to the god, but the city this time has made no preparations'.

(Julian, *Misopogon* 362A–B)

The dream of a 'pagan revival' already shattered, Julian set out into Persia and died there. His reign of just eighteen months did little to halt the growth of Christianity, although psychologically Julian left a deeper legacy and a reminder to Christians that their triumph was not yet assured. The years immediately following Julian's death were a period of relative religious peace, but the early 380s saw increasing tensions. After the emperor Theodosius I (379–395) came to power, a series of Christian attacks upon temples in the eastern Mediterranean provoked the orator Libanius, an old friend and supporter of Julian, into an impassioned defence of the traditional cults.

Such outrages occur in the cities, but especially in the countryside. There are many enemies everywhere, and after innumerable crimes have been perpetrated, the scattered multitude unites and comes together. They require of each other an account of what they have done, and a man is ashamed who cannot tell of some great outrage of which he has been guilty. Thus they spread themselves over the countryside like torrents, and by ravaging the temples, they ravage the estates. For wherever they demolish the temple from an estate, at the same time the estate itself is blinded, declines and dies. Temples, O Emperor, are the soul of the countryside. They mark the beginning of its settlement, and they have subsisted for many ages to this time. In them the farming communities rest all their hopes, for husbands and wives and children, and for oxen and seeds and the plants of the ground. Wherever any estate has lost its temples, that estate is lost and so are the hopes of the community and their inspiration. For they believe that they will labour in vain, when they are deprived of the gods who should bless their labours.

(Libanius, *Pro Templis*, Oration 30.9–10, c.386)

In 384, almost exactly contemporary to Libanius' *Pro Templis*, a parallel debate occurred in the west over the place of traditional religion in an increasingly Christian empire. The focus of the debate was the Altar of Victory, originally erected in the Roman Senate House by the first emperor Augustus to commemorate his defeat of Antony and Cleopatra at Actium. Removed by Constantius II but restored under Julian, the Altar was removed again in 382 by Theodosius' western co-ruler Gratian (367–383). After Gratian's death, the Roman senator and urban prefect Quintus Aurelius Symmachus sent a petition to the new western emperor Valentinian II (375–392) requesting the Altar's restoration. For Symmachus, the Altar was a symbol of the bond between the traditional Roman cults and the Roman state.

Let us suppose that Roma herself stands here in your presence and addresses you with these words, 'Best of emperors, fathers of your country, have respect for my years which the pious observance of our rites has won for me. Permit me to continue to practice my ancestral ceremonies, for I do not repent of them. Permit me to live by my own customs, for I am free. This worship subjected the world to my laws, these sacrifices drove Hannibal from my walls and the Senones from the Capitol. Was I preserved then only for this, that I should be reprimanded in my old age? If I must I will see what manner of innovation might be introduced, but change in old age comes too late and is humiliating'. Thus we ask for peace for the gods of our fathers, the gods of our native land. It is reasonable to believe that whatever is worshipped by each of us is ultimately one and the same. We gaze at the same stars, we share the same sky, the same universe surrounds us. What does it matter what philosophy we each adopt to search for the truth? Not by a single route alone is it possible to reach so great a secret.

(Symmachus, *Third Relatio* 9–10)

Symmachus' plea for religious toleration was met by Ambrose, bishop of Milan where Valentinian II resided.

Roma has given no such charge. She speaks with words of a different character. 'Why do you stain me daily with the useless blood of harmless herds? Trophies of victory derive from the strength of warriors not from the entrails of animals. I subjugated the world through another discipline. Camillus brought back the standards taken from the Capitol by fighting, after he had slain the Gauls who had seized the Tarpeian rock. Valour laid low those whom cults failed to drive away. What shall I say of Atilius [Regulus], who gave service through his death? [Scipio] Africanus won his triumph amongst the battle lines of Hannibal not amongst the altars of the Capitol. Why do you bring forward these examples from our ancestors? I hate the rites of the Neros. Must I speak of emperors who reigned for no more than two months, and of rulers whose accession was immediately followed by their downfall? Or is it perhaps something new for barbarians to march across their boundaries? And what of those two emperors who set a wretched and novel precedent, one of whom was taken captive while in the reign of the other the whole world was taken prisoner? Did they not reveal that their rituals which promised victory were false? Were they too Christians? Was there in those days no Altar of Victory? I am ashamed of my past errors. White-haired with age, I blush at that shameful bloodshed. But I do not blush to be converted in my old age at the same time as the whole world. It is undoubtedly true that no age is too old to learn. Let only that old age blush which cannot mend its ways. It is the character not the years of white-haired age that is to be praised, and there is no shame in changing to better things. That I did not know of God is the one thing that I once had in common with the barbarians. Your sacrifice is a rite of being sprinkled with the blood of beasts. Why do you look for the words of God in dead animals? Come while you are still on earth and learn of the service of heaven, for while we live here, we serve there. Let God Himself, who made the world, teach me the mystery of heaven, not some human being who did not know himself. Whom should I believe concerning God, if not God? How can I possibly believe you, who confess that you are ignorant of what you worship?'. So great a secret, he says, cannot be reached by a single route. But what you do not know, we know from the voice of God, and what you seek in uncertainty we have found with certainty from the very Wisdom and Truth of God. Our aims, therefore, are not the same as yours. You ask for peace for your gods from our emperors, we ask for peace for the emperors themselves from Christ.

(Ambrose of Milan, *Letter* 18.7–8)

The hard-line argument of Ambrose won the day and Symmachus' petition was denied. In truth, the Altar of Victory itself was of little significance to those who did not share the concerns of Rome's educated elite or their respect for the ancient past. But the Altar's fate became a symbol for the decline of the traditional Roman cults and the changing religious world of the fourth century. A few years later, in part again due to Ambrose's influence, Theodosius I took the crucial step of outlawing all forms of traditional 'pagan' worship.

Emperors Valentinian, Theodosius and Arcadius Augusti to Albinus, Prefect of the City. No person shall pollute himself with sacrificial animals; no person shall slaughter an innocent victim; no person shall approach the shrines, shall wander through the temples, or revere the images formed by mortal labour, lest he become guilty by divine and human laws. Judges also shall be bound by the general rule that if any of them should be devoted to profane rites and should enter a temple for the purpose of worship anywhere, either on a journey or in the city, he shall immediately be compelled to pay 15 pounds of gold, and his office staff shall pay a like sum with similar haste, unless they resist the judge and immediately report him by a public attestation. Governors with the rank of consular shall pay 6 pounds of gold each, their office staffs a like amount; those with the rank of corrector or of praeses shall pay 4 pounds each, and their apparitors, by equal lot, a like amount. Given on the sixth day before the kalends of March at Milan in the year of the consulship of Tatianus and Symmachus [24 February 391].

(*Theodosian Code* 16.10.10)

Emperors Valentinian, Theodosius and Arcadius Augusti to Evagrius, Augustal Prefect, and Romanus, Count of Egypt. No person shall be granted the right to perform sacrifices; no person shall go around the temples; no person shall revere the shrines. All persons shall recognize that they are excluded from profane entrance into temples by the opposition of Our law, so that if any person should attempt to do anything with reference to the gods or the sacred rites, contrary to Our prohibition, he shall learn that he will not be exempted from punishment by any special grants of imperial favour. If any judge also, during the time of his administration, should rely on the privilege of his power, and as a sacrilegious violator of the law, should enter polluted places, he shall be forced to pay into Our treasury 15 pounds of gold, and his office staff a like sum, unless they opposed him with their combined strength. Given on the sixteenth day before the kalends of July at Aquileia in the year of the consulship of Tatianus and Symmachus [16 June 391].

(*Theodosian Code* 16.10.11)

The passing of these edicts did not of course mean that all 'pagan' practices immediately ceased. The vehemence of the imperial rhetoric against those who evaded the laws reflected the difficulties involved in their enforcement. Nevertheless, when Theodosius I died in 395 Christianity had become the majority religion of the empire, and at least at the level of law and imperial image the Roman empire was a Christian empire. A subsequent law passed by his grandson Theodosius II (408–450) declared very simply (and inaccurately):

> The regulations of constitutions formerly promulgated shall suppress any pagans who survive, although We now believe that there are none.
>
> (*Theodosian Code*, 16.10.22, AD 423)

Within the Christian Roman empire, Christianity never became the sole and exclusive religion that the imperial laws imagined. Belief in the traditional gods survived, among both the educated elite and the rural population, throughout the fifth century and beyond. Far more importantly, however, when we speak of the 'Christianization' of the Roman empire we cannot look merely at the attitudes of the emperors or at episodes of conflict like the Altar of Victory debate. 'Christianization' is not a straightforward story of Christian triumph or of one religion replacing another, and conflict was the exception not the rule. Across the empire, Christians and non-Christians lived side by side. As more and more converts embraced Christianity, it was inevitable that Christianity would absorb traditional customs and give them new meanings. One such story is recounted by Paulinus of Nola, who described the miraculous offering of a heifer in honour of Felix the martyr-saint of Nola. The farmers who had vowed to present the heifer to Felix attempted to yoke the beast to their wagon for the journey to the martyr's shrine. The animal refused the harness, and yet followed the farmers of its own accord.

> It became friend and guide to the previously hated wagon, until they approached to the sacred shrine of Felix. There voluntarily it came to a halt, and drew close upon being called. As appropriate for one discharging a vow, it rejoiced to stand in the proper place where as victim it owed its death. The one that had rebelled and rejected human bonds was led to a peaceful fate without a struggle. Undefiled by the yoke, it offered its neck to the axe to provide food for the poor from its slaughtered body, and joyfully poured forth its blood in fulfilment of its masters' vows.
>
> (Paulinus of Nola, *Poem* 20.427–436, AD 406)

Paulinus gives us a rare insight into the rural world of early fifth-century Italy. The farmers of his story are Christian, bringing their animal to the martyr's shrine where the meat will be given in charity to the needy. Yet previous generations would have done the same in honour of the traditional gods, offering an animal for sacrifice in fulfilment of a vow. The martyr-saint Felix had replaced the local cult of Apollo, but for the people of Nola and the surrounding countryside little else had changed.

Even Rome's most traditional festivals could survive in a Christian setting. Almost a hundred years after Paulinus, bishop Gelasius of Rome (492–496) found himself in conflict with his own congregation over the ongoing celebration of the Lupercalia. This ancient fertility festival, at which in 44 BC Antony offered a diadem to Julius Caesar, was still celebrated in the 490s under the patronage of Rome's Christian aristocracy. The bishop wrote to one of those aristocrats, warning of dire consequences if the Lupercalia was not abandoned.

> I do not doubt that my predecessors also perhaps did this [i.e. sought to have the festival abolished], and tried at imperial audiences to have these things removed. Because it is not certain that they were heard, since these evils continue even today, this is the reason that the imperial authority itself has failed, and it is for this reason also (that is, since the Lupercalia has not been removed), that the Roman name has reached the very last extremity. And for this reason I now advise that they be removed.
>
> (Gelasius of Rome, *Letter* 31, to Andromachus)

Gelasius associated the Lupercalia's survival with the collapse of the western Roman empire, but there is no evidence that his protest had any practical effect. The distinction between 'Christian' and 'pagan' customs was never as clear-cut as the imperial laws and the writings of bishops would have us believe. Julian 'the Apostate', whose black and white approach to religion paralleled that of his most severe Christian opponents, had a similar shock to Gelasius when he visited the site of Troy (Ilios) back in the 350s and was met by Pegasius, the local Christian bishop.

> Pegasius came to meet me, as I wished to explore the city – this was my excuse for visiting the temples – and he was my guide and showed me all the sights. So now let me tell you what he did and said, and from it one may guess that he was not lacking in right sentiments towards the gods. Hector has a hero's shrine there

and his bronze statue stands in a tiny little temple. Opposite this they have set up a figure of the great Achilles in the unroofed court. If you have seen the spot you will certainly recognize my description of it. You can learn from the guides the story that accounts for the fact that great Achilles was set up opposite to him and takes up the whole of the unroofed court. Now I found that the altars were still alight, I might almost say still blazing, and that the statue of Hector had been anointed till it shone. So I looked at Pegasius and said, 'What does this mean? Do the people of Ilios offer sacrifices?'. This was to test him cautiously to find out his own views. He replied, 'Is it not natural that they should worship a brave man who was their own citizen, just as we worship the martyrs?'. Now the analogy was far from sound; but his point of view and intentions were those of a man of culture, if you consider the times in which we then lived. Observe what followed. 'Let us go', he said, 'to the shrine of Athena of Ilios'. Thereupon with the greatest eagerness he led me there and opened the temple, and as though he were producing evidence he showed me all the statues in perfect preservation, nor did he behave at all as those impious men usually do, I mean when they make the sign on their impious foreheads, nor did he hiss to himself as they do. For these two things are the quintessence of their theology, to hiss at demons and make the sign of the cross on their foreheads.

(Julian, *Letter* 19, to a Priest)

When Julian became emperor, he appointed Pegasius a priest of his 'Pagan Church'. Like Paulinus' farmers and Gelasius' aristocrats, Pegasius' actions reflect the blurring of the lines between what was 'Christian' and what was 'pagan'. One can sympathize with Raedwald, the king of East Anglia (died c.624) who is the strongest candidate to have been buried in the ship at Sutton Hoo. Raedwald was one of the first Anglo-Saxon rulers who converted to Christianity, but he too struggled to recognize his new religion's exclusivity.

Raedwald had long before been initiated into the mysteries of the Christian faith in Kent, but in vain; for on his return home, he was seduced by his wife and by certain evil teachers and perverted from the sincerity of his faith, so that his last state was worse than his first. After the manner of the ancient Samaritans, he seemed to be serving both Christ and the gods whom he had previously served; in the same temple he had one altar for the Christian sacrifice and another small altar on which to offer victims to devils.

(Bede, *Ecclesiastical History of the English People* 2.15)

In the three centuries that separated Constantine and Raedwald, Christianity took firm root as the pre-eminent religion of the Later Roman empire and the post-Roman west. This golden age of 'Christianization', however, was far more than a simple narrative of Christian triumph. As Christianity expanded, the Church absorbed and refashioned the traditional values, customs and rituals of classical Graeco-Roman antiquity. Christian festivals like Christmas gradually superseded 'pagan' holidays such as the Saturnalia, just as the veneration of saints and relics provided a focus for Christian worship to replace the cults of local and household gods. The Christian bishop took on many of the roles played by imperial officials, while the Roman public basilica became the standard design for a western church. All these themes are explored in greater detail in other chapters of this sourcebook. The 'Christianization' of the ancient world was a long and complex process which changed both Christianity and the Roman empire and shaped western history for the next millennium.

Copyright Acknowledgements

Further Reading

P. Athanassiadi, *Julian: An Intellectual Biography* (London and New York 1992)

T. D. Barnes, *Constantine and Eusebius* (Cambridge, Mass. and London 1981)

P. Brown, *Authority and the Sacred: Aspects of the Christianisation of the Roman World* (Cambridge 1995)

Al. Cameron, *The Last Pagans of Rome* (Oxford and New York 2011)

J. Curran, *Pagan City and Christian Capital: Rome in the Fourth Century* (Oxford 2000)

J. Elsner, *Imperial Rome and Christian Triumph: The Art of the Roman Empire* AD *100–450* (Oxford 1998)

R. Fletcher, *The Conversion of Europe: From Paganism to Christianity 371–1386* AD (London 1997)

M. Gaddis, *There Is No Crime for Those Who Have Christ: Religious Violence in the Christian Roman Empire* (Berkeley, Los Angeles and London 2005)

J. N. Hillgarth (ed.), *Christianity and Paganism, 350–750: The Conversion of Western Europe*, revised edition (Philadelphia 1986)

R. MacMullen, *Christianizing the Roman Empire, AD 100–400* (New Haven 1984)

R. MacMullen, *Christianity and Paganism in the Fourth to Eight Centuries* (New Haven and London 1997)

A. Momigliano (ed.), *The Conflict between Paganism and Christianity in the Fourth Century* (Oxford 1963)

M. R. Salzman, *The Making of a Christian Aristocracy: Social and Religious Change in the Western Roman Empire* (Cambridge, Mass. and London 2002)

F. R. Trombley, *Hellenic Religion and Christianization c.370–529*, 2 volumes (Leiden 1993–1994)

D. E. Trout, *Paulinus of Nola: Life, Letters and Poems* (Berkeley, Los Angeles and London 1999)

12

Paideia: Christianity and Classical Culture

Christianity came into existence in a world shaped by the culture of classical Greece and Rome. The Roman empire already ruled the Mediterranean at the time of Christ, and the early Christians lived in Greek and Roman cities and spread their teachings along Roman roads and seaways. From the beginning, Christianity was therefore surrounded by the symbolism of that ruling culture. Classical art and literature were saturated with mythological imagery depicting the gods and heroes of traditional Graeco-Roman religion. This inevitably led to tension for Christian converts, particularly those from the upper classes of society. In the Later Roman empire only the elite received an extensive education, which centred around the great Greek and Latin authors from Homer and Herodotus to Cicero and Virgil. Knowledge of those authors identified a person who possessed *paideia*, the cultural matrix which in turn defined the Roman elite. As Christianity began to attract followers from within the elite, serious questions came to be raised over whether such classical learning could be reconciled with the new religion, questions that had profound consequences for the cultural history of Europe.

During the first three centuries AD, Christianity only gradually began to penetrate the Roman elite. Yet some writers already expressed concern that Graeco-Roman culture might corrupt the Christian message. The North African Tertullian (c.160–c.225) blamed classical philosophy for the errors of heretics like the 'Gnostic' Valentinus, ending with his famous denunciation: What has Athens to do with Jerusalem.

The same themes are discussed over and over again by the heretics and the philosophers; the same arguments are involved. Whence comes evil? Why is it permitted? What is the origin of man? And in what way does he come? Besides the question which Valentinus has very lately proposed: Whence comes God? No doubt from Desire and Abortion! Unhappy Aristotle, who taught these men dialectic, the art which destroys as much as it builds, which changes its opinions like a coat, forces its conjectures, is stubborn in argument, works hard at being contentious and is a burden even to itself. For it reconsiders every point to make sure it never finishes a discussion. From philosophy come those fables and endless genealogies and unprofitable questions, those words which spread like a cancer. When the Apostle would restrain us from all these things, he expressly names philosophy as that which we should be on our guard against. Writing to the Colossians, he says, 'See to it that no one takes you captive through philosophy and empty deceit, according to human tradition' [Colossians 2.8], contrary to the providence of the Holy Spirit. He had been at Athens where he had become acquainted with that human wisdom which pretends to know the truth, while it only corrupts it, and is itself divided into its own manifold heresies by the variety of its mutually repugnant sects. What indeed has Athens to do with Jerusalem? What has the Academy to do with the Church? What have heretics to do with Christians?

(Tertullian, *Prescriptions against Heretics* 7)

Constantine's conversion significantly increased the popularity of Christianity among Rome's educated citizens. Serious debate over Christianity's relationship with classical culture, however, only began in the reign of Julian 'the Apostate' (361–363). The last 'pagan' emperor, Julian insisted that only those who believed in the traditional gods could truly appreciate the literature on which the *paideia* of the educated elite was based. He thus passed an edict banning Christians from teaching, and by doing so forced his Christian subjects to re-examine their culture and beliefs.

All who profess to teach anything whatever ought to be men of upright character, and ought not to harbour in their souls opinions irreconcilable with what they publicly profess; and above all, I believe it is necessary that those who associate with the young and teach them rhetoric should be of that upright character; for they expound the writings of the ancients, whether they be rhetoricians or grammarians, and still more if they are sophists. For these claim to teach, in addition to other things, not only the use of words, but morals also, and they assert that political philosophy is their peculiar field. Let us leave aside for the moment the question whether this is true or not. But while I applaud them for aspiring to such high pretensions, I should applaud them still more if they did not utter falsehoods and convict themselves of thinking one thing and teaching their pupils another. What! Was it not the gods who revealed all their learning to Homer, Hesiod, Demosthenes, Herodotus, Thucydides, Isocrates and Lysias? Did not these men think that they were consecrated, some to Hermes, others to the Muses? I think it is absurd that men who expound the works of these writers should dishonour the gods whom they used to honour.

(Julian, *Letter 36: Rescript on Christian Teachers*)

Reaction to Julian's edict was almost universally hostile, as the importance of education to the Late Roman elite transcended religious differences. Even Ammianus Marcellinus, a strong supporter of Julian and like him a believer in the traditional gods, condemned the measure.

He was guilty of one harsh act which should be buried in lasting oblivion; he banned adherents of Christianity from practicing as teachers of rhetoric or literature.

(Ammianus Marcellinus, *Res Gestae* 22.10)

Some Christians sought to evade the law by combining classical literary models with the Christian Scriptures. Most notable were the efforts of two teachers, a father and son, each named Apollinaris.

Both being skilled in polite learning, the father as a grammarian and the son as a rhetorician, they made themselves serviceable to the Christians at this crisis. For the former, as a grammarian, composed a grammar consistent with the Christian faith. He also translated the Books of Moses into heroic verse; and paraphrased all the historical books of the Old Testament, putting them partly into dactylic measure and partly reducing them to the form of dramatic tragedy. He purposely employed all kinds of verse, that no form of expression peculiar to the Greek language might be unknown or unheard of amongst Christians. The younger Apollinaris, who was well trained in eloquence, expounded the Gospels and apostolic doctrines in the way of dialogue, as Plato among the Greeks had done. Thus showing themselves useful to the Christian cause they overcame the subtlety of the emperor through their own labours.

(Socrates, *Ecclesiastical History* 3.16)

Julian's edict was revoked upon his sudden death in 363, and the Apollinares' works were abandoned and lost. Nevertheless, their efforts highlighted the dilemma that Julian had posed. For the vast majority of educated fourth-century Christians, the literature of the classical past was a crucial part of their cultural identity. Few wished to abandon that identity, and for those few there was no alternative education system to which they could turn, no exclusively Christian counterpart to the *paideia* that defined the Late Roman elite. The prevailing consensus, particularly in the Greek-speaking eastern Church, was that Christians could embrace the traditional classics as long as they remained vigilant against the errors of the 'pagan' authors. The theologian Basil of Cappadocian Caesarea (330–379) laid down the argument in his *Address to Young Men*.

That such pagan learning is not unprofitable for the soul has perhaps been sufficiently demonstrated; I shall therefore discuss next the extent to which one may pursue it. To begin with the poets, since their writings deal with subjects of every kind, you should not study all that they write without exception. When they recount the words and deeds of good men, you should both love and imitate them, earnestly emulating such conduct. But when they portray wicked men, you must flee from them and stop up your ears, as Odysseus is said to have avoided the song of the Sirens. For familiarity with evil words paves the way for evil deeds. Thus the soul must be guarded with great care, lest through pleasure from the poets' words we may receive some contamination unawares, as men drink in poison with honey. We shall not praise the poets when they revile or mock, when they represent fornicators and drunkards, when they define happiness by laden tables and wanton songs. Least of all shall we listen to them when they tell us of their gods, and especially when they represent them as being many and as not in accord even with each other. For at times in their poems brother is at variance with brother, or the father with his children, or the children engage in truceless war against their parents. The adulteries of the gods and their amours, especially those of the one whom they call Zeus, chief of all and most high, are things of which one cannot speak even in connection with brute beasts and which we shall leave to the stage.

I have the same words for the writers of prose, and especially when they make up stories for the amusement of their hearers. And certainly we shall not follow the example of the rhetoricians in the art of lying. For neither in the courts of justice nor in other business affairs is falsehood befitting to us, who have chosen the straight and true path of life and are forbidden by the Gospel to turn to law. On the other hand we shall receive gladly those passages in which they praise virtue or condemn vice. For just as bees know how to extract honey from flowers, which to men are agreeable only for their fragrance and colour, so here also those who look for something more than pleasure and enjoyment in such writers may derive profit for their souls. It is therefore in accordance with the manner of bees that we must use these writings. For the bees do not visit all flowers without discrimination, nor indeed do they seek to carry away entire those upon which they alight, but having taken so much as is suitable to their needs they leave the rest untouched. So we ourselves, if we are wise, shall take from the pagan books what is suitable to us and allied to the truth, and shall pass over the rest.

(Basil of Cappadocian Caesarea, *Address to Young Men* 4)

Yet there was a small but vocal minority of Late Roman Christians who struggled to reconcile their faith with their education. Like Julian, albeit for different reasons, they believed that a true Christian vocation required abandoning the 'pagan' classics. Those who held such views were strongly influenced by the ascetic movement, which encouraged separation from worldly distractions, and were more prominent in the Latin-speaking west than in the east. The psychological turmoil that the conflict between faith and education could arouse received an extreme expression in the dream of Jerome, which he recounted in 383/4 in an open letter to the virgin Eustochium in Rome.

Many years ago for the sake of the kingdom of heaven I cut myself off from home, parents, sister, relations and – harder still – from the dainty food to which I had been accustomed. But even when I was on the way to Jerusalem to fight the good fight there, I still could not bring myself to forgo the library which I had gathered with great care and labour at Rome. And so, miserable man that I was, I would fast, only to read Cicero afterwards. After many nights spent in vigil, after floods of tears called from my innermost heart by the recollection of my past sins, I would once more take up Plautus. Whenever I returned to my right mind and began to read the prophets, their language seemed harsh and barbarous. I failed to see the light with my blinded eyes; but I attributed the fault not to my eyes but to the sun. While the old serpent was thus mocking me, about the middle of Lent a fever attacked my weakened body and spread through my inmost veins. The story seems hardly credible, but it so wasted my unhappy frame that scarcely anything was left of me but skin and bone. Meantime preparations for my funeral went on. My whole body grew gradually colder, and the warmth of life only lingered faintly in my throbbing breast.

Suddenly I was caught up in the spirit and dragged before the Judge's judgement seat. Here the light was so bright, and those who stood around were so radiant, that I cast myself upon the ground and did not dare to look up. I was asked who and what I was, and I replied 'I am a Christian'. But He who presided said: 'You lie; you are a Ciceronian, not a Christian. "For where your treasure is, there will your heart be also" [Matthew 6.21]'. Instantly I became dumb, and amid the strokes of the whip – for He had ordered me to be scourged – I was even more bitterly tortured by the fire of conscience, considering with myself the verse: 'In the grave who shall give you thanks?' [Psalm 6.5]. Yet for all that I began to cry out and to bewail myself, saying 'Have mercy upon me, O Lord, have mercy upon me'. Even amid the sound of the lashes this cry made itself heard. At last the bystanders, falling down before the knees of Him who presided, prayed that He would have pity on my youth and that He would give me opportunity to repent of my error. He might still, they urged, inflict torture upon me, should I ever again read the works of the Gentiles. Under the stress of that awful moment I should have been willing to make even larger promises. Accordingly I took oath and called upon His name, saying: 'O Lord, if ever again I possess worldly books or read them, I have denied you'.

(Jerome, *Letter* 22.30)

Jerome was an exceptional case, and his traumatic dream is open to many different interpretations. But he was not alone in the unease he felt. His contemporary Augustine of Hippo rose from relatively humble North African origins to be a professor and court orator in Rome and Milan through his gifts for education. Looking back after he had committed himself to a Christian ascetic life, however, Augustine renounced Virgil and regretted his wasted studies beyond the essential skills of reading and writing.

Those elementary lessons were far more valuable, because their subjects were practical. Through them I acquired, and still retain, the power of reading whatever I find written and writing myself whatever I wish. In the other lessons I was compelled to learn about the wanderings of a certain Aeneas, oblivious to my own wanderings, and to weep for the dead Dido, who slew herself for love, while at the same time in the midst of those things I looked on with dry eyes at my wretched self dying far from you, my God and my Life. What can be more pitiful than the wretch who does not mourn himself shedding tears over Dido's death for the love of Aeneas, yet shedding no tears over his own death in not loving you, O God, Light of my heart, Bread of my innermost soul, and the Power that binds my mind with my inmost thoughts? I did not love you and committed fornication against you, while those around me applauded. For the friendship of this world is fornication against you, and yet men applaud until one feels ashamed not to be such a man. And for this I shed no tears, though I wept for Dido, who sought death at the sword's point, while I forsook you and sought the lowest of your creatures. If I was forbidden to read these things, how grieved I was that I was not permitted to read what made me sad. This sort of folly is considered a more honourable and more fruitful learning than that by which I learned to read and write.

(Augustine of Hippo, *Confessions* 1.13)

The anxiety of Augustine and Jerome was far from typical. Most educated Christians in the Late Roman west, as in the east, saw no difficulty in combining their religion and their *paideia*. The Proiecta Casket is part of a hoard of silver artefacts discovered on Rome's Esquiline Hill in 1793 and now in the British Museum. The casket appears to have been a wedding gift to the couple depicted on the lid, while on the casket's front face sits Venus on her cockle-shell regarding herself in a mirror. Yet below the goddess runs the inscription that gives the casket its name:

Secunde et Proiecta vivatis in Chri(sto)
'Secundus and Proiecta, may you live in Christ'
(Proiecta Casket, Esquiline Treasure Hoard, late fourth century)

Neither the giver nor the recipients of the casket saw any conflict between the invocation of Christ and the depiction of Venus as the traditional symbol of love and beauty. Nor was it easy for those Christians so comfortable with their *paideia* to understand those who took a more extreme view. The close friendship between the Gallic rhetor Ausonius of Bordeaux and his former protégé Paulinus of Nola collapsed as Paulinus devoted himself to an ascetic lifestyle. Although a sincere Christian, Ausonius pleaded with Paulinus to maintain their relationship in a letter filled with classical imagery.

This yoke is so mild that Mars' horses would endure with obedient neck, and those wild steeds stolen from the stable of Diomedes, and even that team which, when another than the Sun held their reins, plunged lightning-blasted Phaëthon into the Padus. Yet it is being shaken off, Paulinus; and that, not through the fault of both, but of one alone – of you. For my neck will ever bear it gladly.

(Ausonius of Bordeaux, *Letter* 27, to Paulinus)

Paulinus' reply dismissed Ausonius' appeal to the classics as incompatible with the Christian life.

> Why, my father, do you bid the deposed Muses return to my affection? Hearts consecrated to Christ reject the Camenae and are closed to Apollo. Once there was this accord between you and me, equal in zeal if not in resources, to call forth deaf Apollo from his cave at Delphi, to invoke the Muses as divine, to seek from groves or hills the gift of utterance bestowed by divine gift. Now another power inspires my mind, a greater God, who demands another way of life and claims back from man the gift He gave so that we may live for the Father of life. He forbids us to spend time on the empty things of leisure and business or the idle tales of literature, so that we may obey His laws and behold His light which is clouded by the cunning of the sophists, the arts of the rhetoricians, and the inventions of the poets. These steep our hearts in what is false and vain. They train only our tongues, and impart nothing which can reveal the truth or bestow salvation. For what good or truth can they possess who do not have the head of all, God, the enkindler and source of goodness and truth, whom no man sees except in Christ?
>
> (Paulinus of Nola, *Poem* 10, to Ausonius)

For Paulinus, as for his friends Augustine and Jerome, Christian truth stood in direct opposition to classical *paideia*. But an essential difficulty remained. At the end of the fourth century there was still no Christian education system, no alternative for teaching the young except through the traditional authors. Jerome, who in his dream had sworn to abandon all worldly books, nevertheless conceded the enduring value of the classics. His argument followed similar lines to that of Basil of Cappadocian Caesarea, and invoked St Paul as a scriptural guide.

> He [Paul] had learned from the true David to wrench the sword of the enemy out of his hand and with his own blade to cut off the head of the arrogant Goliath. He had read in Deuteronomy the command given by the voice of the Lord that when a captive woman had had her head shaved, her eyebrows and all her hair cut off, and her nails pared, she might then be taken to wife [Deuteronomy 21.10–13]. Is it surprising that I too, admiring the fairness of her form and the grace of her eloquence, desire to make that secular wisdom which is my captive and my handmaid, a matron of the true Israel? Or that shaving off and cutting away all in her that is dead whether this be idolatry, pleasure, error, or lust, I take

her to myself clean and pure and beget by her servants for the Lord of Sabaoth? My efforts promote the advantage of Christ's family, my so-called defilement with an alien increases the number of my fellow-servants.

(Jerome, *Letter* 70.2, to the orator Magnus, AD 397)

Augustine took this argument a stage further. For the first time, he began to consider how to develop an education system based firmly around Christian principles. The model for such a system was laid down in Augustine's *De Doctrina Christiana* (*On Christian Teaching*), composed between 395 and 426.

I think that it is beneficial to warn studious and able youths, who fear God and seek a life of true happiness, not to venture heedlessly into the branches of learning that are encouraged outside the church of Christ, as if these could secure for them the happiness they seek, but to discriminate soberly and carefully among them. Those that they find to have been instituted by men, which vary according to the differing aims of their founders and cause uncertainty through erroneous conjectures, should be utterly rejected and held in detestation, especially if they involve entering into fellowship with demons through contracts and covenants of signs. Likewise avoid such institutions of men as are unnecessary and self-indulgent. It is true that, for the sake of the necessities of this life, we must not neglect those human institutions that enable us to carry on social intercourse with those around us. In the other branches of learning that are found among the pagans, however, I think that there is nothing useful apart from the study of things past or present which relate to the bodily senses, in which are included the experiments and conclusions of the practical arts and the sciences of reasoning and number.

(Augustine of Hippo, *De Doctrina Christiana* 2.39)

The only true function of secular learning, Augustine concluded, was to aid the interpretation and preaching of the Scriptures. Therefore the purpose of education was to prepare the recipient for study of the Scriptures in which all truths are found.

Whatever a person may learn independently of the Scriptures is condemned there if it is harmful but contained there if it is useful. And while a person may find there all the useful knowledge that they have learnt elsewhere, they will also find there in much greater abundance things that are to be found nowhere else, but can be learnt only from the wonderful sublimity and wonderful simplicity of the Scriptures.

(Augustine of Hippo, *De Doctrina Christiana* 2.42)

During Augustine's lifetime, arguments for a Christian scriptural education system exerted only limited influence. The Late Roman elite remained immersed in the classical *paideia* that defined their culture. The crucial change in fact came not through the rise of Christianity, but the collapse of the Roman empire in the west. Knowledge of the great classical poets, orators and philosophers gave the Roman elite not only their *paideia* but also the literacy and rhetorical training required by the bureaucratic imperial government. The western empire's collapse removed the prime need to possess such skills, while the elites of the emerging Germanic kingdoms exalted martial strength over textual learning. Gregory of Tours (c.539–594) opened his *History of the Franks* with a sad invocation of cultural decline.

A great many things keep happening, some of them good, some of them bad. The inhabitants of different countries keep quarrelling fiercely with each other and kings go on losing their temper in the most furious way. Our churches are attacked by the heretics and then protected by the catholics; the faith of Christ burns bright in many men, but it remains lukewarm in others; no sooner are the church-buildings endowed by the faithful than they are stripped bare again by those who have no faith. However, no writer has come to the fore who has been sufficiently skilled in setting things down in an orderly fashion to be able to describe these events in prose or in verse. In fact in the towns of Gaul the writing of literature has declined to the point where it has virtually disappeared altogether. Many people have complained about this, not once but time and time again. 'What a poor period this is!', they have been heard to say, 'If among all our people there is not one man to be found who can write a book about what is happening today, the pursuit of letters really is dead in us!'.

(Gregory of Tours, *History of the Franks*, Preface)

In the post-Roman west, the Church became the chief institution to promote literacy and the preservation of learning. This paved the way for the development of a Christian education system focused upon the Scriptures and the writings of the Church Fathers. Drawing on the earlier work of Jerome and Augustine, and alarmed at the destruction wrought in Italy by emperor Justinian's war against the Ostrogoths, the Roman statesman and monk Cassiodorus (c.485–c.585) completed his *Institutions of Divine and Secular Learning* in the 560s to guide those who sought a scriptural education.

> Together with blessed Pope Agapetus of Rome [bishop 535–536], I made efforts to collect money so that it should rather be the Christian schools in the city of Rome that could employ learned teachers – the money having been collected – from whom the faithful might gain eternal salvation for their souls and the adornment of sober and pure eloquence for their speech. They say that such a system existed for a long time at Alexandria and that the Hebrews are now using it enthusiastically in Nisibis, a city of Syria. But since I could not accomplish this task because of raging wars and violent struggles in the Kingdom of Italy – for a peaceful endeavour has no place in a time of unrest – I was moved by divine love to devise for you, with God's help, these introductory books to take the place of a teacher. Through them I believe that both the textual sequence of holy Scripture and also a compact account of secular letters may, with God's grace, be revealed. These works may seem rather plain in style since they offer not polished eloquence but basic description. But they are of great use as an introduction to the source both of knowledge of this world and of the salvation of the soul.
>
> (Cassiodorus, *Institutions of Divine and Secular Learning* 1.1)

For the history of early medieval education, the *Institutions* proved extremely influential. Cassiodorus emphasized the priority of scriptural over secular learning, and drew upon the older fifth-century author Martianus Capella, whose *De nuptiis Philologiae et Mercurii* (*On the Marriage of Philology and Mercury*) laid down the study of the seven liberal arts: Grammar, Dialectic, Rhetoric, Geometry, Arithmetic, Astronomy and Harmony (music). Despite the influence of these educational treatises, however, western standards of learning were reported to remain in decline even among monks and clergy. Only in the reign of Charlemagne (768–814) did education begin to revive, as the king took steps to prevent falling standards leading his subjects into error.

> Numerous letters have been sent to us in recent years from various monasteries notifying us of the efforts made on our behalf in sacred and pious prayer by the

brothers residing in them; and we have identified in most of these writings of theirs both correct sentiments and uncouth language. For what pious devotion dictated faithfully as regards content, an uneducated tongue was unable, through neglect of learning, to express without fault as regards form. Wherefore it came about that we began to fear lest, as skill in writing was deficient, so also wisdom for understanding the holy Scriptures might perchance be much less than it ought properly to be. And we are all well aware that, although verbal errors are dangerous, errors of understanding are much more so. Wherefore we exhort you not only not to neglect the study of letters but also, with most humble and God-pleasing application, to learn zealously for a purpose, namely, that you may be able the more easily and the more correctly to penetrate the mysteries of divine Scripture.

(Charlemagne, *On Cultivating Letters*, c.790)

Culture and education in the Greek-speaking regions of the Later Roman empire followed a very different path to that of the Latin west. The empire survived in the east, although much reduced by the fifth-century invasions and in the seventh century by the rise of Islam, and thus the imperial bureaucracy survived and with it the need for an educated secular elite. Churches and monasteries remained important educational centres but did not hold the same monopoly on learning, and respect for classical culture never disappeared. As late as the eleventh century, in the reign of Constantine IX Monomachos (1042–1055), a courtier in Constantinople could quote half a line from Homer's *Iliad* and expect to be understood (if not initially by the object of his flattery, the emperor's mistress Sclerena).

One day, when we, the imperial secretaries, were all together, the empress' retinue was taking part in a procession. Zoe herself [Constantine's wife] and her sister Theodora walked in this procession, followed by the Augusta, a new title granted Sclerena by the empresses, at the instigation of Constantine. As they were on their way – the route led them to the theatre, and this was the first time the ordinary people had seen Sclerena in company with Zoe and Theodora – one of the subtle flatterers softly quoted Homer's 'It were no shame . . .' [*Iliad* 3.156–7: 'It were no shame for Trojans and well-greaved Achaeans if for long time they suffer hardship for a woman like this one'] but did not complete the lines. At the time Sclerena gave no sign of having heard these words, but when the ceremony was over, she sought out the man who had uttered them and asked him what

> they meant. She repeated his quotation without a single mistake, pronouncing the words exactly as he had whispered them. As soon as he told her the story in detail, and the crowd showed its approval of his interpretation of the anecdote as well as of the Homeric reference, she was filled with pride and her flatterer was rewarded for his compliment.
>
> (Michael Psellos, *Chronographia* 6.61)

The relationship between Christianity and classical culture was one of the most controversial questions debated in the Later Roman empire. Despite the doubts expressed by some of the leading figures of the age, the majority of educated Late Roman Christians refused to abandon the classical *paideia* that defined their cultural identity. Yet the fall of the western Roman empire led to a parting of the ways between east and west. The Greek-speaking east remained connected to the classical past even as that past was subordinated beneath the triumph of Christianity. In the Latin west Christianity increasingly cut its ties to Graeco-Roman antiquity and a new Christian approach to education replaced the traditional ideal of *paideia*. The first steps had been taken in the western loss and rediscovery of the classical world which culminated in the Renaissance.

Copyright Acknowledgements

Cassiodorus, *Institutions of Divine and Secular Learning*
Translated in J. W. Halporn, *Cassiodorus: Institutions of Divine and Secular Learning* and *On the Soul* (Liverpool 2004), by permission of Liverpool University Press

Gregory of Tours, *History of the Franks*
Translated in L. Thorpe, *Gregory of Tours: The History of the Franks* (Harmondsworth 1974), by permission of Penguin Books Ltd

Michael Psellos, *Chronographia*
Translated in E. R. A. Sewter, *Michael Psellus: Fourteen Byzantine Rulers* (Harmondsworth 1966), by permission of Penguin Books Ltd

Further Reading

J. Bowen, *A History of Western Education. Volume I: The Ancient World* (London 1972)

P. Brown, *Power and Persuasion in Late Antiquity: Towards a Christian Empire* (Madison, Wisconsin 1992)

Av. Cameron, *Christianity and the Rhetoric of Empire: the Development of a Christian Discourse* (Berkeley, Los Angeles and London 1991)

C. N. Cochrane, *Christianity and Classical Culture: A study of Thought and Action from Augustus to Augustine* (Oxford 1944)

J. Elsner, *Imperial Rome and Christian Triumph: The Art of the Roman Empire* AD *100–450* (Oxford 1998)

C. Harrison, *Augustine: Christian Truth and Fractured Humanity* (Oxford 2000)

R. Kaster, *Guardians of Language: The Grammarian and Society in Late Antiquity* (Berkeley 1988)

J. N. D. Kelly, *Jerome* (London 1975)

H. I. Marrou, *A History of Education in Antiquity*, translated by G. Lamb (New York 1956)

J. J. O'Donnell, *Cassiodorus* (Berkeley 1979)

J. H. D. Scourfield (ed.), *Texts and Culture in Late Antiquity: Inheritance, Authority, and Change* (Swansea 2007)

E. J. Watts, *City and School in Late Antique Athens and Alexandria* (Berkeley, Los Angeles and London 2006)

E. G. Weltin, *Athens and Jerusalem: an Interpretative Essay on Christianity and Classical Culture* (Atlanta 1987)

13

Christians, Jews and Manichees

The Later Roman empire may have become a Christian empire, yet the population was never exclusively Christian. At the time of Constantine's conversion in 312 the bulk of his subjects were 'pagan', and only gradually did Christianity become the majority faith. There were also other significant religious minorities, two of which in particular exerted a powerful influence on Late Roman Christians. The Manichees, followers of the Persian prophet Mani, spread their dualist beliefs westward across the Mediterranean. But most important were the Jews, from whom the original Christians had separated and who now faced life under Christian imperial rule.

Judaism had a long and often difficult history within the Roman empire. The cooperation between the Jewish leadership and Pontius Pilate to secure Christ's crucifixion was the exception rather than the rule, and over the next century Roman Judaea repeatedly exploded into violence. The great revolt against Nero in 66 led to the Sack of Jerusalem in 70, interpreted by Christians as retribution for the Jews' crimes against Christ and His apostles.

After the ascension of our Saviour, the Jews had followed their crime against Him by devising as many plots as they could against His disciples. First Stephen was stoned to death by them; and after him James, the son of Zebedee and the brother of John, was beheaded; and finally James, the first who had held the episcopal seat in Jerusalem after our Saviour's ascension, died in the manner already described. The remaining apostles, who were plotted against incessantly with a view to their destruction, were driven out of Judaea and went to every land to preach the Gospel, relying upon the power of Christ who had said to them, 'Go and make disciples of all the nations in my name' [Matthew 28.19].

However, the people of the church in Jerusalem had been commanded by a revelation, received by approved men there before the war, to leave the city and dwell in a certain town in Peraea called Pella. When those who believed in Christ had come there from Jerusalem, then, as if the royal city of the Jews and the whole land of Judaea had been utterly abandoned by holy men, the judgment of God at last overtook those who had committed such outrages against Christ and His apostles, and totally destroyed that generation of impious men.

(Eusebius of Caesarea, *Ecclesiastical History* 3.5.2–3)

The final Jewish rebellion against Roman rule was the Bar Kokhba Revolt (132–135) under Hadrian. The punishment meted out by that emperor after the revolt was crushed had profound implications for Jews and Christians alike.

From this time onwards, the entire Jewish race has been forbidden to ever go up to the country around Jerusalem. For the emperor gave orders that they should not even see from a distance the land of their fathers. Such is the account of Aristo of Pella. When the city had been emptied of the Jewish race and had suffered the total destruction of its ancient inhabitants, it was colonised by an alien race and the Roman city which subsequently arose changed its name and was called Aelia, in honour of the emperor Aelius Hadrianus.

(Eusebius of Caesarea, *Ecclesiastical History* 4.6.3–4)

Hadrian's expulsion of the Jews remained in force at the beginning of the fourth century when Eusebius wrote his *Ecclesiastical History*. In Eusebius' eyes, the fate of the Jews was fitting chastisement for their role in Christ's death. Nevertheless, the initial survival and spread of the Christian message owed much to the Jews. The original disciples were themselves Jewish and many early Christian converts came from the communities of the Jewish Diaspora whose expansion across the empire only increased after the decrees of Hadrian. Early Christian gatherings frequently met in synagogues and drew on Jewish concepts of Scripture, priesthood and charity. There was thus a constant tension within Christianity between the inheritance received from the Jews and the hostility towards those who had condemned Christ. The apostle Paul taught that obedience to the Jewish Law was not required of Christians, a stance that brought him into conflict with Peter and the older disciples.

Listen! I, Paul, am telling you that if you let yourselves be circumcised, Christ will be of no benefit to you. Once again I testify to every man who lets himself be circumcised that he is obliged to obey the entire Law. You who want to be justified by the Law have cut yourselves off from Christ; you have fallen away from grace. For through the Spirit, by faith, we eagerly wait for the hope of righteousness. For in Christ Jesus neither circumcision nor uncircumcision counts for anything; the only thing that counts is faith working through love.

(Galatians 5.2–6)

In the second and third centuries there remained significant numbers of so-called 'Jewish-Christians', who combined Jewish practice with belief in Christ. Such groups were eventually denounced by both Jews and Christians, as we see from the fourth-century Christian writer Epiphanius' attack upon those he names 'Nazoraeans' (from Jesus of Nazareth). But their existence highlighted the blurred lines that still connected the early Christians with their Jewish contemporaries.

They have no different ideas, but confess everything just as it is proclaimed in the Law and in the manner of the Jews, except that they claim to believe in Christ. For they acknowledge both the resurrection of the dead and that the divine power has created all things, and they declare that God is one and that His Son is Jesus Christ. They are very well educated in Hebrew, for they read the entire Law, the Prophets, and the so-called Writings – I mean the poetic books, Kings, Chronicles, Esther, and all the rest – in Hebrew, as of course do the Jews. They differ from both Jews and Christians only in the following ways. They disagree with the Jews because they believe in Christ. But because they are still bound by the Law – circumcision, the Sabbath, and the rest – they are not in accord with Christians.

(Epiphanius of Salamis, *Panarion* 29.7)

This was the complex relationship that the first Christian emperor inherited. Constantine made his personal views on the Jews clear in a letter that he circulated after the Council of Nicaea in 325. The council had debated the dating of Easter, an obvious point of Jewish–Christian conflict, and Constantine criticized those who derived their date from Jewish reckoning.

It was deemed unworthy that in the celebration of this most holy feast we should follow the practice of the Jews, who have impiously defiled their hands with enormous sin and are therefore deservedly afflicted with blindness of the soul. We have it in our power, if we abandon their custom, to prolong the due observance of this festival to future ages through a truer order, which we have preserved from the very day of the Passion until the present time. Let us then have nothing in common with the detestable mob of Jews. We have received from our Saviour a different way, and a course at once lawful and honourable lies open to our most holy religion. Let us with one accord adopt this course, beloved brethren, and withdraw ourselves from all complicity in their wickedness. For it is absurd indeed, that they can boast that we are not able to keep these observances without their instruction. How could they be capable of reaching a sound calculation, who ever since their parricidal guilt in slaying their Lord have been subject to the direction not of reason but of ungoverned passion, and who are swayed by every impulse of the mad spirit that is within them?

(Constantine, *Letter to the churches*, quoted in Eusebius of Caesarea,

Life of Constantine 3.18)

A number of Constantine's laws similarly proclaimed Christianity's superiority over Judaism. The Jews were warned not to hinder those who turned to the Christian faith, and were forbidden from owning and circumcising a Christian slave.

It is Our will that Jews and their elders and patriarchs shall be informed that if, after the issuance of this law, any of them should dare to attempt to assail with stones or with any other kind of madness – a thing which We have learned is now being done – any person who has fled their feral sect and has resorted to the worship of God, such assailant shall be immediately delivered to the flames and burned, with all his accomplices.

(*Theodosian Code* 16.8.1, AD 329)

If any Jew should purchase and circumcise a Christian slave or a slave of any other sect whatever, he shall not retain in slavery such circumcised person. But the person who endured such treatment shall obtain the privilege of freedom.

(*Theodosian Code* 16.9.1, AD 335)

One might easily assume that the emergence of a Christian emperor therefore led inevitably to rising anti-Semitism and violent pogroms. Despite the rhetoric of denunciation against Judaism, however, Constantine in fact passed no laws that directly harmed Jews or their rights to live and worship. Indeed, on one crucial issue he reaffirmed the exemption of Jewish leaders from compulsory public services, a privilege that they shared with the Christian clergy.

If any persons with complete devotion should dedicate themselves to the synagogues of the Jews as patriarchs and priests and should live in the aforementioned sect and preside over the administration of their law, they shall continue to be exempt from all compulsory public services that are incumbent on persons, as well as those that are due to the municipalities.

(*Theodosian Code* 16.8.2, AD 330)

The letters and laws of Constantine reflected the paradoxical status of the Jews within the increasingly Christian Roman empire of the fourth century. On the one hand, the Jews were the subjects of repeated and vicious rhetorical attacks as the betrayers and murderers of Christ. But on the other hand, the Jews remained protected by imperial law and suffered no open persecution. Christians and Jews lived side by side across the empire in relative peace, interrupted only by rare and localized outbreaks of violence. It was against this background that John Chrysostom, as a priest in Antioch in 386/7, composed a set of eight *Homilies against the Jews*. Chrysostom brought the ferocity of anti-Jewish Christian rhetoric to new levels. Yet his very anger was fuelled by the co-existence of Jews and Christians which he condemned.

Many people, I know, respect the Jews and believe that their present way of life is a venerable one. It is for this reason that I hasten to tear out this deadly opinion by the roots. I said that the synagogue is no better than a theatre and as my witness I bring forward a prophet, for surely the Jews are not more worthy of belief than their prophets. 'You have the forehead of a whore, you refuse to be ashamed' [Jeremiah 3.3]. Where a whore has established herself, that place is a brothel. But the synagogue is not only a brothel and a theatre. It is also a den of robbers and a cave for wild beasts. The prophet said: 'Your house has become for me the cave of a hyena' [combining Jeremiah 7.11 and 12.9]. He does not say merely 'of a wild beast' but 'of a filthy wild beast'. And again: 'I have forsaken my house, I have abandoned my heritage' [Jeremiah 12.7]. When God forsakes a people, what hope of salvation is left? When God forsakes a place, that place becomes the dwelling of demons. But the Jews of course claim that they too adore God. May Heaven forbid that this be said! No Jew adores God! Who says so? The Son of God. For He said: 'If you knew my Father, you would know me also. But you know neither me nor my Father' [John 8.19]. What witness could be more trustworthy than the Son of God? Therefore, if the Jews do not know the Father, if they crucified the Son, if they rejected the guidance of the Spirit, who should not make bold to declare openly that the synagogue is a dwelling of demons? God is not worshipped there. Heaven forbid! It is a site of idolatry. And yet some people still pay it honour as a holy place.

(John Chrysostom, *Homilies against the Jews* 1.3)

This vitriol from the preacher's pulpit was an obvious incitement to violence. And Chrysostom, although exceptional in the power of his language, was not alone in expressing such views. In 388 a Christian mob destroyed a synagogue in the town of Callinicum on the Euphrates river. The initial response of emperor Theodosius I was to order the local clergy to repair the damage. But he was persuaded to reverse his decision by bishop Ambrose of Milan, who maintained that a Christian emperor could not be seen to favour the Jews.

What could a synagogue in a remote fortified settlement in the back of beyond possess, when all there is in the place is inconsiderable, and nothing is of value and little in quantity? Of what then could the fire have robbed the treacherous Jews? These are the tricks of Jews eager to spread slander, so that an extraordinary inquiry of a military court should be set up, because they are making these complaints, and that a soldier should be sent out – who, emperor, will quite possibly say what he said here some time before your arrival: 'How will Christ be able to help, when we are in the service for the Jews against Christ, when we are sent to exact punishment on behalf of the Jews? They have lost their own armies, they wish to destroy ours'. What other slanders will they not zealously take up, these people who have defamed Christ Himself with false evidence? What other slanders will they not zealously embark upon, these men who lie even in matters relating to God? Whom will they not accuse of being instigators of this disturbance? Whom will they not inform against even though they do not know them at all, so that they can witness innumerable files of chained members of the Christian community, see the necks of the faithful people yoked in captivity, so that the servants of God are buried in darkness, smitten with axes, delivered to the flames, or sent to the mines, so that their punishment should not be brief. Will you give the Jews this triumph over the Church of God? This trophy at the expense of the community of Christ? This rejoicing, emperor, to the faithless?

This celebration to the synagogue? This grief to the Church? The Jewish people will enter this feast-day into their calendar, and will assuredly rank it with the days on which they triumphed over the Amorites, or over the Canaanites, or over Pharaoh, the king of Egypt, or that on which they succeeded in freeing themselves from the hand of Nebuchadnezzar, king of Babylon. They will now add this festival, signifying that they have celebrated a triumph over the people of Christ.

(Ambrose of Milan, *Letter* 40.18–20)

Callinicum was an isolated incident, and it is significant that Ambrose had to work hard to prevent Theodosius I from taking action on the Jews' behalf. Even at the end of the fourth century, when Christianity stood unchallenged as the official imperial religion, the Christian emperors actively defended the rights of the Jews. Theodosius I reaffirmed Judaism's status as a legal sect in 393, and this was repeated by his son Honorius in 412.

It is sufficiently established that the sect of the Jews is forbidden by no law. Hence We are gravely disturbed that their assemblies have been forbidden in certain places. Your Sublime Magnitude will therefore, after receiving this order, restrain with proper severity the excesses of those persons who, in the name of the Christian religion, presume to commit certain unlawful acts and attempt to destroy and to despoil the synagogues.

(*Theodosian Code* 16.8.9, AD 393)

If it should appear that any places are frequented by conventicles of the Jews and are called by the name of synagogues, no one shall dare to violate or to occupy and retain such places, since all persons must retain their own property in undisturbed right without any argument of religion or worship. Moreover, since indeed ancient custom and practice have preserved for the aforesaid Jewish people the consecrated day of the Sabbath, We also decree that it shall be forbidden that any man of the aforesaid faith should be constrained by any summons on that day under the pretext of public or private business.

(*Theodosian Code* 16.8.20, AD 412)

The Jews thus received much greater legal protection under the Christian empire than did either 'pagans' or heretics, and it was far from inevitable that Christian rule had to lead inexorably to persecution. Yet the need for such laws was itself evidence that there was a threat, and the sheer weight of anti-Jewish rhetoric created an environment in which further attacks could occur. During the fifth century violence never became widespread, but the outbreaks became more common and on a larger scale. Two infamous episodes in the 410s cast a long shadow for later generations. In 414/15 a series of Jewish–Christian skirmishes in Alexandria allegedly culminated in the Jews being driven from the city by the bishop Cyril and his Christian mob.

Cyril sent for the principal Jews, and threatened them with the utmost severities unless they desisted from their molestation of the Christians. The Jewish populace on hearing these menaces, instead of suppressing their violence, only became more furious and were led to form conspiracies for the destruction of the Christians; one of these was of so desperate a character as to cause their entire expulsion from Alexandria as I shall now describe. Having agreed that each one of them should wear a ring on his finger made of the bark of a palm branch, for the sake of mutual recognition, they determined to make a nightly attack on the Christians. They therefore sent persons into the streets to raise an outcry that the church named after Alexander was on fire. Thus many Christians on hearing this ran out, some from one direction and some from another, in great anxiety to save their church. The Jews immediately fell upon and slew them; readily distinguishing each other by their rings. At daybreak the authors of this atrocity could not be concealed; and Cyril, accompanied by an immense crowd of people, going to their synagogues – for so they call their house of prayer – took them away from them, and drove the Jews out of the city, permitting the multitude to plunder their goods. Thus the Jews who had inhabited the city from the time of Alexander the Macedonian were expelled from it, stripped of all they possessed, and dispersed some in one direction and some in another.

(Socrates, *Ecclesiastical History* 7.13)

This was followed in early 418 by perhaps the only example from the Later Roman empire of the forcible conversion of an entire Jewish population. On the Balearic island of Minorca, the Christian community dominated the town of Jamona (modern Ciutadella) while the Jews were most numerous in Majona (Mahon). Exploiting the zeal aroused by the arrival on the island of the relics of Stephen the protomartyr, bishop Severus of Jamona rallied his congregation to march against the Jews of Majona. The synagogue was destroyed and over the next week the entire Jewish community were converted, an achievement that Severus celebrated (and justified) in a letter circulated to the wider Church.

Although the eight days in which these events occurred were before the beginning of Lent, they were celebrated by us as if it were Easter. For it is confirmed that 540 souls were added to the Church. Moreover, I do not think it frivolous or superfluous (though I will have omitted many things due to my endless supply) to recollect in closing that of the great multitude of people from Jamona who had come so many days before on a journey of thirty miles, not one placed concern for his house, or plans for his daily sustenance, or personal affections before this task. All the more joy should be felt at the following marvel, namely that we see the land of the Jewish people, barren for so long, producing manifold fruits of righteousness, now that the thorns of unbelief have been cut down and the seed of the Word implanted, so that we rejoice for ourselves in the hope of new crops. Where we uprooted an infamous forest of unbelief, the most fertile works of faith have flourished. For not only are the Jews bearing the expense, first for levelling the very foundations of the synagogue and then for constructing a new basilica, but they even carry the stones on their own shoulders.

(Severus of Minorca, *Letter on the Conversion of the Jews* 29–30)

We must be cautious in accepting the reported events in Alexandria and Minorca at face value, but the rhetoric of violence set a tone that would continue throughout the long tragic history of anti-Semitism. Yet the Christian emperors upheld a policy of toleration and legal protection towards the Jews rather than persecution, and many Christians and Jews still lived as neighbours unaffected by either imperial laws or episcopal rabble-rousing. It was a balance of tension that shaped the place of Jews and Judaism in medieval Christian Europe.

By comparison to the Jews, the Manichees (or Manichaeans) were a relatively recent sect who faced persecution almost immediately within the Later Roman empire. The Persian prophet Mani (c.216–276) proclaimed himself the apostle of Christ, and combined Jewish–Christian ideas with concepts from Zoroastrianism (the chief religion of the Sassanian Persian empire) and Buddhism. His message was dualist rather than monotheistic, teaching of two principles of light and darkness in whose struggle the true believers, the elect, served the forces of light.

In the years of Ardashir the king of Persia (224–240), I was tended and grew tall and attained the fullness of the season. In that same year, when Ardashir the king was crowned, the living Paraclete came down to me. He spoke with me. He unveiled to me the hidden mystery, the one that is hidden from the worlds and the generations, the mystery of the depths and the heights. He unveiled to me the mystery of the light and the darkness; the mystery of the calamity of conflict, and the war, and the great . . . the battle that the darkness spread about. Afterwards, he unveiled to me also how the light . . . the darkness, through their mingling this universe was set up . . . He opened my eyes also to the way that the ships were constructed; to enable the gods of light to be in them, to purify the light from creation. Conversely, the dregs and the effluent . . . to the abyss. The mystery of the fashioning of Adam, the first man. He also informed me about the mystery of the tree of knowledge, which Adam ate from; his eyes saw. Also, the mystery of the apostles who were sent to the world, to enable them to choose the churches. The mystery of the elect, with their commandments. The mystery of the catechumens their helpers, with their commandments. The mystery of the sinners with their deeds; and the punishing that lies hidden for them. This is how everything that has happened and that will happen was unveiled to me by the Paraclete.

(*Kephalaia* 14.29–15.20)

Mani spread his message widely across the Persian empire from Mesopotamia to India. As his followers increased he came to be seen as a threat to imperial Sassanian and Zoroastrian authority. The prophet was imprisoned and died under Shah Vahram I (273–276), but after his martyrdom Manichaeism continued to spread both eastward and into the Roman empire to the west.

Just like a sovereign who takes off armour and garment and puts on another royal garment, thus the apostle of light took off the warlike dress of the body and sat down in a ship of light and received the divine garment, the diadem of light, and the beautiful garland. And in great joy he flew together with the light gods that are going to the right and to the left (of him), with harp and song of joy, in divine miraculous power, like a swift lightning and a shooting star, to the Pillar of Glory, the path of the light, and the moon-chariot, the meeting-place of the gods. And he stayed with god Ohrmezd the father [i.e. the First Man]. And he left the whole herd of righteousness [the Manichaean community] orphaned and sad, because the master of the house had entered *parinirvana*.

(Turfan fragment M5569)

The primary evidence for Manichaeism is scattered and fragmentary. The *Kephalaia* text quoted above was preserved in the Coptic language of Egypt, while the fragment from Turfan in Chinese Turkestan was translated into Parthian from Syriac and uses the Buddhist term *parinirvana* (a blessed state of death freed from the cycle of birth and rebirth). Such testimony underlines the geographical and cultural extent of Mani's teachings, but its fragmentary survival reflects the ongoing persecution that his followers endured. Within the Later Roman empire, the Manichees were condemned by 'pagans' and Christians alike. Diocletian issued an anti-Manichaean edict shortly before he began the Great Persecution (see Chapter 2), and the later Christian emperors passed similar edicts.

> Emperors Valentinian and Valens Augusti to Ampelius, Prefect of the City. Wherever an assembly of Manichaeans or such a throng is found, their teachers shall be punished with a heavy penalty. Those who assemble shall also be segregated from the company of men as infamous and ignominious, and the houses and habitations in which the profane doctrine is taught shall undoubtedly be appropriated to the resources of the fisc.
>
> (*Theodosian Code* 16.5.3, AD 372)

Yet the Manichees continued to draw new converts. The law of 372 was addressed to the Urban Prefect of Rome, attesting to their presence in the old imperial city. And it was in the 370s that Manichaeism acquired its most famous Roman adherent: Augustine of Hippo. One of the greatest fathers of the Church, Augustine was attracted by the Manichaean emphasis upon asceticism and above all by how Mani's dualist theology explained the origin of evil and human suffering through his principle of darkness.

> Even at Rome I joined those deluding and deluded 'saints', and associated not only with their 'hearers', one of whose number was he in whose house I had fallen ill and recovered, but also with those whom they designate the 'elect'. For it still seemed to me that it was not we who sin but that some other unknown nature sinned in us. It gratified my pride to be free from blame and, after I had committed any fault, not to confess my guilt so that you might 'bring healing to a soul that had sinned against you' [Psalm 41.4]. I preferred to excuse myself and to accuse this unknown thing which was with me, but was not me. Of course, in truth, it was wholly I. My impiety had divided me against myself, and that sin was all the more incurable in that I did not deem myself a sinner.
>
> (Augustine of Hippo, *Confessions* 5.10)

Augustine eventually broke with the Manichees and became one of their most determined foes. The fact that Manichaeism could attract so gifted a man as Augustine bears eloquent witness to the religion's appeal, but under the weight of continual persecution Manichaeism in the Later Roman empire gradually declined. Laws denouncing the Manichees were still passed by Justinian in the sixth century and further afield by Chinese and Islamic rulers of the ninth and tenth centuries. Even then Mani's teachings survived in Central Asia until at least the twelfth century, while in medieval Europe the legacy of Manichaean dualism endured in groups as diverse as the Bogomils of Bulgaria and the Albigensian Cathars.

This sect with which we are concerned undoubtedly owes its origin to the heresiarch Mani, whose teaching was poisonous and accursed, rooted in an evil people. They have added much to the teachings of their master which is not to be found among his heresies, and they are divided among themselves, for some of them assert what others deny. Manichaeus, if I may speak of him for a moment, was born in Persia. He was called Mani at first, but his disciples later called him Manichaeus to prevent him from being thought mad, for his name, Mani, derived from mania, which means madness. For all that, he was mad. He said he was the Holy Spirit, and had been sent to the world by Christ, as He has promised when He ascended to the throne of Heaven. Therefore he called himself an apostle of Christ, because he had been sent by Him. Hence his disciples boasted that Christ's promise of the Holy Spirit was fulfilled in their master.

I will now show that the teaching of Manichaeus and his followers is fundamentally opposed to the Christian faith. We believe and confess that there is one God who made heaven and earth and all that is in them, and this is the root of our faith. They teach that there were two creators, one good and one evil: God and the prince of darkness – I am not sure how accurately we could call him the Devil. They are said to have had two quite opposite natures from the beginning of time, one good and the other evil, and they created the universe. The souls of men and all the other living animals and the quality which gives life to trees, plants and seeds owed their beginning to God, and were created from His good nature – or rather they hold that each of such things is a part of God. Everything of flesh which lives on the earth, whether man or animal, originates from the prince of darkness, the Devil, and is founded in his evil nature – this is why, as I have said, they avoid eating meat. The message which these children of the Devil have concocted for the damnation of all those who believe them and turn their minds away from the pure truth of the holy Scriptures is alien to every human feeling: it must be spurned.

(Eckbert of Schönau, *First Sermon against the Cathars*, c.1163)

Copyright Acknowledgements

Ambrose of Milan, *Letter* 40
Translated in J. H. W. G. Liebeschuetz, *Ambrose of Milan: Political Letters and Speeches* (Liverpool 2005), by permission of Liverpool University Press

Eckbert of Schönau, *First Sermon against the Cathars*
Translated in R. I. Moore, *The Birth of Popular Heresy: Documents of Medieval Heresy I* (London 1975)

Kephalaia 14
Turfan fragment M5569
Translated in I. Gardner and S. N. C. Lieu, *Manichaean Texts from the Roman Empire* (Cambridge 2004), by permission of Cambridge University Press

Severus of Minorca, *Letter on the Conversion of the Jews*
Translated in S. Bradbury, *Severus of Minorca: Letter on the Conversion of the Jews* (Oxford 1996), by permission of Oxford University Press

Theodosian Code
Translated in C. Pharr, *The Theodosian Code and Novels and the Sirmondian Constitutions* (Princeton 1952, © 1952 in the name of the author, 1980 renewed in the name of Roy Pharr, executor), by permission of Princeton University Press

Further Reading

A. H. Becker and A. Y. Reed (eds), *The Ways that Never Parted: Jews and Christians in Late Antiquity and the Early Middle Ages* (Tübingen 2003)

S. Bradbury, *Severus of Minorca: Letter on the Conversion of the Jews* (Oxford 1996)

L. H. Feldman, *Jew and Gentile in the Ancient World: Attitudes and Interactions from Alexander to Justinian* (Princeton 1993)

J. G. Gager, *The Origins of Anti-Semitism: Attitudes towards Judaism in Pagan and Christian Antiquity* (Oxford 1983)

I. Gardner and S. N. C. Lieu, *Manichaean Texts from the Roman Empire* (Cambridge 2004)

M. Goodman, *Rome and Jerusalem: The Clash of Ancient Civilizations* (London 2007)

W. Horbury, *Jews and Christians in Contact and Controversy* (Edinburgh 1998)

S. N. C. Lieu, *Manichaeism in the Later Roman Empire and Medieval China: A Historical Survey*, 2nd edition (Tübingen 1992)

S. N. C. Lieu, *Manichaeism in Mesopotamia and the Roman East* (Leiden 1994)

S. N. C. Lieu, *Manichaeism in Central Asia and China* (Leiden 1998)

A. Linder, *The Jews in Roman Imperial Legislation: Edited with introductions, translations and commentary* (Detroit 1987)

P. Mirecki and J. D. BeDuhn (eds), *The Light and the Darkness, Studies in Manichaeism and its World* (Leiden 2001)

F. E. Peters, *The Children of Abraham: Judaism, Christianity, Islam*, new edition (Princeton 2006)

L. V. Rutgers, *The Hidden Heritage of Diaspora Judaism* (Leuven 1998)

R. L. Wilken, *John Chrysostom and the Jews: Rhetoric and Reality in the Late Fourth Century* (Berkeley and London 1983)

14

Gender and Society

> In Christ Jesus you are all children of God through faith. As many of you as were baptized into Christ have clothed yourselves with Christ. There is no longer Jew or Greek, there is no longer slave or free, there is no longer male and female; for all of you are one in Christ Jesus.
>
> (Galatians 3.26–28)

> Women should be silent in the churches. For they are not permitted to speak, but should be subordinate, as the law also says. If there is anything they desire to know, let them ask their husbands at home. For it is shameful for a woman to speak in church.
>
> (1 Corinthians 14.34–35)

The place of women in early Christian history has long been a subject of controversy. A number of female figures play prominent roles in the Gospel narratives, and Christ's message offered salvation for all as Paul wrote in Galatians. But Christianity has also been accused of restricting women's rights and increasing their subordination. The first Christians lived in a strongly patriarchal society, and while the command that women should not speak in church may well have been added to 1 Corinthians by a later editor, it expressed a view that many of Paul's followers would have shared. We are further limited by the nature of our evidence, for barely a handful of works actually written by early Christian women survive and we must frequently view those women through male eyes. Nevertheless, in the crucial formative years that followed Constantine's conversion, Christianity offered women no less than men new challenges and new opportunities.

During the early Christian centuries, women played a fundamental part in the new religion's success. Indeed, there are some indications that women comprised the majority of early converts, drawn by Christianity's promise of community and salvation. One famous example was the martyr Perpetua, who died in Carthage in c.203. A text survives that claims to be Perpetua's own diary, which may be one of the earliest extant writings by a Christian woman. Perpetua describes the days leading up to her death, including a vision of herself fighting in the arena as a man.

> There came out against me a certain ill-favoured Egyptian with his seconds, to fight with me. Also there came to me handsome young men to be my seconds and assistants. And I was stripped naked, and I became a man. My seconds began to rub me with oil as is their custom before a contest; and over against me I saw that Egyptian wallowing in the dust. Next there came forth a man of very great stature, so that he surpassed the very top of the amphitheatre, wearing an ungirdled robe and beneath it between the two stripes over the breast a tunic of purple, and having shoes curiously wrought in gold and silver. He bore a rod like a master of gladiators, and a green branch on which were golden apples. And he called for silence and said 'The Egyptian, if he shall conquer this woman, shall slay her with the sword; but if she shall conquer him, she shall receive this branch'. And he withdrew. We drew close to each other, and began to strike one another. He tried to trip up my feet, but I with my heels smote upon his face. Then I rose up into the air and began to smite him as if I trod not the earth. When I saw that there was a lull, I joined my hands, setting finger against finger of them. And I caught his head and he fell upon his face, and I trod upon his head. The people began to shout, and my assistants began to sing. And I went up to the master of gladiators and received the branch. He kissed me and said to me 'Daughter, peace be with you'. And I began to go in triumph to the gate called the Gate of Life. I awoke, and I understood that I should fight not with beasts but against the Devil, but I knew that mine was the victory.
>
> (*Passion of Perpetua* 10)

A hundred years after Perpetua's death, at the time of the Great Persecution, the Christians in the North African city of Cirta were forced to surrender their church's possessions. The inventory of the clothing seized strongly suggests that women outnumbered men in the local Christian community.

The inventory in brief was as follows: two gold chalices, six silver chalices, six silver urns, a silver cooking-pot, seven silver lamps, two wafer-holders, seven short bronze candle-sticks with their own lights, eleven bronze lamps with their own chains, 82 women's tunics, 38 capes, 16 men's tunics, 13 pairs of men's shoes, 47 pairs of women's shoes, 19 peasant clasps.

(preserved in the *Gesta apud Zenophilum*, quoted in turn by Optatus, *Against the Donatists*, Appendix 1)

It is impossible to generalize from such individual examples, both of which happen to survive from Roman North Africa. But there can be no doubt that women were integral to Christianity's initial growth and remained so after the conversion of Constantine. The public profile that Christianity now possessed was promoted by the emperor's female relatives, notably Constantine's mother Helena through her pilgrimage to the Holy Land (see Chapter 16). So how did imperial patronage of the Church impact on the daily lives of ordinary Christian women?

For the majority of the Roman empire's female population, imperial support for Christianity had little practical effect. Rome remained a patriarchal world, and while in reality women ran households, farms and shops, in principle they were regarded as inferior. Christianity's emphasis on charity improved some women's lives, particularly for the sick, widows, and orphaned daughters. However, perhaps the one aspect of daily life that Christian emperors did improve for women concerned marriage. The value that Christianity placed on marriage as an institution helped to prompt Constantine to tighten the grounds on which either party might seek divorce. In doing so, the emperor gave women greater marital rights than they had previously held, although the language of Constantine's law does not suggest that he did so out of respect for the female condition.

It is Our pleasure that no woman, on account of her own depraved desires, shall be permitted to send a notice of divorce to her husband on trumped up grounds, as, for instance, that he is a drunkard or a gambler or a philanderer, nor indeed shall a husband be permitted to divorce his wife on every sort of pretext. But when a woman sends a notice of divorce, the following criminal charges only shall be investigated, that is, if she should prove that her husband is a homicide, a sorcerer, or a destroyer of tombs, so that the wife may thus earn commendation and at length recover her entire dowry. For if she should send a notice of divorce to her husband on grounds other than these three criminal charges, she must leave everything, even to her last hairpin, in her husband's home, and as punishment for her supreme self-confidence, she shall be deported to an island. In the case of a man also, if he should send a notice of divorce, inquiry shall be made as to the following three criminal charges, namely, if he wishes to divorce her as an adulteress, a sorceress, or a procuress. For if he should cast off a wife who is innocent of these crimes, he must restore her entire dowry, and he shall not marry another woman. But if he should do this, his former wife shall be given the right to enter and seize his home by force and to transfer to herself the entire dowry of his later wife in recompense for the outrage inflicted upon her.

(*Theodosian Code* 3.16.1, AD 331)

Christian law thus strengthened the bond of marriage, even if that bond was by no means one of equality (adultery was grounds to divorce a wife, but not a husband). In his autobiographical *Confessions*, Augustine of Hippo described how his mother Monica coped with her marriage to his father Patricius. Monica was the driving force behind Augustine's Christian upbringing and eventually succeeded in converting even her husband. Her acceptance of Patricius' behaviour may horrify a modern reader, but Monica provides us with a rare insight into the lives of the countless unnamed Christian women who by their teachings and example spread their faith to their families and beyond.

My mother was brought up in modesty and temperance, and was rather made subject to her parents by you than to you by her parents. When she had arrived at a marriageable age, she was given to a husband whom she served as her lord. She constantly sought to gain him for you, preaching you to him by her behaviour through the virtues by which you adorned her and made her loved and admired by her husband. She so endured the wronging of her marriage bed that this never became a subject of dissension with her husband. For she trusted in your mercy for him, that by believing in you he might become chaste. Though he was earnest in friendship so too he was violent in anger, yet she had learned that an angry husband should not be resisted in deed or even in word. As soon as he had grown calm and tranquil, and she saw a fitting moment, she would give him a reason for her conduct should he have been excited without cause. Many matrons, whose husbands were more gentle, carried the marks of blows on their dishonoured faces and would in private conversation criticise the lives of their husbands. She would blame their tongues, admonishing them gravely, as if in jest, that from the hour that they had heard the marriage contract read out to them they should have regarded it as binding them like servants, and being always mindful of their condition they ought not to set themselves in opposition to their masters.

(Augustine of Hippo, *Confessions* 9.9)

If imperial law did little to impact upon Christian women's lives, on one crucial issue the imperial Church acted decisively to restrict female involvement. The first Christian communities were highly diverse, and while the leadership was always primarily male there were women in positions of influence. Paul paid tribute to one such figure, the deaconess Phoebe.

I commend to you our sister Phoebe, a deacon of the church at Cenchreae, so that you may welcome her in the Lord as is fitting for the saints, and help her in whatever she may require from you, for she has been a benefactor of many and of myself as well.

(Romans 16.1–2)

The position of deaconess existed in a number of early Christian communities, although the precise functions of that office seem to have varied. The strongest justification for why a female minister was required is provided in the third-century Syrian text known as the *Didascalia Apostolorum*.

Wherefore, O bishop, appoint yourself workers of righteousness as helpers who may cooperate with you for salvation. Those that please you out of all the people you shall choose and appoint as deacons: a man for the performance of most things that are required, but a woman for the ministry of women. For there are houses to which you cannot send a deacon to the women, on account of the gentiles, but you may send a deaconess. Also, because in many other matters the office of a woman deacon is required. In the first place, when women go down into the water, those who go down into the water ought to be anointed by a deaconess with the oil of anointing; and where there is no woman at hand, and especially no deaconess, he who baptizes must of necessity anoint her who is being baptized. But where there is a woman, and especially a deaconess, it is not fitting that women should be seen by men; but with the imposition of the hand do you anoint the head only. As of old the priests and kings were anointed in Israel, do you in like manner, with the imposition of the hand, anoint the head of those who receive baptism, whether of men or of women; and afterwards – whether you yourself baptize or you command the deacons or presbyters to baptize – let a woman deacon, as we have already said, anoint the women. But let a man pronounce over them the invocation of the divine Names in the water. And when she who is being baptized has come up from the water, let the deaconess receive her, and teach and instruct her how the seal of baptism ought to be [kept] unbroken in purity and holiness. For this cause we say that the ministry of a woman deacon is especially needful and important. For our Lord and Saviour also was ministered to by women ministers, Mary Magdalene, and Mary the daughter of James and mother of Joses, and the mother of the sons of Zebedee, with other women beside. And you also have need of the ministry of a deaconess for many things; for a deaconess is required to go into the houses of the gentiles where there are believing women, and to visit those who are sick, and to minister to them in that of which they have need, and to bathe those who have begun to recover from sickness.

(*Didascalia Apostolorum* 16)

Deaconesses continued to appear in the fourth and fifth centuries, but in the increasingly institutionalized imperial Church efforts were made to enforce uniformity and limit female authority. John Chrysostom as bishop of Constantinople became a close friend of the deaconess Olympias who supported his career. But a deaconess was not regarded as an official member of the clergy, and Chrysostom's attitude towards women in the Christian ministry was explicit and hostile.

The divine law indeed has excluded women from the ministry, but they endeavour to thrust themselves into it; and since they can effect nothing of themselves, they do all through the agency of others; and they have become invested with so much power that they can appoint or eject priests at their will. Things in fact are turned upside down, and the proverbial saying may be seen realized – 'The ruled lead the rulers'. Would that it were men who do this instead of women, who have not received a commission to teach. Why do I say teach? For the blessed Paul did not suffer them even to speak in the church. But I have

> heard someone say that they have obtained such a large privilege of free speech, as even to rebuke the prelates of the churches, and censure them more severely than masters do their own domestics.
>
> (John Chrysostom, *On the Priesthood* 3.9)

In the eyes of many male Christian writers, female priests and women holding authority became characteristic indicators of heresy. This was particularly true in writings against Montanism. Also known as the New Prophecy, the Montanist movement began in Phrygia in Asia Minor in the later second century, and taught that spiritual gifts like prophecy and speaking in tongues were open equally to men and women. The founder Montanus was accompanied by two prophetesses, Prisca and Maximilla, and it is possible that Perpetua of Carthage was also a Montanist. The fourth-century viewpoint on such ideas was forcibly expressed in the *Panarion* (*Medicine Chest*) of Epiphanius of Salamis.

> They cite many irrelevant proof texts, and offer thanks to Eve because she was the first to eat from the tree of wisdom. As evidence in support of their ordination of women as clergy, they say that Moses' sister was a prophetess and also that Philip had four daughters who prophesied. In their church seven virgins dressed in white and carrying lamps often enter to prophesy to the people. By displaying a kind of frenzy they deceive the congregation, and by shedding tears and claiming to mourn for humanity they cause everyone to weep as if encouraging the lamentations of repentance. They have women bishops, presbyters and the rest, which they assert is entirely in accord with 'In Christ Jesus there is neither male nor female' [Galatians 3.28].
>
> (Epiphanius of Salamis, *Panarion* 49.2)

Epiphanius then lays down his judgement on the proper relationship between man and woman.

> Even though it is because of Eve that they ordain women to be bishops and presbyters, they should heed the Lord when He says, 'Your desire shall be for your husband, and he shall rule over you' [Genesis 3.16]. And they have ignored the command of the Apostle, 'I permit no woman to teach, or to have authority

over a man' [1 Timothy 2.12], and again, 'Man was not made from woman, but woman from man' [1 Corinthians 11.8], and 'Adam was not deceived, but the woman was deceived and became a transgressor' [1 Timothy 2.14]. Such great error exists in this world!

(Epiphanius of Salamis, *Panarion* 49.3)

During the fifth century, the Church further defined what would remain the official position on women and clerical office throughout the medieval period. In 451 the Council of Chalcedon confirmed the position of deaconess and regulated who could be appointed. But a deaconess was not a member of the clergy and did not share the authority of bishops, presbyters and male deacons.

A woman is not to be ordained deacon before she is forty, and this after a strict investigation. If after receiving ordination and exercising her ministry for some time she gives herself in marriage, insulting the grace of God, she is to be anathematized together with her partner.

(Council of Chalcedon, canon 15)

Women could not under any circumstances act as formal clergy. This was repeated again by Gelasius of Rome (bishop 492–496) in a letter to the bishops of southern Italy. Although the vehemence of Gelasius' tone suggests that the reality was not as clear-cut as the official Church would have preferred.

We have heard with impatience that such contempt has been shown for divine matters that women are encouraged to minister at the sacred altars, and to carry out all the tasks entrusted to the male gender, to which they do not belong.

(Gelasius of Rome, *Letter* 14, to the bishops of Lucania, Calabria and Sicily)

Women were thus barred from the official clergy, a debate that continues to rage to this day. Yet in one sphere the changing nature of Christianity in the fourth and fifth centuries did open new female opportunities. This was the rise of the ascetic movement (see Chapter 10). A life of virginity and ascetic discipline to bring oneself closer to God appealed to women no less than men, and for some exceptional women provided an avenue to distinction and independence. The fourth-century Cappadocian theologian Gregory of Nyssa wrote a panegyric in praise of his elder sister Macrina, who devoted herself and their mother to asceticism.

The life of the virgin became her mother's guide and led her on to this philosophic and spiritual manner of life. And weaning her from all accustomed luxuries, Macrina drew her on to adopt her own standard of humility. She induced her to live on a footing of equality with the staff of maids, so as to share with them in the same food, the same kind of bed, and in all the necessities of life, without any regard to differences of rank. Such was the manner of their life, so great the height of their philosophy, and so holy their conduct day and night, as to make verbal description inadequate. For just as souls freed from the body by death are saved from the cares of this life, so was their life far removed from all earthly follies and ordered with a view of imitating the angelic life. For no anger or jealousy, no hatred or pride, was observed in their midst, nor anything else of this nature, since they had cast away all vain desires for honour and glory, all vanity, arrogance and the like. Continence was their luxury, and obscurity their glory. Poverty, and the casting away of all material superfluities like dust from their bodies, was their wealth. In fact, of all the things after which men eagerly pursue in this life, there were none with which they could not easily dispense. Nothing was left but the care of divine things and the unceasing round of prayer and endless hymnody, co-extensive with time itself, practised by night and day. So that to them this meant work, and work so called was rest. What human words could make you realize such a life as this, a life on the borderline between human and spiritual nature? For that nature should be free from human weaknesses is more than can be expected from mankind. But these women fell short of the angelic and immaterial nature only in so far as they appeared in bodily form.

(Gregory of Nyssa, *Life of Macrina* 970B–972A)

The ascetic women of this period on whom we are best informed are the circle that gathered around Jerome. When he arrived in Rome in 382, Jerome gained renown as an ascetic and scriptural expert and attracted numerous pupils. The most devoted of all were the widow Paula and her daughters Blaesilla and Eustochium. Blaesilla, herself widowed young, died in 384 in part due to her commitment to Jerome's ascetic teachings.

Who can recall with dry eyes the glowing faith which induced a girl of twenty to raise the standard of the Cross, and to mourn the loss of her virginity more than the death of her husband? Who can recall without a sigh the earnestness of her prayers, the brilliancy of her conversation, the tenacity of her memory, and the quickness of her intellect? Had you heard her speak Greek you would have deemed her ignorant of Latin; yet when she used the tongue of Rome her words were free from a foreign accent. She even rivalled the great Origen in those acquirements which won for him the admiration of Greece. For in a few months, or rather days, she so completely mastered the difficulties of Hebrew as to emulate her mother's zeal in learning and singing the psalms. Her attire was plain, but this plainness was not, as it often is, a mark of pride. Indeed, her self-abasement was so perfect that she dressed no better than her maids, and was only distinguished from them by the greater ease of her walk. Her steps tottered with weakness, her face was pale and quivering. Her slender neck scarcely upheld her head.

(Jerome, *Letter* 39.1, to Paula, late 384)

Jerome continued his letter by warning Paula against excessive mourning for her dead daughter. His argument strikes modern readers as harsh, and Blaesilla's fate contributed to Jerome being forced to leave Rome in 385. Yet when he settled in Bethlehem, he was joined again by Paula and Eustochium. Paula died there in 404, and Jerome recounted her virtues in one of his most powerful letters.

Humility is the first of Christian graces, and hers was so pronounced that one who had never seen her, and who on account of her celebrity had desired to see her, would have believed that he saw not her but the lowest of her maids. When she was surrounded by companies of virgins she was always the least remarkable in dress, in speech, in gesture, and in gait. From the time that her husband died until she fell asleep herself she never sat at meat with a man, even though she might know him to stand upon the pinnacle of the episcopate. She never entered a bath except when dangerously ill. Even in the severest fever she rested not on an ordinary bed but on the hard ground covered only with a mat of goat's hair; if that can be called rest which made day and night alike a time of almost unbroken prayer. Well did she fulfil the words of the Psalter, 'All the night make I my bed to swim; I water my couch with my tears' [Psalm 6.6]. Her tears welled forth as it were from fountains, and she lamented her slightest faults as if they were sins of the deepest dye. Constantly did I warn her to spare her eyes and to keep them for the reading of the Gospel; but she only said 'I must disfigure that face which contrary to God's commandment I have painted with rouge, white lead, and antimony. I must mortify that body which has been given up to many pleasures. I must make up for my long laughter by constant weeping. I must exchange my soft linen and costly silks for rough goat's hair. I who have pleased my husband and the world in the past, desire now to please Christ'.

Were I to select her chastity among her great and signal virtues as a subject of praise, my words would seem superfluous. Even when she was still in the world, she set an example to all the matrons of Rome, and bore herself so admirably that the most slanderous never ventured to couple scandal with her name. No mind could be more considerate than hers, or none kinder towards the lowly. She did not court the powerful; at the same time, if the proud and the vainglorious sought her, she did not turn from them with disdain. If she saw a poor man, she supported him, and if she saw a rich one, she urged him to do good. Her liberality alone knew no bounds.

(Jerome, *Letter* 108.15, to Eustochium, AD 404)

Paula, Eustochium and Macrina attained widespread fame, their purity and devotion admired by men and women alike. But their ascetic lifestyle was not one that every woman would wish to embrace, and many of the leading female ascetics came from the wealthy educated classes who possessed the leisure to turn to God rather than from the wider population. There were also fears that ascetic values might lead to social revolution. Jerome encouraged the women in his circle to reject feminine concerns of fashion and appearance, and preaching chastity threatened to undermine family values. The canons passed by the fourth-century Council of Gangra reflected the concerns excessive asceticism inspired.

(13) If any woman, under pretence of asceticism, shall change her apparel and, instead of a woman's accustomed clothing, shall put on that of a man, let her be anathema.

(14) If any woman shall forsake her husband, and resolve to depart from him because she abhors marriage, let her be anathema.

(17) If any woman from pretended asceticism shall cut off her hair, which God gave her as the reminder of her subjection, thus annulling as it were the ordinance of subjection, let her be anathema.

(Canons of the Council of Gangra)

Nevertheless, female ascetics remained a small but significant minority in eastern and western Christianity. Houses of nuns emerged alongside male monasteries, while despite Gangra's concerns a number of holy women contrived to live and dress as men, only to be revealed upon their deaths. Even an empress embraced the ascetic life, Pulcheria, whose younger brother Theodosius II (emperor 408–450) came to power as an infant.

This princess was not yet fifteen years of age, but had received a mind most wise and divine above her years. She first devoted her virginity to God, and instructed her sisters in the same course of life. To avoid all cause of jealousy and intrigue, she permitted no man to enter her palace. In confirmation of her resolution, she took God, the priests, and all the subjects of the Roman empire as witnesses to her self-dedication. In token of her virginity and the headship of her brother, she consecrated in the church of Constantinople a holy table, a remarkable fabric and very beautiful to see for it was made of gold and precious stones, and she inscribed these things on the front of the table so that it might be patent to all. After quietly resuming the care of the state, she governed the Roman empire excellently and with great orderliness.

(Sozomen, *Ecclesiastical History* 9.1)

All the ascetic women whose virtues were celebrated by our male sources were by definition exceptional. The vast majority of Christian women from the Late Roman period remain hidden from us, their ordinary lives revealed only in brief glimpses such as Augustine's stories of Monica. The Late Roman world was dominated by men, and Christianity's rise arguably reaffirmed the prevailing view of female subordination by providing a theological justification. Women inherited the sin of Eve, who had led Adam into error in the Garden of Eden. Ambrosiaster, an anonymous late fourth-century author whose works survived under the name of Ambrose of Milan, offers a concise summary of this influential argument in his commentary on the text of 1 Corinthians.

A woman ought to cover her head, because she is not the likeness of God but is under subjection. Because transgression began with her, she ought to indicate this by covering her head in church out of reverence for the bishop. Nor should she speak, because the bishop takes the place of Christ. In front of him, and because he is the representative of Christ, she ought to appear as she would before a judge, as one under subjection, because of the way the sin of which we are guilty originated.

(Ambrosiaster, *Commentary on 1 Corinthians* 11.8–10)

Yet there was also hope. As Christ sacrificed Himself for Adam's sin, so the Virgin Mary corrected the error of Eve and offered both a celebration of female virtue and a role model for Christian women.

Let the life of Mary, the bearer of God, be for all of you, as it is written, an [image and likeness of] her virginity. For it is best for you to recognize yourselves in her as in a mirror and so govern yourselves. Complete the good deeds you have forgotten, and increase the things you have done well, so that your life too might serve for a time as an image for others; continually look to the instruction of others. Thus, Mary was a holy virgin, having the disposition of her soul balanced and doubly increasing. For she desired good works, doing what is proper, having true thoughts in faith and purity. And she did not desire to be seen by people; rather, she prayed that God would be her judge. Nor did she have an eagerness to leave her house, nor was she at all acquainted with the streets; rather, she remained in her house being calm, imitating the fly in honey. She virtuously spent the excess of her manual labour on the poor. And she did not acquire eagerness to look out the window, rather to look at the Scriptures. And she would pray to God privately, taking care about these two things: that she not let evil thoughts dwell in her heart, and also that she not acquire curiosity or learn hardness of heart.

(Athanasius of Alexandria, *First Letter to Virgins* 12–13)

For Christian women today, the appeal of such a call to emulation is a question they must decide themselves. But many Late Roman women did find comfort and inspiration in the Christian message of their times, from ascetics like Paula and mothers like Monica to the countless unknown women who lived Christian lives beyond the lens of our patriarchal sources. Faltonia Betitia Proba (c.322–c.370) offers a rare female voice expressing her faith in her own words. An aristocrat who converted to Christianity and may have influenced her family to do likewise, Proba retold the stories of the Garden of Eden and the life of Christ through verses taken from the Roman poet Virgil. Her *De Laudibus*

Christi is the earliest extant Christian work written indisputably by a woman and was widely read in the Middle Ages.

Gardens breathing with saffron-coloured flowers attract
amid an open wood scented of laurel, and earth herself
kept bearing all freely without being asked.
Blessed pair, if the mind of the unspeakable wife had not been
stupid; afterwards the mighty exodus taught.
And now the unspeakable day was at hand; through the fields of flowers
look, a snake, abominable, hostile, with immeasurable circles,
seven huge coils, twisting with seven rolls
not easily seen nor courteous in speech to anyone,
it hung with hidden hatred from sprouting branch
breathing a viper's breath, in its heart sad wars
and anger and treachery and harmful crimes.
The Father Himself hated it; it changed itself so many times in its face
and it bristled with its steep scales and, so as not to leave
neither wickedness nor trickery undared nor untried,
first it approached like this with words and showed itself of its own accord.
It said, 'Tell me, maiden – I live in the dark woods
and river banks and dwell in meadows refreshed by streams –
what great cowardice has come upon your courage?
Fruits lie scattered everywhere, each beneath its own tree
the cups are springs of water. It is wicked to touch
the heavenly gifts. That one thing the world lacks.
What prevents you testing reasons hidden far away?
It is empty superstition. The other part of the world has been withdrawn.
Why did He give eternal life? Why have the arrangements for death
been withdrawn? If you think that what I said was not futile,
I the author of what should be dared annul the sacred laws.
You are his wife, it is right for you to test his soul by pleading.
I shall be your leader. If your choice of me is sure,
we will heap up the couches and feast on sumptuous banquets'.
It said this, and quicker than its speech, what was prohibited by law,
the once hallowed tree they submitted to their banquets
and began the meal, and defiled everything with their contact.
The especially unlucky woman, devoted to future ruin,
admired the new leaves and fruit that was not hers,
the cause of such great wrong-doing, she touched with her lips.
After venturing upon a very great crime, she rose to an even greater madness,

alas, the wife pushed the fruit from the tree that was not theirs
on the wretched man and moved his soul with sudden sweetness.
At once a new light shone from their eyes; but
they were frightened by their sudden vision and without delay
they shaded their bodies beneath the spreading of leafy branches;
they fastened together a covering. No hope of help was given.

Now I return to you and your great decrees, Father.
I begin my greater work. I take up the predictions of the older prophets,
although the end of a slender life awaits,
I have to attempt the path by which I too could lift me
from the ground and carry your name in fame through countless years,
because your Son came down from high heaven,
the age brought to us as we prayed for something
the help and advent of God, whom a woman first
wearing the face and clothing of a virgin – marvellous to relate –
gave birth to a boy not of our race nor blood.
And alarming prophets sang the late omens
that a magnificent man was coming to the people and to the earth
from heavenly seed, who would seize the world by His might.
And then the promised day was at hand, when for the first time
the source of divine progeny revealed His holy face.

(Proba, *De Laudibus Christi* 167–209 and 333–347)

Copyright Acknowledgements

Ambrosiaster, *Commentary on 1 Corinthians*
Translated in G. L. Bray, *Ambrosiaster: Commentaries on Romans and 1–2 Corinthians*
(Downers Grove, Ill. 2009, © by Gerald L. Bray, Thomas C. Oden, Michael Glerup and
the Institute of Classical Christian Studies (ICCS)), by permission of InterVarsity Press

Athanasius of Alexandria, *First Letter to Virgins*
Translated in D. Brakke, *Athanasius and the Politics of Asceticism* (Oxford 1995), by
permission of the author

Optatus, *Against the Donatists*
Translated in M. Edwards, *Optatus: Against the Donatists* (Liverpool 1997), by
permission of Liverpool University Press

Proba, *De Laudibus Christi*
Translated in I. M. Plant, *Women Writers of Ancient Greece and Rome: An Anthology* (London 2004, © Equinox Publishing Ltd), by permission of Equinox Publishing Ltd

Theodosian Code
Translated in C. Pharr, *The Theodosian Code and Novels and the Sirmondian Constitutions* (Princeton 1952, © 1952 in the name of the author, 1980 renewed in the name of Roy Pharr, executor), by permission of Princeton University Press

Further Reading

E. A. Clark and D. F. Hatch, *The Golden Bough, the Oaken Cross: The Virgilian Cento of Faltonia Betitia Proba* (Chicago 1981)

G. Clark, *Women in Late Antiquity: Pagan and Christian Lifestyles* (New York and Oxford 1993)

G. Cloke, *This Female Man of God: Women and Spiritual Power in the Patristic Age,* AD *350–450* (London 1995)

K. Cooper, *The Virgin and the Bride: Idealized Womanhood in Late Antiquity* (Cambridge 1996)

C. S. Keener, *Paul, Women and Wives: Marriage and Women's Ministry in the Letters of Paul* (Peabody 1992)

J. N. D. Kelly, *Jerome* (London 1975)

R. S. Kraemer, *Her Share of the Blessings: Women's Religions among Pagans, Jews and Christians in the Greco-Roman World* (Oxford and New York 1992)

A. G. Martimort, *Deaconesses: An historical study,* translated by K. D. Whitehead (San Francisco 1986)

P. Pantel (ed.), *A History of Women in the West, Volume I: From Ancient Goddesses to Christian Saints* (Cambridge, Mass. 1992)

J. E. Salisbury, *Perpetua's Passion: the Death and Memory of a Young Roman Woman* (London and New York 1997)

R. Stark, *The Rise of Christianity: A Sociologist Reconsiders History* (Princeton 1996)

15

Holy Men and Holy Women

The rise of the 'holy man', or more accurately of holy men and holy women, is one of the characteristic features of the increasingly Christian Later Roman empire. These blessed individuals were venerated in their own times for their ascetic piety and commemorated as saints after their deaths. Examples of holy men and women can be drawn from every region of the empire and beyond the frontiers. Their fame was preserved through hagiographies (*hagios* 'holy', 'saint'; *graphein* 'to write') which described their lives and miracles, and such writings were extremely popular throughout the late antique and medieval periods. The historical value of these texts is often controversial, particularly due to the prominence of miracles that the reader must take on faith. But whatever our personal beliefs, the hagiographies of the Late Roman holy men and women offer a priceless insight into the mentality of their age and the world in which they lived and died.

The first true hagiography is the *Life of Antony* attributed to Athanasius of Alexandria. Antony (d.356) was a key figure in early Christian asceticism (see Chapter 10), and the *Life* (or *Vita*) set the model for the biography of a holy man. After describing Antony's upbringing and his decision to become a hermit, the *Life* speaks at length of the abuse that Antony suffered as the Devil sought to tempt him away from his ascetic commitment.

First the Devil tried to lead Antony away from the discipline, whispering to him the remembrance of his wealth, his care for his sister, the bonds of kinship, love of money and of glory, the various pleasures of food, the relaxations of life, and, finally, the difficulty of virtue and the labour that earns it, suggesting also the infirmity of the body and the length of time involved. Thus the Devil raised in

Antony's mind a great dust cloud of debate, wishing to call him back from his settled purpose. But the enemy saw himself to be too weak to break Antony's resolve, and that rather he was conquered by the other's firmness, overthrown by his great faith and falling before his constant prayers. Then he put his trust in the weapons which are 'in the navel of his belly', and boasting in these (for they are his first snare for the young) he attacked the young man, disturbing him by night and harassing him by day, so that even onlookers saw the struggle which was going on between them. The one would suggest foul thoughts and the other countered them with prayers; the one fired him with lust, the other, as one who seemed to blush, fortified his body with faith, prayers, and fasting. And the unhappy Devil one night even took the shape of a woman and imitated all her acts solely in order to beguile Antony. But he, his mind filled with Christ and the nobility inspired by Him, and considering the spirituality of the soul, quenched the fire of the other's deceit.

(Athanasius of Alexandria, *Life of Antony* 5)

The conflict of the saint with the temptations of the Devil is a recurring theme of hagiography. Victory revealed Antony's spiritual strength and the divine blessing that he had received. His reputation drew disciples and supplicants to his desert mountain, where he debated with philosophers and healed the sick.

There was a man named Fronto, from Palatium, and he had a terrible disease, for he used to bite his own tongue and was in danger of injury to his eyes. Having come to the mountain, he asked Antony to pray for him. Having done this, Antony said to him, 'Depart and you shall be healed'. When he grew worse and remained there for several days, Antony said again, 'If you stay here, you cannot be healed. Go, and when you come into Egypt you shall see the sign wrought in you'. And he believed and departed. As soon as he set eyes on Egypt his sufferings ceased and the man became whole, according to the word of Antony, which the Saviour had revealed to him in prayer.

(Athanasius of Alexandria, *Life of Antony* 57)

Such miraculous occurrences are difficult for some modern readers to accept, yet Antony's healing of Fronto highlights two concepts crucial to understanding the importance of the holy man in Late Roman society. Firstly, the holy man acts as a living mediator between earth and heaven. It was not Antony who healed Fronto, but God working through Antony and his prayers. Secondly, even a solitary desert hermit like Antony was never entirely cut off from the social world around him. Holy men and women played a vital pastoral role, as teachers, healers, counsellors and spiritual guides. Near the end of the *Life*, Athanasius paid tribute to Antony's achievements.

> It was as if a physician had been given by God to Egypt. For who went to Antony in grief and did not return rejoicing? Who came mourning for the dead and did not immediately put off their sorrow? Who came in anger and was not converted to friendship? What poor and low-spirited man met him who, hearing him and looking upon him, did not despise wealth and console himself in his poverty? What monk, having become discouraged, did not come to him and become all the stronger? What young man, having come to the mountain and seen Antony, did not immediately renounce pleasure and love moderation? Who, when tempted by a demon, came to him and did not find relief? And who came troubled with doubts and did not find quietness of mind?
>
> (Athanasius of Alexandria, *Life of Antony* 87)

The earliest western holy man whose fame rivalled that of Antony was Martin of Tours (d.397). His *Life* was written by his admirer Sulpicius Severus shortly before Martin's death and tells the story of the soldier Martin's arrival at Amiens in Gaul.

> One day, in the middle of a winter more bitterly cold than usual (so much so that many perished as a result of the severity of the icy weather), when Martin had nothing with him apart from his weapons and a simple military cloak, he came across a naked beggar at the gate of the city of Amiens. The man begged the people who were passing to have pity on him but they all walked past him. Then Martin, who was filled with God's grace, understood that this man had been reserved for him, since the others were not showing him any mercy. But what was he to do? He had nothing apart from the cloak he was wearing, for he had already used up the rest of his things for a similar purpose. So he seized the sword which he wore at his side, divided the cloak in two, gave half to the beggar and then put the remaining piece on again. Some of the bystanders began to laugh because he looked odd with his chopped-up cloak, but many who were more sensible sighed deeply because they had not done the same.
>
> (Sulpicius Severus, *Life of Martin* 3.1–2)

After leaving the army to dedicate himself to Christ, Martin lived for several years as a monk and gained renown for miraculous healings and his opposition to the 'Arian' heresy. Eventually, against his will according to the *Life*, he was elected bishop of Tours. Martin devoted himself to promoting Christianity and suppressing 'pagan' rites, although at times his zeal may have been excessive.

> While he was on a journey he came across the corpse of a pagan which was being carried out for burial in accordance with superstitious funeral rites. Seeing in the distance a crowd of people coming towards him, he stopped for a while, not knowing what it was. For he was about five hundred paces away so it was difficult to make out what he was seeing. However, because he could see a group of peasants and the linen cloths laid over the corpse fluttering in the wind, he thought that they were performing pagan sacrificial rites, for it was the custom for the peasants of Gaul, in their pitiable delusion, to carry demonic representations, covered with a white veil, over their fields. And so Martin raised his hand and made the sign of the cross against those who were coming towards him. He ordered the crowd to stop and to set down what they were carrying. And now you would have seen an amazing thing. These miserable people first became rigid like rocks; then, when they made a great effort to move forward, they found that they were unable to move any further and went spinning round in a ridiculous whirling movement until they were overcome with dizziness and set down the burden of the corpse. They looked round at each other in amazement, wondering in silence what had happened. But when the holy man understood that these people had gathered for a funeral, not for a religious ceremony, he raised his hand once more and granted them the power to depart and to carry the corpse.
>
> (Sulpicius Severus, *Life of Martin* 12.1–5)

On this occasion Martin's aim may have been slightly awry. But the holy man as a leading figure in Christianity's triumph over 'paganism' is another recurring hagiographic theme, and the *Life of Martin* is a valuable if difficult source for the survival of traditional religious practices in fourth-century rural Gaul. As a bishop, Martin was more directly involved in secular affairs than the hermit Antony. Other saints came from still more worldly backgrounds. A number of prominent holy women are depicted as prostitutes who repented and found their true calling. Pelagia the Harlot of Antioch (fourth–fifth century) is one example. Her *Life* claims to have been written by Jacob, a deacon serving the bishop Nonnos who inspired Pelagia's conversion.

> This prostitute then appeared before our eyes, sitting prominently on a riding donkey adorned with little bells and caparisoned; in front of her was a great throng of her servants and she herself was decked out with gold ornaments, pearls, and all sorts of precious stones, resplendent in luxurious and expensive clothes. On her hands and feet she wore armbands, silks, and anklets decorated with all sorts of pearls, while around her neck were necklaces and strings of pendants and pearls. Her beauty stunned those who beheld her, captivating them in their desire for her.
>
> (Jacob, *Life of Pelagia of Antioch* 4)

Pelagia's exotic description fits her other name of Margarito ('pearl'), and makes her repentance all the more striking. Moved by hearing Nonnos preach, she humbled herself and sought baptism. She gave her fortune to charity and disappeared. Three years later, Jacob went on pilgrimage to Jerusalem and was advised by Nonnos to visit the monk Pelagios.

> I learnt that he dwelt on the Mount of Olives, where our Lord used to pray with His disciples. Accordingly I went up to the Mount of Olives and kept on asking until I discovered his cell. He was very well known in the area and held in high honour. As I approached his cell, I saw it had no door to it; on close examination I espied a small window in the wall in front of me. I knocked, and Pelagia, the handmaid of God, opened it. She was dressed in the habit of a venerable man. She came up and greeted me with great humility, clasping my hands and kissing them from within. She was overjoyed at my arrival, for the moment she saw me she recognized me. She was inside, and I outside, and I failed to recognize her because she had lost those good looks I used to know. Her astounding beauty had all faded away, her laughing and bright face that I had known had become ugly, her pretty eyes had become hollow and cavernous as the result of much fasting and the keeping of vigils. The joints of her holy bones, all fleshless, were visible beneath her skin through emaciation brought on by ascetic practices. Indeed the whole complexion of her body was coarse and dark like sackcloth, as the result of her strenuous penance. The whole of Jerusalem used to call her 'the eunuch', and no one suspected anything else about her; nor did I notice anything about her that resembled the manner of a woman. I received a blessing from her as if from a male eunuch who was a renowned monk, a perfect and righteous disciple of Christ.
>
> (Jacob, *Life of Pelagia of Antioch* 44–45)

The *Lives* of holy women are almost without exception written by men. Pelagia is presented as surpassing her female weakness and achieving sanctity in the guise of a man, with the truth only discovered upon her death. In comparison to Pelagia the Harlot, her approximate contemporary Melania the Younger (d.439) came from the highest western senatorial aristocracy. Inspired by her grandmother Melania the Elder, herself a controversial holy woman, the younger Melania persuaded her husband Pinianus that together they should abandon their wealthy aristocratic lifestyle and devote themselves to chastity and asceticism.

> I shall report on their property by just skimming the surface of things I heard from the mouth of the blessed Pinianus. He said that he had as an annual income 120,000 pieces of gold, more or less, not counting that derived from his wife's property. Their movable goods were such that they were too many to be counted. Immediately they began, with zeal, to distribute these, entrusting to the holy men the administration of alms. They sent money to different regions, through one man 40,000 coins, through another 30,000, by another 20,000, through another 10,000, and the rest they distributed as the Lord helped them do. The saint herself said to her blessed husband and brother, 'The burden of life is very heavy for us, and we are not competent in these circumstances to take on the light yoke of Christ. Therefore let us quickly lay aside our goods, so that we may gain Christ'. Pinianus received the admonition of the blessed woman as if it came from God, and with generous hands they distributed their goods.
>
> (Gerontius, *Life of Melania the Younger* 15)

Melania and Pinianus left Italy shortly before the Gothic Sack of Rome in 410 and travelled to Sicily and on to North Africa, where they associated with Augustine of Hippo and founded a convent and a monastery. Eventually they settled in Jerusalem, where Melania created a second house for virgins on the Mount of Olives and later (following Pinianus' death in 431/2) a second monastery. Gerontius, who succeeded Melania as the head of her Jerusalem communities, wrote her *Life* and recalled the example that she set for the virgins gathered around her.

> Fulfilling the work of Martha, she began henceforth to imitate Mary, who was extolled in the Gospel as having chosen the good part. Indeed, in the beginning,

Melania would just taste a little oil and take a bit of something to drink in the evening (she had never used wine during her worldly life, because the children of the Roman senatorial class were raised in this way). Then after that she began to mortify her body with strenuous fasting. At first she took food without oil every two days, then every three days, and then every five, so that it was only on Saturday and Sunday that she ate some mouldy bread. She was zealous to surpass everyone in asceticism. She was by nature gifted as a writer and wrote without mistakes in notebooks. She decided for herself how much she ought to write every day, and how much she should read in the canonical books, how much in the collections of homilies. And after she was satisfied with this activity, she would go through the *Lives* of the fathers as if she were eating dessert. Then she slept for a period of about two hours. Straightway after having gotten up, she roused the virgins who were leading the ascetic life with her, and said 'Just as the blessed Abel and each of the holy ones offered first-fruits to God, so we as well in this way should spend the first-fruits of the night for God's glory. We ought to keep awake and pray at every hour, for, just as it is written, we do not know at what hour the thief comes'. She gave strict rules to the sisters with her that no idle word or reckless laughter should come forth from their mouths. She also patiently inquired about their thoughts and refused to allow filthy imaginations to dwell in them in any way.

(Gerontius, *Life of Melania the Younger* 22–23)

All holy men and women were mediators. They acted as impartial judges in human disputes and as intermediaries for supplicants who sought divine aid. The physical symbol for that mediatory role was the stylite, the holy man on his pillar between earth and heaven (see Chapter 10). The multiple *Lives* of the first great stylite, Symeon the Elder (d.459), describe the miracles he achieved through God's grace. Many were cases of miraculous healing, but Symeon also aided entire villages in need.

A priest from the region of Samosata came a great distance to him. He told him about a spring in his village which irrigated all their fields and from which by the Lord's design their lives were sustained. All of a sudden it failed and dried up, and they were exhausted from thirst and hunger. They had brought workmen. They had dug and laboured and spent a good deal of money and they did not find one drop of water in it. When the priest came and told the whole matter just as it was, the saint said, 'I trust in our Lord Jesus that when you start to leave this enclosure our Lord will make it return to normal. But go, keep vigil and celebrate the eucharist and give thanks to our Lord'. The priest noted the time the saint spoke to him and our Lord did a favour. The priest went and found that the spring had gushed forth and overflowed and irrigated all the fields of the village. When he asked the villagers they told him that on such and such a day it suddenly gave a violent sound and gushed forth and watered all the fields of the village double what it used to. He took out the note he had written and saw that the spring had gushed forth into its canal at the very moment the saint blessed him.

(Syriac *Life of Symeon Stylites* 85)

In a world where the vast majority of the population were dependent on subsistence agriculture to survive, water shortage meant starvation. Hence the desperate appeal to the holy man a week's journey away. Although rooted to his pillar, Symeon came into contact with people from every walk of life, and through his miracles sheds light on this rural world which our literary sources (written by the urban educated elite) too often ignore.

Symeon was not the only prominent stylite, and some of his emulators established their pillars closer to centres of worldly affairs. Daniel (d.493) was one of those inspired by Symeon's example, and set up his pillar within a few miles of the imperial city of Constantinople. So great was Daniel's reputation that even the emperor Leo I (457–474) came to the pillar to seek the holy man's protection for his son-in-law Zeno (emperor 474–491).

About that time [AD 468] the pious emperor Leo married his daughter Ariadne to Zeno and also created him consul. And shortly afterwards when the barbarians created a disturbance in Thrace, he further appointed him commander-in-chief in Thrace. And in solemn procession he went up to Anaplus to the holy man and besought him as follows: 'I am sending Zeno as general to Thrace because of the war which threatens; and now I beg you to pray on his behalf that he may be kept safe'. The holy man said to the emperor, 'As he has the holy Trinity and the invincible weapon of the Holy Cross on his side he will return unharmed. However, a plot will be formed against him and he will be sorely troubled for a short time, but he shall come back without injury'. The emperor said, 'Is it possible, I beg you, for anyone to survive a war without some labour and trouble?'. When they had received a blessing and taken their leave they returned to the city.

(*Life of Daniel the Stylite* 65)

Other holy men found themselves drawn into military conflict under more dramatic circumstances. The *Life* of Severinus of Noricum (d.482) describes the collapse of the Roman frontier on the Upper Danube in the 460s and 470s. As imperial power in the region disintegrated under repeated barbarian attacks, the holy man took the lead and rallied the defenders.

Barbarian robbers made an unexpected plundering incursion, and led away captive all the men and cattle they found outside the walls. Then many of the citizens flocked weeping to the man of God, recounted to him the destructive calamity that had come upon them, and showed him evidence of the recent rapine. But he directly questioned Mamertinus, then a tribune, who afterwards was ordained bishop, whether he had with him any armed men with whom to institute an energetic pursuit of the robbers. Mamertinus replied, 'I have soldiers, a very few. But I dare not contend with such a host of enemies. However, if you command it, venerable father, though we lack the aid of weapons yet we believe that through your prayers we shall be victorious'. And the servant of God said, 'Even if your soldiers are unarmed, they shall now be armed from the enemy. For neither numbers nor fleshly courage is required, when everything proves that God is our champion. Only in the name of the Lord advance swiftly, advance confidently. For when God in His compassion goes before, the weakest shall seem the bravest. The Lord shall fight for you, and you shall be silent. Then make haste; and this one thing observe above everything, to conduct unharmed into my presence those of the barbarians whom you shall take'.

Then they went forth. At the second milestone, by a brook which is called Tiguntia, they came upon the foe. Some of the robbers escaped by hasty flight, abandoning their weapons. The soldiers bound the rest and brought them captive to the servant of God, as he had commanded. He freed them from chains, refreshed them with food and drink, and briefly addressed them. 'Go', he said, 'and command your confederates not to dare to approach this place again in their lust for booty. For the judgment and retribution of heaven shall straightway punish them, since God fights for His servants, whom His celestial power is wont so to protect that hostile missiles do not inflict wounds upon them, but rather furnish them with arms'.

(Eugippius, *Life of Severinus* 4)

Holy women too were drawn into the violence of the fifth century as Goths, Vandals and Huns invaded the western territories of the Roman empire. Genovefa (Genevieve) of Paris was a devout virgin who is said to have saved Paris from Attila the Hun in 451.

When it was noised abroad that Attila the king of the Huns, overcome with savage rage, was laying waste the province of Gaul, the terror-stricken citizens of Paris sought to save their goods and money from his power by moving them to other, safer cities. But Genovefa summoned the matrons of the city and persuaded them to undertake a series of fasts, prayers, and vigils in order to ward off the threatening disaster, as Esther and Judith had done in the past. Agreeing with Genovefa, the women gave themselves up to God and laboured for days in the baptistery – fasting, praying and keeping watch as she directed. Meanwhile she persuaded the men that they should not remove their goods from Paris because the cities they deemed safer would be devastated by the raging Huns while Paris, guarded by Christ, would remain untouched by her enemies.

(*Life of Genovefa* 3.10)

In this age of uncertainty, the need for a mediator to secure divine favour was greater than ever. Genovefa continued to offer charity and miraculous healings for the next half-century, and was remembered as the patron saint of Paris. When she died in the early 500s she was buried in the church built by Clovis, the first Christian king of the Franks, which would become the Church of St Genevieve.

By the end of the fifth century, Roman power in Gaul and Britain had entirely collapsed. Christianity, however, continued to spread across the former Roman territories. Missionary holy men played a key role in Christianity's ongoing success, particularly Irish monks whose efforts spanned from Britain through Gaul and Germany and as far as Italy. Such a monk was Columba, who founded the monastery of Iona and was hailed as an apostle to the Picts of Scotland. In one encounter, Columba impressed a Pictish band by driving away an aquatic beast, a miracle that has been interpreted as the earliest historical reference to the Loch Ness monster.

When the blessed man stayed for some days in the land of the Picts, he had to cross the River Ness. When he reached its bank, he saw some of the local people burying a poor fellow. They said they had seen a water beast snatch him and maul him savagely as he was swimming not long before. Although some men had put out in a little boat to rescue him, they were too late, but, reaching out with hooks, they had hauled in his wretched corpse. The blessed man, having been told all this, astonished them by sending one of his companions to swim across the river and sail back to him in a dinghy that was on the further bank. At the command of the holy and praiseworthy man, Luigne moccu Min obeyed without hesitation. He took off his clothes except for a tunic and dived into the water.

But the beast was lying low on the riverbed, its appetite not so much sated as whetted for prey. It could sense that the water above was stirred by the swimmer, and suddenly swam up to the surface, rushing open-mouthed with a great roar towards the man as he was swimming midstream. All the bystanders, both the heathen and the brethren, froze in terror, but the blessed man looking on raised his holy hand and made the sign of the cross in the air, and invoking the name of God, he commanded the fierce beast, saying: 'Go no further. Do not touch the man. Go back at once'. At the sound of the saint's voice, the beast fled in terror so fast one might have thought it was pulled back with ropes. But it had got so close to Luigne swimming that there was no more than the length of a pole between man and beast. The brethren were amazed to see that the beast had gone and that their fellow-soldier Luigne returned to them untouched and safe in the dinghy, and they glorified God in the blessed man. Even the heathen natives who were present at the time were so moved by the greatness of the miracle they had witnessed that they too magnified the God of the Christians.

(Adomnán of Iona, *Life of Columba* 2.27)

Columba died in 597, the same year that Augustine of Canterbury reached Kent on his mission to England. The efforts of Columba and other Irish monks ensured a surviving Christian presence in Britain when Augustine arrived, although conflict would arise between the Irish Christianity of the monks and the Roman Christianity of Augustine. This missionary activity was continued by further generations of Anglo-Saxon holy men and women. The *Life of Cuthbert*, by the Venerable Bede, is one of the earliest hagiographies of an English saint. Cuthbert (d.687) was a hermit and miracle-worker closely associated with the monastery of Lindisfarne. His sanctity was expressed not only by his achievements while alive, but after his death.

The sublimity of the saint's earthly life was well attested by his numerous miracles. Almighty God in His providence now chose to give further proof of Cuthbert's glory in Heaven by putting it into the minds of the brethren to dig up his bones. They expected to find the bones quite bare (as is usual with the dead), the rest of the body having dwindled away to dust. They were going to put them in a light casket in some fitting place above ground in order to give them their due veneration. Bishop Eadberht was informed of their decision sometime in mid-Lent and expressed his agreement, ordering them to carry out the ceremony on the 20th of March, the anniversary of the burial. This they did. On opening the coffin they found the body completely intact, looking as though still alive, and the joints of the limbs still flexible. It seemed not dead but sleeping. The vestments, all of them, were not merely unfaded but crisp and fresh like new, and wonderfully bright.

(Bede, *Life of Cuthbert* 42)

Copyright Acknowledgements

Adomnán of Iona, *Life of Columba*
Translated in R. Sharpe, *Adomnán of Iona: Life of St Columba* (London 1995), by permission of Penguin Books Ltd

Bede, *Life of Cuthbert*
Translated in J. F. Webb, *Lives of the Saints* (Harmondsworth 1965), by permission of Penguin Books Ltd

Gerontius, *Life of Melania the Younger*
Translated in E. A. Clark, *The Life of Melania the Younger* (New York 1984), by permission of The Edwin Mellen Press

Jacob, *Life of Pelagia of Antioch*
Translated in S. P. Brock and S. A. Harvey, *Holy Women of the Syrian Orient* (Berkeley 1987, © by the Regents of the University of California), by permission of the University of California Press

Life of Daniel the Stylite
Translated in E. Dawes and N. H. Baynes, *Three Byzantine Saints: Contemporary Biographies of St. Daniel the Stylite, St. Theodore of Sykeon and St. John the Almsgiver* (Crestwood, New York 1977)

Life of Genovefa
Translated in J. A. McNamara and J. E. Halborg, with E. G. Whatley, *Sainted Women of the Dark Ages* (Durham and London 1992)

Sulpicius Severus, *Life of Martin*
Translated in C. White, *Early Christian Lives* (London 1998), by permission of Penguin Books Ltd

Syriac *Life of Symeon Stylites*
Translated in R. Doran, *The Lives of Simeon Stylites* (Kalamazoo 1992, © by Cistercian
Publications. Published by Liturgical Press, Collegeville, Minn.), by permission of
Liturgical Press

Further Reading

D. Brakke, *Athanasius and the Politics of Asceticism* (Oxford 1995)

S. P. Brock and S. A. Harvey, *Holy Women of the Syrian Orient* (Berkeley 1987)

P. Brown, *Society and the Holy in Late Antiquity* (London 1982)

P. Brown, *Authority and the Sacred: Aspects of the Christianisation of the Roman World*
(Cambridge 1995)

L. L. Coon, *Sacred Fictions: Holy Women and Hagiography in Late Antiquity*
(Philadelphia 1997)

P. Cox Miller, *Biography in Late Antiquity: A Quest for the Holy Man* (Berkeley 1983)

R. Doran, *The Lives of Simeon Stylites* (Kalamazoo 1992)

J. M. Petersen, *Handmaids of the Lord: Holy Women in Late Antiquity and the Early
Middle Ages* (Kalamazoo 1996)

D. W. Rollason, *Saints and Relics in Anglo-Saxon England* (Oxford 1989)

C. Stancliffe, *St. Martin and His Hagiographer* (Oxford 1983)

R. Van Dam, *Saints and their Miracles in Late Antique Gaul* (Princeton 1993)

16

Pilgrimage and Relics

When Constantine converted to Christianity almost three centuries had already elapsed since the time of Jesus and the apostles. The passing of the years aroused in many Christians a growing reverence for the places most closely associated with the living Christ. The Christian message is rooted in the historical existence of Jesus who was crucified and rose from death, and celebrating the physical setting in which Christ lived and died reaffirmed that truth and brought believers closer to Him. Imperial patronage gave the Church wealth to promote the sacred sites and allowed Christian travellers greater freedom of movement. Christian pilgrimage expanded beyond the Holy Land to celebrate the lives and deaths of the apostles, martyrs and holy men, and became closely intertwined with the veneration of relics that preserved the memory of Christ, the saints, and the Virgin Mary.

The Christian practice of pilgrimage had existed on a lesser scale long before Constantine. But the first imperial pilgrim was Constantine's own mother Helena, whose visit to Palestine in 327 bore witness to the new status of the Holy Land under a Christian emperor.

This lady had resolved to discharge the duties of pious devotion to God, the King of kings, and believed that she ought to offer thanksgiving with prayers on behalf both of her own son, now so mighty an emperor, and of his sons, her grandchildren, the divinely favoured Caesars. Thus she came, advanced in years yet with the eagerness of youth and gifted with no common measure of wisdom, to behold this venerable land and at the same time to visit the eastern provinces, cities, and people with a truly imperial solicitude. As soon as she had rendered due reverence to the ground which the Saviour's feet had trodden, according to the prophetic word which says, 'Let us worship at His footstool' [Psalm 132.7], she immediately bequeathed the fruit of her piety to future generations.

Without delay she dedicated to the God she adored two churches, one at the cave which had been the scene of the Saviour's birth and the other on the mountain of His ascension. For the God with us submitted Himself to be born even in a cave of the earth, and the place of His nativity was called Bethlehem by the Hebrews. Accordingly the pious empress honoured the scene of the pregnancy of she who bore this heavenly child with rare monuments and beautified the sacred cave with all possible splendour. The emperor himself soon afterwards testified to his own reverence for the site with princely offerings, and added to his mother's magnificence through costly presents of silver and gold and embroidered hangings. Likewise the mother of the emperor raised a stately monument on the Mount of Olives also, in memory of the ascent to heaven of the Saviour of mankind, erecting a sacred church and shrine on the very summit of the mountain where authentic history informs us that in this cave the Saviour imparted His secret revelations to His disciples. And here also the emperor affirmed his reverence for the King of kings with diverse and costly offerings.

(Eusebius of Caesarea, *Life of Constantine* 3.42–43)

According to subsequent Christian tradition, it was during her visit to Jerusalem that Helena discovered the relics of the True Cross. Neither Eusebius of Caesarea nor any other contemporary of Helena, however, makes any allusion to such a discovery. The earliest reference to Helena's legendary achievement appeared more than a generation later in Ambrose of Milan's funeral oration for emperor Theodosius I in 395.

She opens up the earth; she clears away the soil; she lays bare three forked gibbets tangled together, which rubble had covered up, and the Enemy had concealed. But the triumph of Christ could not be effaced. Doubtfully, she hesitates, woman-like she hesitates, but the Holy Spirit inspires a particular line of investigation, because of the fact that two thieves had been crucified with the Lord. So she picks out the middle piece of wood; but it was possible that the rubble had jumbled up the crosses and accidentally interchanged their positions. She goes back to the Gospel passage, she finds that on the middle gibbet there had been an inscription: 'Jesus of Nazareth, King of the Jews' [John 19.19]. From this, a true line of reasoning was deduced: the inscription revealed the cross of salvation. This is what Pilate answered to the Jews when they protested: 'What I have written, I have written' [John 19.22], that is: 'I have not written these things to please you, but that future ages may know them, I have not written for you, but for posterity'. He was virtually saying, 'Let Helena have something to read, by which she can identify the cross of the Lord'. So now, she found the inscription; she adored the king – most definitely not the wood, for this is Gentile error and the folly of the impious, but she adored Him, who hung on the tree, whose name was cited on the inscription.

(Ambrose of Milan, *On the Death of Theodosius I* 45–46)

The True Cross is the relic most strongly associated with Helena's name, but it was not the only relic that she is reported to have discovered in the cave.

She hunted for the nails with which the Lord was crucified, and found them. From one nail she ordered a bridle to be made, and from a second she fashioned a diadem; she converted one to ornamental, the other to devotional use. Mary was visited to set Eve free; Helena was visited so that emperors should be redeemed. That is why she sent to her son Constantine a diadem brilliant with jewels, which were embedded in the more precious jewel of divine redemption bound in the iron of the cross; that is why she also sent the bridle. Constantine used both, and passed on the faith to subsequent rulers. Thus the holy object on the bridle is the foundation of the belief of emperors. From this came faith, in order that persecution should end and true religion take its place.

(Ambrose of Milan, *On the Death of Theodosius I* 47)

Helena is commemorated as a saint in both eastern and western Christianity, and is invariably depicted with the True Cross in her hands. While doubts remain concerning the accuracy of the later legends, she was remembered as a key figure in the emerging cult of relics and her visit to the Holy Land in 327 is well documented and an important milestone in the history of Christian pilgrimage. Less than ten years after Helena's journey, the earliest first-hand account by a Holy Land pilgrim is preserved in the work known as the *Bordeaux Itinerary*. The author, who is anonymous, travelled from Bordeaux to Jerusalem and then back to Milan in the year 333. The text is very exact in its directions, but the precision of the detail does not detract from the wonders that are described.

As you leave Jerusalem to climb Sion, you see down in the valley on your left, beside the wall, the pool called Siloam. It has four porticoes and a second pool outside, and it flows for six days and six nights; but the seventh day is the Sabbath, and then it does not flow at all either by night or day. Climbing Sion from there you can see the place where once the house of Caiaphas used to stand, and the column at which they fell on Christ and scourged Him still remains there. Inside Sion, within the wall, you can see where David had his palace. Seven synagogues were there, but only one is left – the rest have been ploughed and sown as was said by the prophet Isaiah. As you leave there and pass through the wall of Sion towards the Gate of Neapolis, down in the valley on your right you have some walls where Pilate had his house, the Praetorium where the Lord's case was heard before He suffered. On your left is the hillock Golgotha where the Lord was crucified, and about a stone's throw from it the vault where they laid His body, and He rose again on the third day. By order of the emperor Constantine there has now been built there a basilica – I mean a place for the Lord – which has beside it cisterns of remarkable beauty, and beside them a baptistery where children are baptized. When you have arrived at the gate of Jerusalem which faces the east, and are about to climb the Mount of Olives, there is what is called the Valley of Jehoshaphat. On your left, where there are vineyards, is a rock where Judas Iscariot betrayed Christ, and on the right is the palm tree from which children took branches and strewed them in Christ's path.

(*Bordeaux Itinerary* 592–5)

Some fifty years later, another westerner left an extensive account of her pilgrimage to the east. The female ascetic Egeria, who came either from Spain or more probably southern Gaul, travelled widely across Syria-Palestine, Egypt and the Sinai in the 380s. Although incomplete, her diary is one of the few extant works written by an early Christian woman and a priceless guide to the diverse forms of prayer and liturgical worship that she encountered on her journeys. Egeria attests to the increasing scale and organization of Christian pilgrimage in the late fourth century, not only to places identified in the Gospels but to Old Testament locations which revealed the power of God.

Impelled by God, I conceived the desire to go once more into Arabia, to Mount Nebo. It is the mountain which God told Moses to climb, in the words 'Ascend this mountain Araboth, Mount Nebo, which is in the land of Moab over against Jericho, and view the land of Canaan, which I give to the people of Israel for a possession; and you will die on that mountain which you ascend' [Deuteronomy 32.49–50]. And Jesus our God, who never fails those who hope in Him, saw fit to grant my desire. With us came some holy men from Jerusalem, a presbyter and deacons and several brothers, and we reached the place on the Jordan where holy Joshua the son of Nun sent the children of Israel across, and they passed over, as we are told in the Book of Joshua the son of Nun. We were also shown a slightly raised place on the Jericho side of the river, where the children of Reuben and Gad and the half-tribe of Manasseh made an altar. After crossing the river we came to the city of Livias, in the plain where the children of Israel encamped in those days. The foundations of the camp and dwellings of the Israelites are still to be seen there today. It is a vast plain stretching from the foot of the Arabian mountains to the Jordan.

(*Itinerary of Egeria* 10.1–4)

The Holy Land and other Biblical locations provided a natural focus for early Christian pilgrimage. But over the fourth and fifth centuries pilgrimage centres emerged across the Mediterranean world. Some sites were associated with New Testament figures, such as Patmos where John is said to have composed the book of Revelation. Other centres emerged around local cults, either of martyrs or living saints. The transfer of relics allowed physical representations of the sacred to be brought to cities that lacked existing claims to Christian identity. The new imperial capital of Constantinople was such a city, despite later stories that ancient Byzantion had been visited by the apostle Andrew. Helena is said to have sent relics to her son, and Constantinopolitan tradition believed that Constantine enclosed a fragment of the True Cross within the statue whose column base still stands today in Istanbul.

The emperor, being persuaded that the city would be perfectly secure where that relic should be preserved, privately enclosed it in his own statue, which stands on a large column of porphyry in the forum called Constantine's at Constantinople. I have written this from report indeed; but almost all the inhabitants of Constantinople affirm that it is true.

(Socrates, *Ecclesiastical History* 1.17)

Additional relics were also brought to Constantinople by Constantine and his successors, including the remains of the apostle Andrew, Luke the evangelist, and the missionary Timothy. The New Rome on the Bosporus thus acquired a Christian presence to rival at least in some degree the Old Rome with its apostles Peter and Paul. In the west no city could challenge Rome's pre-eminence. Pilgrims flocked to St Peter's church on the Vatican Hill and to the numerous martyr shrines, while Helena reportedly brought relics from the Holy Land to be preserved in the Roman church of Santa Croce in Gerusalemme. Other western cities sought their own focal points of sanctity, sometimes influenced by the pressures of urban competition and ecclesiastical politics. Ambrose of Milan (bishop 374–397) was a prominent if controversial figure who founded a number of churches. The discovery of relics enabled Ambrose to promote his foundations and reinforced his own episcopal position. One such miraculous discovery occurred in 386 when Ambrose sought relics to consecrate the church that would bear his name.

> I want you also to know that we have found holy martyrs. This was how: when I had consecrated the basilica, a large number of people as with one accord began to interrupt the proceedings shouting: 'Consecrate the basilica as you did the basilica in Romana'! I replied: 'I will if I find relics of martyrs'. And immediately I felt a thrill as if of foresight. To be brief: the Lord was gracious to me. Though even the clergy were nervous, I ordered the area in front of the rails of Saints Felix and Nabor to be dug up. I found promising signs. When some persons were brought up on whom I was to perform the laying on hands, the martyrs began to make their presence felt to such effect that instantly, without a word from me, a woman was seized and flung headlong towards the site of the tomb. We found two men of amazing stature, such as were produced in the old days. All the bones were intact. There was abundance of blood. There was a great thronging together of people throughout that two-day period. To be brief: we tidied up the remains, taking care to leave them intact, and as evening was falling transferred them to the basilica of Fausta. All night there was a vigil and laying on of hands. On the following day we transferred the relics to the basilica which is known as the Ambrosian. During the transfer a blind man was healed.
>
> (Ambrose of Milan, *Letter* 22.1–2, to his sister Marcellina)

The bodies were those of Protasius and Gervasius, brothers and martyrs who became the patron saints of Milan and themselves a focus for later pilgrimage. Living saints too were a magnet for pilgrims. Some travelled in the hope of healing or spiritual guidance from the holy men and women they visited, others wished only to show reverence and satisfy their curiosity. Travellers came from throughout the Roman world and beyond to behold the stylite Symeon the Elder on his pillar at Qal'at Sim'ān, where an entire industry emerged to cater for pilgrims and tourists alike.

As his [Symeon's] reputation spread everywhere, all hurried to him – not just those in the neighbourhood, but also those who lived many days' journey distant. Some brought those with weakened bodies, others sought health for the sick, others were entreating that they might become fathers, and what they could not receive from nature they begged to receive from him. When they received it and their prayers had been heard, they joyfully returned and, by proclaiming the benefits they had obtained, they sent back many more with the same demands. As they all come from every quarter, each road is like a river: one can see collected in that spot a human sea into which rivers from all sides debouche. For it is not only inhabitants of our part of the world who pour in, but also Ishmaelites, Persians and the Armenians subject to them, the Iberians, the Homerites, and those who live even further in the interior than these. Many came from the extreme west: Spaniards, Britons, and the Gauls who dwell between them. It is superfluous to speak of Italy, for they say that he became so well-known in the great city of Rome that small portraits of him were set up on a column at the entrances of every shop to bring through that some protection and security to them.

(Theodoret of Cyrrhus, *History of the Monks* 26.11)

The popularity of pilgrimage and the cult of relics in the Christian Roman empire did not mean that everyone approved. Critics believed that the excessive veneration of particular locations and objects undermined the universality of God and could easily lead into superstition. Credulous believers might fall victim to charlatans and relic sellers and lose sight of the true faith. In 386, the year when Ambrose discovered the remains of Protasius and Gervasius, the first of many laws was passed which tried unsuccessfully to control the translation and sale of relics.

Emperors Valentinian, Theodosius, and Arcadius Augusti to Cynegius, Praetorian Prefect. No person shall transfer a buried body to another place. No person shall sell the relics of a martyr; no person shall traffic in them. But if anyone of the saints has been buried in any place whatever, persons shall have it in their power to add whatever building they may wish in veneration of such a place, and such building must be called a martyry. Given on the fourth day before the kalends of March at Constantinople in the year of the consulship of Emperor Designate Honorius and of Evodius [26 February 386].

(*Theodosian Code* 9.17.7)

One leading fourth-century theologian who offered cautious criticism of those who flocked to the Holy Land was the Cappadocian father Gregory of Nyssa. What did the pilgrim gain, Gregory asked, and were the sites they visited truly more sacred than those they left behind?

What advantage is gained by that person who has been to those celebrated places themselves, as if the Lord was still living there in the body but is keeping away from us foreigners or as if the Holy Spirit is in abundance at Jerusalem but unable to travel as far as us? If it is really possible for the presence of God to be shown through visible symbols, one might more justly think that He dwelt among the Cappadocian people rather than in any of the foreign places. The number of shrines there are here, on which the name of our Lord is glorified, one could hardly count so many in all the rest of the world. And again, if the divine grace was more abundant around Jerusalem than elsewhere, sin would not be so frequent among those who live there; yet as it is there is no form of uncleanness that is not perpetrated among them: fornication, adultery, theft, idolatry, poisoning, jealousy and murder. Evil is so prevalent there that nowhere else in the world are people so ready to kill each other as in that place, where kinsmen attack each other like wild beasts and spill each other's blood merely for the sake of lifeless plunder. In a place where such things go on, what proof is there of an abundance of divine grace?

(Gregory of Nyssa, *On Pilgrimages* 8–10)

Gregory was writing in the 380s, at approximately the same time as Egeria's travels in the east. Two decades later in the early fifth century, a Gallic presbyter named Vigilantius attacked the prevailing reverence for saints and relics. His argument is lost and can only be reconstructed from the viciously polemical response of Jerome, who condemned Vigilantius in no uncertain terms.

Among other blasphemies, he is heard to say this: 'What need is there for you not only to pay such honour but even to worship that thing, whatever it may be, which you carry around in a little vessel?'. And again, in the same pamphlet: 'Why do you kiss and adore a bit of dust wrapped up in a cloth?'. And again: 'Under the cloak of religion we see what is almost a pagan ceremony introduced into the churches. While the sun is still shining, vast numbers of candles are lit and everywhere a tiny bit of dust, wrapped up in a costly cloth, is kissed and worshipped. Great honour do men of this sort pay to the blessed martyrs, who, they think, are to be made glorious by cheap candles, when it is the Lamb in the midst of the throne who with the brightness of His majesty gives them light'.

You madman, who in the world has ever worshipped the martyrs? Who has thought man was God? When the people of Lycaonia thought Paul and Barnabas to be Jupiter and Mercury, and would have offered sacrifices to them, did they not rend their clothes and declare that they were men? Not that they were not better than Jupiter and Mercury, who were but men long dead, but it was through the mistaken ideas of the Gentiles that the honour due to God was being paid to them. And we read that the same Peter, when Cornelius wished to worship him, raised him by the hand and said, 'Get up, for I too am a man' [Acts 10.26]. And have you the audacity to speak of 'whatever it is that you carry around in a little vessel and worship'? I would like to know what it is that you call 'whatever it is'. Tell us more clearly, that there may be no restraint on your blasphemy, what you mean by 'a tiny bit of dust, wrapped up in a costly cloth'. It is nothing less than the relics of the martyrs which he deplores being covered with a costly veil, rather than being bound up with rags or hair-cloth or thrown on the midden, so that Vigilantius alone in his drunken slumber may be worshipped.

(Jerome, *Against Vigilantius* 4–5)

The critical voices of those like Gregory of Nyssa and Vigilantius never entirely disappeared, but they always remained a distinct minority. The breakdown of the Roman empire in the fifth century and the growing separation of eastern and western Christianity had no significant impact on the enduring popularity of pilgrimage and the cult of relics. In c.570 an anonymous pilgrim from Piacenza set out for the Holy Land, just as the Bordeaux pilgrim and Egeria had done two hundred years before. The Piacenza account attests both to the progressive accumulation of sites and relics on the pilgrimage trail through Jerusalem and to the awe that those wonders still inspired in those who made the long and arduous journey.

We went to the basilica of Holy Sion, which contains many remarkable things, including the corner stone which the Bible tells us was rejected by the builders. The Lord Jesus entered this church, which used to be the House of Saint James, and found this ugly stone lying about somewhere, so He took it and placed it in the corner. You can hold it in your hands and lift it. Then put your ear in the corners and the sound is like the murmuring of a crowd. In this church is the column at which the Lord was scourged, and it has on it a miraculous mark. When He clasped it, His chest clove to the stone, and you can see the marks of both His hands, His fingers, and His palms. They are so clear that you can use them to take measures for any kind of disease, and people can wear them round their neck and be cured. On this column is the horn from which kings were anointed, including David, and the church also contains the crown of thorns with which they crowned the Lord, and the lance with which they struck Him in the side. There are also many of the stones with which they stoned Stephen, and the small column in which they set the cross on which blessed Peter was crucified at Rome. The Cup of the Apostles is there, with which they celebrated mass after the Lord had risen again, and many other remarkable things which I cannot remember.

(*The Piacenza Pilgrim* 22)

Eastern respect for the Holy Land and for the sanctity of relics remained equally strong. Constantinople became a beacon of holiness, New Jerusalem as well as New Rome. In the eastern empire's most desperate hour, when the invading Sassanian Persians conquered Egypt, Syria-Palestine and Asia Minor between 603 and 626, the defenders of Constantinople paraded icons on the walls and attributed their survival to Christ and the Virgin Mary. After the emperor Heraclius (610–641) miraculously brought the war to a victorious end, he celebrated his triumph by restoring to Jerusalem the fragments of the True Cross which the Persians had looted, in a ceremony that prefigured the later Crusades.

When the blessed, pious, and late-lamented king Heraclius had received the Lord's holy Cross, he gathered his army with ardent and happy heart. He set out with all the royal retinue, honouring the holy, wonderful, and heavenly discovery, and brought it to the holy city, with all the vessels of the church which had been saved from the hands of the enemy in the city of Byzantium. There was no little joy on that day as they entered Jerusalem. [There was] the sound of weeping and wailing; their tears flowed from the awesome fervour of the emotion of their hearts and from the rending of the entrails of the king, the princes, all the troops, and the inhabitants of the city. No one was able to sing the Lord's chants from the fearful and agonizing emotion of the king and the whole multitude. He set it back up in its place, and put all the vessels of the churches in their places, and distributed alms and money for incense to all the churches and inhabitants of the city.

(*The Armenian History attributed to Sebeos* 41)

It is not always easy for those of us living in today's western world to understand the early Christian pilgrims, or their veneration for relics whose authenticity modern historians regard with scepticism. Yet the forces that drove those early pilgrims and the devotion that surrounded the True Cross and other relics have played a crucial role in shaping Christian history, and for many believers continue to provide a source of inspiration to this day. Nor was Christianity alone in inspiring such commitment. The emperor Heraclius would live to witness the coming of Islam, which brought a new vision of pilgrimage and of a sacred landscape that united Jerusalem and Mecca.

Copyright Acknowledgements

Ambrose of Milan, *Letter 22*
Ambrose of Milan, *On the Death of Theodosius I*
Translated in J. H. W. G. Liebeschuetz, *Ambrose of Milan: Political Letters and Speeches* (Liverpool 2005), by permission of Liverpool University Press

The Armenian History attributed to Sebeos
Translated in R. W. Thomson with J. Howard-Johnston and T. Greenwood, *The Armenian History attributed to Sebeos* (Liverpool 1999), by permission of Liverpool University Press

Bordeaux Itinerary
Itinerary of Egeria
Translated in J. Wilkinson, *Egeria's Travels*, 3rd edition (Warminster 1999), by permission of Oxbow Books Ltd

The Piacenza Pilgrim
Translated in J. Wilkinson, *Jerusalem Pilgrims before the Crusades*, 2nd edition (Warminster 2002), by permission of Oxbow Books Ltd

Theodoret of Cyrrhus, *History of the Monks*
Translated in R. Doran, *The Lives of Simeon Stylites* (Kalamazoo 1992, © by Cistercian Publications. Published by Liturgical Press, Collegeville, Minn.), by permission of Liturgical Press

Theodosian Code
Translated in C. Pharr, *The Theodosian Code and Novels and the Sirmondian Constitutions* (Princeton 1952, © 1952 in the name of the author, 1980 renewed in the name of Roy Pharr, executor), by permission of Princeton University Press

Further Reading

B. Bitton-Ashkelony, *Encountering the Sacred: The Debate on Christian Pilgrimage in Late Antiquity* (Berkeley and London 2005)

S. Borgehammar, *How the Holy Cross was Found: From Event to Medieval Legend* (Stockholm 1991)

J. W. Drijvers, *Helena Augusta: The Mother of Constantine the Great and the Legend of Her Finding of the True Cross* (Leiden 1992)

J. Elsner and I. Rutherford (eds), *Pilgrimage in Graeco-Roman and Early Christian Antiquity: Seeing the Gods* (Oxford 2005)

G. Frank, *The Memory of the Eyes: Pilgrims to Living Saints in Christian Late Antiquity* (Berkeley 2000)

E. D. Hunt, *Holy Land Pilgrimage in the Late Roman Empire AD 312–460* (Oxford 1982)

F. E. Peters, *Jerusalem: The Holy City in the Eyes of Chroniclers, Visitors, Pilgrims, and Prophets from the Days of Abraham to the Beginnings of Modern Times* (Princeton 1985)

S. Sora, *Treasures from Heaven: Relics from Noah's Ark to the Shroud of Turin* (Hoboken, New Jersey 2005)

E. Thunø, *Image and Relic: Mediating the Sacred in Early Medieval Rome* (Rome 2002)

J. Wilkinson, *Jerusalem Pilgrims before the Crusades*, 2nd edition (Warminster 2002)

17

Missionaries and Kings

Go and make disciples of all nations, baptising them in the name of the Father and of the Son and of the Holy Spirit, and teaching them to obey everything that I have commanded you.

(Matthew 28.19–20)

Christianity from its very beginnings was a missionary religion. Jesus' words at the end of Matthew's Gospel preached a message for all races and peoples. His followers obeyed the call. The most famous apostolic missionary was Paul, whose Epistles bear testimony to his untiring efforts to promote the faith from Asia Minor and Greece to Italy and perhaps as far as Spain. But the original disciples too devoted themselves to spreading Christ's teachings and many gave their lives in His service. Eusebius of Caesarea recorded the Church's memory of those original missions.

The holy apostles and disciples of our Saviour were scattered throughout the world. Parthia, according to tradition, was allotted to Thomas as his field of labour, Scythia to Andrew, and Asia to John, who after he had lived some time there died at Ephesus. Peter appears to have preached in Pontus, Galatia, Bithynia, Cappadocia, and Asia to the Jews of the dispersion. At last, having come to Rome, he was crucified, head downwards as he had requested. What do I need to say concerning Paul, who preached the gospel of Christ from Jerusalem to Illyricum, and afterwards suffered martyrdom in Rome under Nero?

(Eusebius of Caesarea, *Ecclesiastical History* 3.1.1–2)

After the generation of the apostles, however, there is surprisingly little evidence for early Christian missionary activity. Within the Roman empire, the new religion spread chiefly through word of mouth and the promise of community and salvation. Active missions were rare, not least as Christianity remained illegal and open to public persecution across the second and third centuries. Beyond the imperial borders our knowledge is extremely limited. A few Christian communities existed north of the Black Sea and in the Sassanian Persian empire of Iran and Iraq. Contact between Christians on different sides of the Roman frontiers was sparse, and the missionary zeal of the apostolic age appeared to have faded away.

Constantine's conversion brought renewed energy to the expansion of Christianity. Although the first Christian emperor did not sponsor organized missionary activity, the increased prestige and resources of the Church offered support to those who promoted the faith. Nevertheless, the spread of Christianity has always depended upon the efforts and sacrifices of special individuals. In the Constantinian age, the work of the original apostles was taken up by men and women who by chance or design found themselves in the right place at the right time. Rufinus of Aquileia described how during the fourth century Christianity took root in two regions on the fringes of the Roman world, regions that have remained strongly Christian down to the present day.

One of those regions was the kingdom of Aksum, in modern Ethiopia. Two young Christians from Tyre, named Frumentius and Aedesius, were captured while on a voyage and brought to the Aksumite king. Recognizing their ability, the king appointed both young men to high office, and upon the king's death Frumentius became advisor to the queen and her son.

> While Frumentius had the helm of the kingdom, God put it into his mind and heart to begin making careful inquiries if there were any Christians among the Roman merchants and to give them extensive rights, which he urged them to use to build places of assembly in each location in which they might gather for prayer in the Roman manner. Not only that, but he himself did far more along these lines than anyone else and in this way encouraged the others, invited them with his support and favours, made available whatever was suitable, furnished sites for buildings and everything else that was necessary, and bent every effort to see that the seed of Christians should grow up there.
>
> (Rufinus of Aquileia, *Ecclesiastical History* 10.9)

When the new king reached maturity, the two travellers were allowed to return to the Roman empire.

> Aedesius hastened to Tyre to see his parents and relatives again, but Frumentius journeyed to Alexandria saying that it was not right to conceal what the Lord had achieved. He therefore explained to the bishop everything that had been done and urged him to provide some worthy man to send as bishop to the already numerous Christians and churches built on barbarian soil.
>
> (Rufinus of Aquileia, *Ecclesiastical History* 10.10)

Athanasius, the bishop of Alexandria, listened to Frumentius' report and immediately sent him back as the first bishop of Aksum. The close relationship between Athanasius and Frumentius laid the basis for the bond that still exists between the churches of Egypt and Ethiopia.

Also in the fourth century, Christianity began to spread through the people of Georgia on the eastern coast of the Black Sea.

> The cause of this great benefit was a woman captive who lived among them and led such a faithful, sober and modest life, spending all of her days and nights in sleepless supplications to God, that the very novelty of it began to be wondered at by the barbarians. Their curiosity led them to ask what she was about. She replied with the truth: that in this manner she simply worshipped Christ as God.
>
> (Rufinus of Aquileia, *Ecclesiastical History* 10.11)

Rufinus does not identify the woman whose efforts he celebrates, although later Georgian tradition gives her name as Nino. Through her piety she healed first a sick child and then the queen, which drew the attention of the Georgian king. At first, however, the king resisted his wife's appeals that he adopt the faith of her healer.

> It happened one day when the king was hunting in the woods with his companions that a thick darkness fell upon the day, and with the light removed there was no longer any way for his blind steps through the grim and

awful night. Each of his companions wandered off a different way, while he, left alone in the thick darkness which surrounded him, did not know what to do or where to turn. Then suddenly there arose in his heart, which was near to losing hope of being saved, the thought that if the Christ preached to his wife by the woman captive were really God, He might now free him from this darkness so that he could from then on abandon all the others and worship Him. No sooner had he vowed to do so, not even verbally but only in his mind, than the daylight returned to the world and guided the king safely to the city. He explained directly to the queen what had happened. He required that the woman captive be summoned at once and hand on to him her manner of worship, insisting that from then on he would venerate no god but Christ. The captive came, instructed him that Christ is God, and explained, as far as it was lawful for a woman to disclose such things, the way of making petition and offering reverence. She advised that a church be built and described its shape.

(Rufinus of Aquileia, *Ecclesiastical History* 10.11)

The attempt to build the first church in Georgia was delayed by engineering problems, but these were resolved through the captive woman's prayers. And so the Georgians followed their king and embraced Christianity.

We must of course be wary in accepting such traditional stories at face value. Yet archaeological as well as literary evidence confirms an expanding Christian presence in Ethiopia and Georgia during the fourth century, even if the religion's spread in those regions was more gradual and uneven than our texts might suggest. The same caution has to be borne in mind concerning the most important Christian mission of the fourth century: the conversion of the Goths.

Gothic tribes from north of the Black Sea had first threatened the Roman empire during the third century. Among the captives whom they took home as slaves were a number of Christians, from whom was descended Ulfila, the apostle to the Goths and their first bishop.

Ulfila was appointed in the following circumstances: sent with others by the ruler of the race of the Goths on an embassy in the time of Constantine (for the barbarian peoples in those parts owed allegiance to the emperor), Ulfila was elected by Eusebius [bishop of Constantinople] and the bishops of his party as bishop of the Christians in the land of the Goths. Among the matters which he attended to among them, he was the inventor for them of their own letters, and translated all the Scriptures into their language – with the exception, that is, of Kings. This was because these books contain the history of wars, while the Gothic people, being lovers of war, were in need of something to restrain their passion for fighting rather than to incite them to it.

(Philostorgius, *Ecclesiastical History* 2.5)

Ulfila's mission received patronage from the imperial court, particularly from Constantine's son Constantius II (337–361), and from the bishop of Constantinople. As tensions between Goths and Romans mounted, many Goths regarded Christianity as a dangerous foreign influence and Ulfila and his followers were expelled. Nevertheless, Ulfila and his Gothic Bible (fragments of which still survive) continued to exert influence. When Gothic tribes entered the Roman empire in the 370s, it was Ulfila's Christian teachings that they adopted as their religion. One of his pupils celebrated Ulfila's achievement:

Flourishing gloriously for forty years in the bishopric, he preached unceasingly with apostolic grace in the Greek, Latin and Gothic languages, in the one and only church of Christ; for one is the church of the living God, 'the pillar and ground of the truth' [1 Timothy 3.15], asserting and bearing witness that there is but one flock of Christ our Lord and God, one worship and one edifice, one virgin and one bride, one queen and one vine, one house, one temple, one assembly of Christians, and that all other assemblies are not churches of God but 'synagogues of Satan' [Revelation 2.9]. And that all he said, and all I have set down, is from the divine Scriptures, 'let him that reads understand' [Matthew 24.15]. He left behind him several tracts and many interpretations in these three languages for the benefit and edification of those willing to accept it, and as his own eternal memorial and recompense. It is beyond my powers to praise this man according to his merits; yet I dare not be silent altogether, for I owe him a debt greater than does any other man, in that he spent upon me a greater share of labour. He received me from my parents as his disciple in the earliest years of my life; he taught me the holy Scriptures and made plain the truth, and through the mercy of God and the grace of Christ he raised me in the faith, as his son in body and spirit.

(*Letter* of Auxentius of Durostorum 33–4)

The Christianity of the Goths proved crucial as they migrated across the empire into western Europe, and when they sacked Rome in 410 they spared the churches and those who sheltered inside. But tensions remained. The teachings of Ulfila that the Goths had embraced preached the 'Homoian' doctrine that the Son was 'like' (*homoios*) to the Father (see Chapter 6). When Ulfila had set out on his mission this doctrine was recognized as imperial orthodoxy, yet by the early fifth century the 'Homoian' position was widely condemned as 'Arian'. The Goths were thus seen as heretics by the Roman population, as were the other Germanic peoples who shared the Goths' beliefs (notably the Vandals in North Africa). One Germanic tribe, however, did not embrace 'Arian' Christianity. They were the Franks, whose adoption of the 'catholic' orthodoxy of their Roman Christian neighbours helped to lay the foundation for the most successful Germanic kingdom of the post-Roman west.

Gregory of Tours in his *History of the Franks* tells a story of how the Franks became Christian that closely resembles Rufinus' account of the conversion of Georgia. The Frankish king Clovis (c.481–c.511) had married Clothild, a Christian Burgundian princess, but he refused to share her religion.

Queen Clothild continued to pray that her husband might recognize the true God and give up his idol-worship. Nothing could persuade him to accept Christianity. Finally war broke out against the Alamanni and in this conflict he was forced by necessity to accept what he had refused of his own free will. It so turned out that when the two armies met on the battlefield there was great slaughter and the troops of Clovis were rapidly being annihilated. He raised his eyes to heaven when he saw this, felt compunction in his heart and was moved to tears. 'Jesus Christ', he said, 'You who Clothild maintains to be the Son of the living God, you who deign to give help to those in travail and victory to those who trust in you, in faith I beg the glory of your help. If you will give me victory over my enemies, and if I may have evidence of that miraculous power which the people dedicated to your name say that they have experienced, then I will believe in you and I will be baptized in your name. I have called upon my own gods, but as I see only too clearly they have no intention of helping me. I therefore cannot believe that they possess any power, for they do not come to the assistance of those who trust in them. I now call upon you. I want to believe in you, but I must first be saved from my enemies'. Even as he said this the Alamanni turned their backs and began to flee.

(Gregory of Tours, *History of the Franks* 2.30)

There are certain historical problems with this dramatic narrative. Gregory wrote several generations after Clovis, and his desire to construct a perfect conversion story led him to make a number of chronological errors. In Gregory's version, Clovis converted to Christianity in 496 and became an orthodox champion, leading a crusade against the 'Arian' Visigoths and driving them from Gaul. Yet Clovis' marriage to Clothild did not take place until c.500, while his defeat of the Alamanni probably occurred in 506. There is no contemporary evidence that Clovis embraced Christianity during a battle as Gregory described, and his conversion and baptism likely took place only in 508, after Clovis' victories over the Alamanni and Visigoths and shortly before his death in 511. What is not in dispute is that Clovis did indeed convert and accepted orthodox rather than 'Arian' teachings. For we possess the letter that the Burgundian bishop Avitus of Vienne wrote to Clovis praising his decision to embrace the true faith.

> Many in this very situation, seeking true belief, if they are moved to the suggestion, encouraged by priests or their friends, usually invoke the custom of their race and the rites of ancestral observance as stumbling-blocks. Thus, to their own detriment, they prefer due reverence to salvation ... You [alone] among your ancient clan, content with nobility alone, wished whatever could adorn all your lofty ancestry to start from you for the benefit of your race. You have ancestors who did good [deeds], but you wished to be the author of better ones. You are the equal of your great-grandfathers in that you reign in the temporal world; for your descendants you have established your rule in heaven. Therefore let Greece, to be sure, rejoice in having an orthodox ruler, but she is no longer the only one to deserve so great a gift. Now her bright glory adorns your part of the world also, and in the west, in the person of a new king, the ray of an age-old light shines forth.
>
> (Avitus of Vienne, *Letter* 46 to Clovis)

Contrary to the rhetoric of our sources, a king's conversion did not automatically inspire the wider population to follow their ruler's lead. The expansion of Christianity in the Germanic kingdoms, as in Ethiopia and Georgia, was a long and gradual process. Nevertheless, through the Franks and Goths, Burgundians and Vandals, Christianity not only survived the fall of the Roman empire in the west but flourished. Only in one territory formerly under Roman control did the Christian presence decline. The Anglo-Saxons who invaded

Britain had never shared the Roman cultural or religious influence experienced by the other Germanic peoples. A Christian presence endured in the British Isles through the unceasing efforts of Irish monks, whose legacy is preserved in Bede's *Ecclesiastical History of the English People* and in artwork such as the Book of Kells. But at the end of the sixth century a famous mission arrived to convert the Anglo-Saxons to Roman Christianity, the first mission sent by a Pope who now claimed some of the authority of the old western emperors.

The race of the Angli, who live in a corner of the world, remained up to this time faithless in their worship of trees and stones. Through the aid of your prayers for me, I determined to send there a monk of my monastery [Augustine] to preach to them. With my approval he was elected bishop by the bishops of Germany, and with their support also he crossed over to the aforesaid people at the end of the world. Already letters have reached us telling us of his safety and his work, stating that he or those that have been sent with him are resplendent with such great miracles among that same race that they seem to imitate the powers of the apostles in the signs which they display. And at the solemnity of our Lord's nativity, which was celebrated during this first indiction [AD 597], more than ten thousand Angli are reported to have been baptized by our brother and fellow-bishop.

(Gregory the Great, *Letter* 8.29, to Eulogius of Alexandria)

The monk Augustine took office as the inaugural bishop of Canterbury, the chief town of king Aethelberht of Kent who was the first Anglo-Saxon king to embrace Christianity. Thus the mission to Britain took root, which began according to legend with a chance encounter in a market.

It is reported that one day, soon after some merchants had arrived in Rome, many things were offered for sale in the market-place and crowds of people came to buy and Gregory too amongst them. As well as other merchandise he saw some boys put up for sale, with fair complexions, handsome faces and lovely hair. On seeing them he asked, so it is said, from what region or land they had been brought. He was told that they came from the island of Britain, whose inhabitants were like that in appearance. He asked again whether those islanders were Christians or still entangled in the errors of heathenism. He was told that they were heathen. Then with a deep-drawn sigh he said 'Alas that the author of darkness should have men so bright of face in his grip, and that minds devoid of inward grace should bear so graceful an outward form'. Again he asked for the name of the race. He was told that they were called *Angli*. 'Good', he said, 'they have the face of angels and such men should be fellow-heirs of the angels in heaven'. 'What is the name', he asked, 'of the kingdom from which they have been brought?'. He was told that the men of the kingdom were called *Deiri*. '*Deiri*', he replied, '*De Ira!* Good! Snatched from the wrath of Christ and called to His mercy. And what is the name of the king of the land?'. He was told that it was Aelle; and playing on the name, he said, 'Alleluia! The praise of God the Creator must be sung in those parts'.

(Bede, *Ecclesiastical History of the English People* 2.1)

Perhaps the most remarkable missionary achievement of the Late Roman period, however, took place far beyond Britain or any other region ever claimed by imperial Rome. The Church of the East, often referred to inaccurately as the 'Nestorian Church', emerged in the course of the fifth-century Christological controversies (see Chapter 19). Driven from Roman territory, this Church spread eastward from Persia into India and beyond. A Tang dynasty monument erected in 781 preserves the 'Memorial of the Propagation in China of the Luminous Religion from Daqin' ('Daqin' was a Chinese term used to refer both to the Roman empire and to the Church of the East itself). The text records in Chinese and Syriac script the arrival of the Church of the East's mission in 635, led by the holy man Olopun, and their successful promotion of the first Christian communities in China.

In the time of the accomplished emperor Tai-tsung [626–649], the illustrious and magnificent founder of the dynasty, among the enlightened and holy men who arrived was the most-virtuous Olopun, from the country of Syria. Observing the azure clouds, he bore the true sacred books; beholding the direction of the winds, he braved difficulties and dangers. In the year of our Lord [635] he arrived at Chang-an; the emperor sent his prime minister, duke Fang Hiuen-ling; who, carrying the official staff to the west border, conducted his guest into the interior; the sacred books were translated in the imperial library, the sovereign investigated the subject in his private apartments; when becoming deeply impressed with the rectitude and truth of the religion, he gave special orders for its dissemination. In the seventh month of the year [638] the following imperial proclamation was issued:

'Right principles have no invariable name, holy men have no invariable station; instruction is established in accordance with the locality, with the object of benefiting the people at large. The greatly virtuous Olopun, of the kingdom of Syria, has brought his sacred books and images from that distant part, and has presented them at our chief capital. Having examined the principles of this religion, we find them to be purely excellent and natural; investigating its originating source, we find it has taken its rise from the establishment of important truths; its ritual is free from perplexing expressions, its principles will survive when the framework is forgot; it is beneficial to all creatures; it is advantageous to mankind. Let it be published throughout the Empire, and let the proper authority build a Syrian church in the capital in the I-ning May, which shall be governed by twenty-one priests. When the virtue of the Chau Dynasty declined, the rider on the azure ox ascended to the west; the principles of the great Tang becoming resplendent, the Illustrious breezes have come to fan the East'.

('Memorial of the Propagation in China of the Luminous Religion from Daqin' or 'Nestorian Stele')

Copyright Acknowledgements

Avitus of Vienne, *Letter* 46
Translated in D. Shanzer and I. Wood, *Avitus of Vienne: Letters and Selected Prose* (Liverpool 2002), by permission of Liverpool University Press

Bede, *Ecclesiastical History of the English People*
Translated in J. McClure and R. Collins, *Bede: The Ecclesiastical History of the English People* (Oxford and New York 1994), by permission of Oxford University Press

Gregory of Tours, *History of the Franks*
Translated in L. Thorpe, *Gregory of Tours: The History of the Franks* (Harmondsworth 1974), by permission of Penguin Books Ltd

Philostorgius, *Ecclesiastical History*
Letter of Auxentius of Durostorum
Translated in P. Heather and J. Matthews, *The Goths in the Fourth Century* (Liverpool 1991), by permission of Liverpool University Press

Rufinus of Aquileia, *Ecclesiastical History*
Translated in P. R. Amidon, *The Church History of Rufinus of Aquileia, Books 10 and 11* (Oxford 1997), by permission of Oxford University Press

Further Reading

D. Braund, *Georgia in Antiquity: A History of Colchis and Transcaucasian Iberia, 550 BC–AD 562* (Oxford 1994)

R. Fletcher, *The Conversion of Europe: From Paganism to Christianity 371–1386 AD* (London 1997)

P. Heather and J. Matthews, *The Goths in the Fourth Century* (Liverpool 1991)

M. Heinzelmann, *Gregory of Tours: History and Society in the Sixth Century*, translated by C. Carroll (Cambridge 2001)

H. Mayr-Harting, *The Coming of Christianity to Anglo-Saxon England*, 3rd edition (London 1991)

S. Munro-Hay, *Ethiopia and Alexandria: the Metropolitan Episcopacy of Ethiopia* (Warsaw and Wiesbaden 1997)

Li Tang, *A Study of the History of Nestorian Christianity in China and its Literature in Chinese, together with a new English translation of the Dunhuang Nestorian Documents*, 2nd revised edition (Frankfurt am Main 2004)

E. A. Thompson, *The Visigoths in the Time of Ulfila* (Oxford 1966)

I. Wood, *The Merovingian Kingdoms 450–571* (London 1994)

I. Wood, *The Missionary Life: Saints and the Evangelisation of Europe 400–1050* (Harlow 2001)

18

The City of God

The Gothic Sack of Rome in 410 sent tremors rippling across the Mediterranean world. Refugees from Italy fled to North Africa and the eastern provinces, while Christians and non-Christians alike sought divine explanations for the catastrophe. Amidst accusations that abandoning the ancient gods had caused Rome's fall and Christians struggling to come to terms with why God would permit such a disaster, Augustine of Hippo began to compose one of the most influential Christian works ever written: the *City of God* (*De Civitatis Dei*).

Augustine stands among the select pantheon of the greatest men and women in western and Christian history. Hundreds of his treatises, letters and sermons survive (although the famous words of Isidore of Seville (c.560–636), 'he is a liar who confesses to have read the whole [of Augustine's works]', refers to the difficulty in obtaining all those works as well as their sheer scale). Augustine's life spanned a momentous period. He was born in Thagaste in Roman North Africa in 354 and died with the Vandals besieging his episcopal city of Hippo in 430. The story of his early religious experiences and his ultimate decision to devote himself entirely to Christianity is well-known, for Augustine left to posterity the work he called the *Confessions*, one of the first true autobiographies.

> Even as a boy I had heard of the eternal life promised to us through the humility of the Lord our God who came down amongst us proud sinners. I was blessed with the sign of the cross and was seasoned with God's salt from the womb of my mother, who greatly trusted in you. You saw, O Lord, how once while I was yet a boy I was suddenly seized with pains in my stomach and was at the point of death. You saw, O my God, for even then you were my keeper, with what emotion of mind and with what faith I solicited from the piety of my mother and of your

Church, the mother of us all, the baptism of your Christ, my Lord and my God. At this the mother of my flesh was much troubled, for she with a heart pure in your faith was in greater labour for my eternal salvation than she had been at my birth. Had I not quickly recovered, she would have without delay ensured that I was initiated and washed clean by your life-giving sacraments, confessing you, O Lord Jesus, for the remission of sins. So my cleansing was deferred, for should I live I must inevitably be further polluted and indeed the guilt contracted by sin would, after baptism, be greater and more perilous. At that time I believed with my mother and the whole household except for my father, and he did not overcome the influence upon me of my mother's piety so as to prevent my believing in Christ because he did not yet believe in Him.

(Augustine of Hippo, *Confessions* 1.11)

Monica, Augustine's mother, exerted a strong influence upon him and ensured that he was raised with Christian beliefs. Infant baptism was not universal practice, however, and after surviving his childhood illness Augustine was not baptized. Moreover, despite his mother's influence, Augustine initially struggled to reconcile Christianity with his worldly dreams and his understanding of God.

I studied the books of eloquence, for it was my ambition to be eminent for the unhallowed and empty purpose of delighting human vanity. In the ordinary course of study, I lighted upon a certain book of Cicero, whose language, though not his spirit, almost all admire. This book of his contains an exhortation to philosophy, and is called the *Hortensius*. This book changed my outlook on life. It turned my prayers to you, O Lord, and gave me new hopes and aspirations.

(Augustine of Hippo, *Confessions* 3.4)

His pursuit of a successful career as a teacher and orator took Augustine to Carthage, the greatest city in North Africa, and then to Rome. But like his contemporary Jerome, Augustine felt tension between his Christian inclinations and his knowledge of classical culture. Of still greater concern were the limits of his Christian understanding. Augustine believed implicitly in God's love for His creation, but how could a loving God have allowed evil to exist and how should man conceive of God's being? In his search for reassurance, Augustine associated with the Manichees, whose dualist theology divided the universe between good and evil. Looking back on these years in the *Confessions*, Augustine mourned his error.

> I was ignorant as to that which really is, and was moved to give my support to foolish deceivers who asked me what was the origin of evil, whether God is limited by a bodily shape, whether He has hair and nails, and whether those men are to be esteemed righteous who had many wives at once and killed men and sacrificed living creatures? At these questions I in my ignorance was much disturbed and, retreating from the truth, I appeared to myself to be going towards it. As yet I did not know that evil was nothing but the removal of good until in the end no good remains. How could I see this, when the sight of my eyes saw no further than material bodies and the sight of my mind no further than a phantasm? I knew not that God is Spirit, a being without bulk and not one with limbs defined in length and breadth.
>
> (Augustine of Hippo, *Confessions* 3.7)

Over time Augustine found answers to ease his concerns. In 384 he accepted a teaching post in Milan, the residence of the western imperial court. There he was inspired by the preaching of the bishop Ambrose and by the spiritual philosophy of Neoplatonism. Yet still he hesitated to commit to a pure Christian life. The chastity that Augustine believed such a life required remained a stumbling block in his quest for true happiness.

> Still I hesitated to reject mere worldly joys and to devote myself to seek out that happiness of which the very search, let alone its discovery, I ought to have preferred over possessing the treasures and kingdoms of this world and over enjoying at will the pleasures of the body. But I, a miserable young man even in the very outset of my youth, had entreated you for chastity and said, 'Grant me chastity and continence, but not yet'. For I was afraid that you might hear me too soon and deliver me from the disease of lust, which I desired to have satisfied rather than extinguished.
>
> (Augustine of Hippo, *Confessions* 8.7)

Augustine's anguish reached its climax in August 386 in the garden attached to his house in Milan. Flinging himself down beneath a fig tree:

In my misery I sent up these sorrowful cries, 'How long, how long? Tomorrow, and tomorrow? Why not now? Why is there not at this moment an end to my uncleanness?'. I was saying these things and weeping in the most bitter contrition of my heart, when suddenly I heard the voice of a boy or girl, I know not which, coming from a neighbouring house and chanting again and again, 'Take up and read; take up and read' (*tolle lege*). Immediately my countenance changed, and I began most earnestly to consider whether it was usual for children in any kind of game to sing such words, but I could not remember ever to have heard the like. Restraining the torrent of my tears, I therefore rose up, interpreting it in no other way than as a command to me from Heaven to open my book of Scripture and read the first passage that I should light upon.

(Augustine of Hippo, *Confessions* 8.12)

The verse was:

Not in revelry and drunkenness, not in debauchery and licentiousness, not in quarrelling and jealousy. Instead, put on the Lord Jesus Christ, and make no provision for the flesh to gratify its desires.

(Romans 13.13–14)

At Easter 387, Augustine and his lifelong friend Alypius presented themselves to Ambrose for baptism.

Now we were ready to be educated in your ways. We were baptized, and concern for our past lives left us. My days were full with the wondrous joy of contemplating the depth of your providence for the salvation of the human race.

(Augustine of Hippo, *Confessions* 9.6)

Augustine returned to North Africa and eventually settled in Hippo where he became bishop in 395. An active participant in the debates that divided North African Christianity, he wrote several treatises against the Manichees and was a prominent figure at the Conference of Carthage in 411 opposing the Donatists. He was also drawn into the controversy over the British monk Pelagius whose insistence that man could and should seek perfection in service to God challenged Augustine's emphasis on original sin and the need for divine grace. All these issues came together in the *City of God*. Following the Sack of Rome, many looked to Augustine for guidance. One such man was Flavius Marcellinus, a high-ranking official who also oversaw the Conference of 411, and it was Marcellinus whom Augustine addressed in the opening words of his *magnum opus*.

> The glorious City of God is the theme of my work, my dearest son Marcellinus, which I owed to you in fulfilment of my promise. I have undertaken its defence against those who prefer their own gods to the Founder of this city, a city surpassingly glorious whether we view it as it exists through faith in this fleeting world of time and sojourns as a stranger in the midst of the ungodly, or as it shall dwell in the fixed security of its eternal seat. This security it now awaits with patience, until 'justice will return to the righteous' [Psalm 94.15] and it shall obtain hereafter, by virtue of its excellence, with the final victory and perfect peace. The task is great and arduous, but God is my helper.
>
> (Augustine of Hippo, *City of God* Preface)

The *City of God* was begun in 412 and completed in 426/7. Augustine divided the vast work into twenty-two books which were published in instalments. We are fortunate to possess a letter that Augustine wrote to Firmus, a priest who acted as his literary agent, describing how the finished work should be organized for publication.

> There are twenty-two books, too many to combine in a single volume. If you wish to make two volumes, they should be so divided that one volume contains ten books, the other twelve. In those ten, the empty teachings of the pagans have been refuted, while in the remainder our own religion has been demonstrated and defended – although naturally the latter subject has been addressed in the former books where appropriate, and the former subject in the latter. If you want more than two volumes, then you must make five. The first should contain the opening five books, written against those who maintain that the worship of the gods, or rather of demons, leads to happiness in this present life. The second volume should contain the next five books, written against those who think that such deities are to be worshipped by rites and sacrifices for the sake of the life to come. The remaining three volumes should contain four books each. This part of the work has been arranged so that four books describe the origin of that City, four its progress or development, and the final four its appointed ends.
>
> (Augustine of Hippo, *Letter to Firmus*)

In the first book of the *City of God*, Augustine turned immediately to the Sack of Rome.

> To this world's city belong the enemies against whom I must defend the City of God. Many of them, indeed, have been reclaimed from their ungodly error and become useful citizens of this City, but many are inflamed with hatred against it and are ungrateful to its Redeemer for His unmistakeable benefits. They forget that they would now be unable to utter a single word against the City, had they not found in its sacred places, as they fled from the enemy's steel, that safety on which they now congratulate themselves. These very Romans, who were spared by the barbarians for Christ's sake, have become enemies to Christ's name. The sacred places of the martyrs and the churches of the apostles bear witness to this; for in the sack of Rome they offered sanctuary to all who fled to them, Christian and pagan alike.
>
> (Augustine of Hippo, *City of God* 1.1)

Like his contemporaries, both Christian and non-Christian, Augustine believed strongly in divine providence. The course of this world is directed by the divine will, and so God determined the fate of Rome and the survivors. But Augustine's conception of providence was far more complex than that of other Christian authors such as Eusebius of Caesarea. *City of God* books 1–5 place the Sack of Rome in the context of wider Roman history, tracing the triumphs and disasters that had befallen the Romans before and after Christ's Incarnation and then Constantine's conversion. Whereas Eusebius glorified the first Christian emperor as God's representative on earth, Augustine knew well that not all Christian rulers prospered as Constantine did. A more nuanced understanding of God's will was required, for the true reward for Christians comes not in this world but in the next.

> We do not say that certain Christian emperors were 'happy' because they ruled for a long time, or died a peaceful death leaving their sons to succeed them, or subdued the state's enemies, or were able to guard against and suppress those who rose against them. These and other gifts or consolations of this sorrowful life even some worshippers of demons have deserved to receive, who do not belong to the kingdom of God to which these Christian emperors belong. This was due to the mercy of God, who would not have those who believe in Him desire such things as the highest good.
>
> (Augustine of Hippo, *City of God* 5.24)

This vision of providence underlay Augustine's doctrine of the two cities, the earthly city and the City of God. These cities are not physical structures, nor are they divided simply between those inside or outside the Church. They exist throughout time, from the original angels to the last age when the members of the two cities will stand revealed. In *City of God* books 6–10, Augustine first denounces the errors of traditional Roman religion and Graeco-Roman philosophy. The remaining twelve books then trace the parallel stories of the two cities.

> I have classified the human race into two branches: the one consisting of those who live according to man, the other of those who live according to God. These we also call allegorically the two cities or two communities, of which the one is predestined to reign eternally with God, and the other to suffer eternal punishment with the Devil. This, however, is their final destiny, which I will speak of later. At present, as we have said enough about the origins of these cities, whether among the angels, whose numbers are unknown to us, or in the first two human beings, it seems appropriate that I should attempt to trace their development from the time when our first two parents began to propagate the race until the time when all human generation shall cease. For the development of these two cities which are my subject spans this whole period or age of the world, in which the dying give place to the newly born who succeed them.
>
> (Augustine of Hippo, *City of God* 15.1)

Books 11–14 begin with creation and explore the original sin and the fall of Adam and Eve from the Garden of Eden. Books 15–18 follow the two cities from the conflict between Cain and Abel through scriptural and classical history. The two cities will continue to exist until the end, which is the focus of books 19–22. But Augustine warns against those who in his own time (and still to this day) try to predict when the end will come.

> In vain do we attempt to compute and define the years that may remain for this world, since we hear from the mouth of Truth itself that it is not for us to know this. And yet some claim that 400, some that 500, and others that a 1000 years may be completed between the ascension of the Lord and His final coming. But to point out how each of them supports their own opinion would take too long and is not necessary, for they rely upon human conjectures and bring forward nothing certain from the authority of the canonical Scriptures. Indeed, all those

> who make such calculations on this subject are ordered to put aside their figures and be silent, by He who says, 'It is not for you to know the times or periods that the Father has set by His own authority' [Acts 1.7].
>
> (Augustine of Hippo, *City of God* 18.53)

The *City of God* is a remarkable achievement. The argument is dense and heavily scriptural, too much so for many of Augustine's contemporaries as well as modern readers. Yet the fundamental message is one of reassurance. In the imperfect world in which we live, the good will suffer evil and bad things will happen to those who deserve better. As long as we hold true to our path, which for Augustine is the path of Christ, then due reward will come in the world hereafter.

> There will be true honour, for it shall be denied to none who are worthy and yielded to none who are unworthy. Nor shall anyone unworthy court honour, for none but the worthy shall be there. And there will be true peace, where none shall suffer opposition from within themselves or from any other. God Himself, who is the giver of virtue, shall be virtue's reward, for there is nothing greater or better as He Himself has promised.
>
> (Augustine of Hippo, *City of God* 22.30)

Whether we accept the reassurance that Augustine seeks to offer is a decision we each make for ourselves. But it is difficult to find fault with his closing words.

> I think that I have now, by God's help, discharged my debt with the completion of this huge work. Some may believe that I have said too little, others that I have said too much. Of both these groups I ask forgiveness. Let those for whom I have said enough join me in giving thanks to God. Amen. Amen.
>
> (Augustine of Hippo, *City of God* 22.30, postscript)

Further Reading

G. Bonner, *St Augustine of Hippo. Life and Controversies*, 3rd edition (Norwich 2002)
P. Brown, *Augustine of Hippo*, revised edition (London 2000)

H. Chadwick, *Augustine* (Oxford 1986)

S. Lancel, *St Augustine*, translated by A. Nevill (London 2002)

R. A. Markus, *Saeculum: History and Society in the Theology of St Augustine* (Cambridge 1970)

G. O'Daly, *Augustine's City of God: A Reader's Guide* (Oxford 1999)

J. J. O'Donnell, *Augustine's Confessions*, 3 volumes (Oxford 1992)

J. J. O'Donnell, *Augustine, Sinner and Saint: A New Biography* (London 2005)

J. J. O'Meara, *The Young Augustine*, revised edition (New York 2001)

E. Stump and N. Kretzmann (eds), *The Cambridge Companion to Augustine* (Cambridge 2001)

M. Vessey with S. Reid (eds), *A Companion to Augustine* (Chichester and Malden 2012)

19

The Christological Controversies

The fifth and sixth centuries witnessed the break-up of the Roman empire in the west and the rise of the Germanic kingdoms. Yet for the future of Christianity, equally dramatic events were unfolding in the east. Here the crisis involved not invading barbarians, but the definition of the Christian faith. The theological controversies of the fourth century concerned the doctrine of the Trinity, but by the end of that century they were drawing to a close (see Chapter 6). At the councils of Nicaea in 325 and Constantinople in 381, the Son was upheld as consubstantial (*homoousios*) with the Father and the Trinity defined as three equal persons in one divine essence (three *hypostases* in one *ousia*). The fourth-century Trinitarian debates, however, led in turn to new controversies in the fifth and sixth centuries which centred around questions of Christology: the humanity and divinity of the incarnate Christ. Like the fourth-century debates, these Christological questions may appear arcane to many modern readers but concern issues fundamental to Christianity as a living religion. And to a far greater extent than the Trinitarian debates, the Christological controversies shaped later Christian history. For the divisions that emerged in the Church during the fifth and sixth centuries still exist within Christianity to this day.

At the heart of the Christian message lies the salvation of humanity through the Incarnation of the Son as Jesus Christ. The fourth-century bishop Athanasius of Alexandria encapsulated that message as a process of 'deification' or 'divinization', that the Son became human so that we might become divine.

> Just as if someone who should wish to see God, who is invisible by nature and not seen at all, may understand and know Him from His works, so likewise let he who does not see Christ with his mind learn of Him from the works of His body,

and let him test whether they be human works or the works of God. And if they be human, let him mock. But if they are not human but of God, let him recognise this and not laugh at what is no matter for mockery. Rather let him marvel that through such ordinary means these divine things have been revealed to us, and that through death immortality has reached to all, and through the Word becoming human the universal providence has been made known and its giver and creator the very Word of God. For He became human that we might become divine; and He revealed Himself through a body that we might receive an idea of the invisible Father; and He endured the insolence of human beings that we might inherit immortality.

(Athanasius of Alexandria, *On the Incarnation* 54)

Athanasius was particularly concerned to emphasize the Son's full divinity against those like his older contemporary Arius who subordinated the Son to the Father. But it is no less essential for Christian salvation that the incarnate Christ was fully human and so took on all our sins. This argument was laid down explicitly by the Cappadocian Gregory of Nazianzus in refuting Apollinaris of Laodicea, who taught that the Son took the place of Jesus' human mind in the Incarnation.

If anyone has put his trust in Him as a man without a human mind, he is really bereft of mind himself and quite unworthy of salvation. For that which He has not assumed, He has not healed; but that which is united to His Godhead is also saved. If only half Adam fell, then that which Christ assumes and saves may be half also; but if the whole of Adam fell, he must be united to the whole nature of Him that was begotten, and so be saved as a whole. Let them not then begrudge us our complete salvation, or clothe the Saviour only with bones and nerves and the portraiture of man.

(Gregory of Nazianzus, *Letter* 101)

The central paradox of the fourth-century Trinitarian controversies had been how to reconcile the divine Trinity with the monotheistic belief in One God that Christianity proclaimed. Now a second paradox had to be resolved: how could the incarnate Son be both fully God and fully man? This was the debate that came to a head in the early decades of the fifth century, a conflict further fuelled by the rivalry between the great eastern cities of Constantinople, Antioch and

Alexandria. In 428 the Antiochene Nestorius was appointed as bishop of Constantinople. It was the teachings there of one of his followers which lit the spark of discord within the eastern Church.

Nestorius had an associate whom he had brought from Antioch, a presbyter named Anastasius; for this man he had the highest esteem, and consulted him in the management of his most important affairs. This Anastasius preaching one day in the church said, 'Let no one call Mary *Theotokos* ['God-bearer']: for Mary was but a woman; and it is impossible that God should be born of a woman'. These words created a great sensation and troubled many both of the clergy and laity, as they had been taught heretofore to acknowledge Christ as God, and by no means to separate His humanity from His divinity on account of the economy of the Incarnation, heeding the voice of the Apostle when he said, 'Though we once knew Christ after the flesh, we know Him no longer in that way' [2 Corinthians 5.16] and again, 'Therefore, leaving the word of the beginning of Christ, let us go on towards perfection' [Hebrews 6.1]. While great offense was taken in the church, as we have said, at what was thus propounded, Nestorius, eager to establish Anastasius' proposition – for he did not wish to have the man who was esteemed by himself found guilty of blasphemy – delivered several public discourses on the subject, in which he assumed a controversial attitude and totally rejected the epithet *Theotokos*.

(Socrates, *Ecclesiastical History* 7.32)

The title *Theotokos* or 'God-bearer' was given to Mary by a number of fourth-century theologians as an expression of the union of humanity and divinity in the Incarnation. For Nestorius, such language threatened to blur the distinction between the divine Son and the human Jesus. For Nestorius' opponents, his rejection of *Theotokos* implied a denial of the Incarnation as a true union. Those opponents were led by Nestorius' chief ecclesiastical rival, Cyril of Alexandria (bishop 412–444). A gifted theologian and ambitious politician, Cyril exploited the controversy over the *Theotokos* to assert himself as the champion of orthodoxy and Nestorius' instructor in the correct faith.

We acknowledge one Christ and Lord, not worshipping a man together with the Word, lest a semblance of division might secretly creep in through the use of the word 'with', but worshipping Him as one and the same, because His body with which He is seated with the Father is not alien to the Word; it is again not the case that two sons are seated with the Father, but one is, in virtue of His union with the flesh. But if we reject the hypostatic union as incomprehensible or unseemly, we fall into saying two sons, for it becomes inevitable to draw a distinction and to speak of the one as individually a man, honoured with the title of 'son', and again of the other as individually the Word from God, possessing by nature both the name and reality of sonship. We must therefore not divide into two sons the one Lord Jesus Christ, for doing so will in no way assist the right expression of the faith, even though some allege a union of persons; for Scripture did not say that the Word united to Himself the person of a man, but that He became flesh. The Word becoming flesh means nothing other than that 'He partook of blood and flesh like us' [Hebrews 2.14], and made our body His own, and came forth a human being from a woman, not laying aside His being God and His generation from God the Father, but even in His assumption of flesh remaining what He was. This is what the account of the true faith everywhere proclaims; this we shall find to be the belief of the holy fathers. Accordingly they confidently called the holy Virgin *Theotokos*.

(Cyril of Alexandria, *Second Letter to Nestorius*)

Nestorius reacted angrily to Cyril's arguments on ecclesiastical and theological grounds. He particularly opposed Cyril's attribution of human properties such as suffering to the divine Son through the principle known as the communication of idioms. In Nestorius' eyes, the teachings of Cyril confused Christ's humanity and divinity and compromised the Godhead of the Son.

It is correct and worthy of the Gospel traditions to confess that the body is the temple of the Son's Godhead and a temple joined to the Godhead through a sublime and divine union, so that the nature of the Godhead takes as its own the characteristics of the temple. But to attribute also to the Godhead, through the expression of this relationship, the properties of the flesh that is united with it – I mean birth, suffering, and death – this, my brother, is the error either of a pagan mentality or of a mind diseased with the madness of Apollinaris, Arius, and the other heresies, or even worse than theirs. For those who are led into such error by this idea of relationship must necessarily through this relationship associate God the Word with being fed on milk, with growing gradually, with fear at the time of His passion, and with being in need of angelic assistance. I make no mention of circumcision, sacrificing, sweat and hunger, all of which belong to the flesh and are honoured as they were taken on for our sake, but which are entirely false if attributed to the Godhead and would give cause for our just condemnation as slanderers. These are the traditions of the holy fathers. These are the precepts of the holy Scriptures.

(Nestorius, *Reply to Cyril's Second Letter*)

Both Cyril and Nestorius thus claimed to represent the traditional and scriptural faith of the Church. Their rivalry climaxed when the emperor Theodosius II (408–450) summoned a council to meet at Ephesus in 431. Although remembered as the third ecumenical council, the full council never actually met. Cyril reached Ephesus first, and passed judgement against Nestorius before the latter's main supporter John of Antioch had arrived. John then held his own council which denounced Cyril. When the dust finally settled, Nestorius was deposed and exiled to an Egyptian monastery and the doctrines associated with him were condemned. Beyond the Roman empire's eastern borders, however, a theological tradition endured that upheld Nestorius' insistence on the distinct natures of Christ. This was the Church of the East, which in the following centuries expanded across Persia as far as India and China (see Chapter 17) and has survived to the present day. Sometimes wrongly called the 'Nestorian Church', the Church of the East recognizes Nestorius as a saint but does not share all his teachings. The early theology of the Church of the East is well represented by the verse homilies of the poet Narsai in the second half of the fifth century.

Let not the hearer suppose
by the fact that I have distinguished the natures
that I am speaking of two prosopa
which are distant from one another.
I am talking of one prosopon,
of the Word and the temple He chose,
and I confess one Son,
but I preach in two natures:
the venerated and glorious nature of the Word,
the Being from His Father,
and our nature which He took
in accordance with the promises He made.
Perfect in His divinity,
for He is equal with His begetter,

and complete in His humanity,
with soul and body of mortal beings.
Two that became, in the union,
a single love and a single will.

(Narsai, *Homily* 56)

Within the eastern empire, the Christological controversies continued. Following Nestorius' deposition, Cyril of Alexandria and John of Antioch came to a temporary understanding. The document that they approved in 433 is known as the Formula of Reunion.

We acknowledge our Lord Jesus Christ, the only-begotten Son of God, perfect God and perfect man made up of a rational soul and body, begotten from the Father before the ages in respect of the Godhead and the same on the last day for us and for our salvation from the Virgin Mary in respect of His manhood, the same consubstantial with the Father in respect of the Godhead and consubstantial with us in respect of the manhood. For there has occurred a union of two natures, and therefore we acknowledge one Christ, one Son, one Lord. By virtue of this understanding of the union which involves no merging, we acknowledge the holy Virgin to be *Theotokos*, because God the Word was enfleshed and became man and from the very conception united to Himself the temple taken from her. As regards the sayings concerning the Lord in the Gospels and the apostolic writings we know that theologians treat some as common, as relating to one person, and distinguish others, as relating to two natures, attributing the ones worthy of God to the Godhead of Christ and the lowly ones to His manhood.

(Formula of Reunion, 433)

The Formula was composed by John and his followers. They abandoned their defence of Nestorius and conceded the term *Theotokos*, but insisted upon a clear statement of the incarnate Christ as having two natures, human and divine. Cyril accepted the Formula as the price of reconciliation, but he preferred to qualify such language with greater emphasis upon the unity of Christ. Thus he described the Incarnation as occurring 'out of two natures' and adopted the expression 'one incarnate nature of the Word' (Cyril attributed this phrase to his illustrious predecessor Athanasius of Alexandria when it was actually inspired by the heretic Apollinaris of Laodicea).

If we consider the manner of the Incarnation, we see that two natures have united without confusion and without alteration in an indivisible union. Thus the flesh is flesh and not Godhead, even though it has become God's flesh; and likewise the Word is God and not flesh even though He made the flesh His own in the fulfilment of God's plan. When we understand this, we do not damage the concurrence into unity when we declare that it was achieved out of two natures. After the union, however, we do not divide the natures from each other and do not separate the one and indivisible into two sons, but we say that there is one Son and, in accordance with the holy fathers, one incarnate nature of the Word.

(Cyril of Alexandria, *First Letter to Succensus of Diocaesarea*)

With the Formula of Reunion, peace appeared to have been restored. Yet crucial theological questions remained unresolved, particularly concerning Christ's two natures and their relationship after the Incarnation. Cyril of Alexandria died in 444, allegedly provoking Nestorius' old friend Theodoret of Cyrrhus to urge someone:

To tell the guild of undertakers to lay a very big heavy stone upon his grave, for fear he should come back again.

(Theodoret of Cyrrhus, *Letter* 180)

Renewed controversy broke out within five years of Cyril's death. In 448 the presbyter Eutyches, a leading opponent of Nestorius, was examined and denounced at a council led by bishop Flavian of Constantinople. Eutyches claimed to follow the teachings of Cyril, and affirmed that Christ following the Incarnation had only one nature.

I have read in the blessed Cyril, in the holy fathers and in Saint Athanasius that they said 'from two natures' before the union, but after the union and the Incarnation they no longer affirmed two natures but one.

(Eutyches, at the Council of Constantinople (448),
quoted in the *Acts of Chalcedon* 1.542)

Eutyches' condemnation sparked further debate across the eastern Church, and angered Cyril's successor Dioscorus of Alexandria. Emperor Theodosius II's response was to summon a second great council to Ephesus to re-examine Flavian and Eutyches.

It was our wish to keep the holy churches of God free from disturbance, and that you should stay in your most holy churches to serve the cult of the Almighty as usual and not be burdened with such labour and trouble. But when the most God-beloved bishop Flavian decided to raise some questions about the holy faith in opposition to the most devout archimandrite Eutyches, summoned a tribunal and initiated proceedings, we wrote to the same most God-beloved bishop repeatedly in an attempt to still the turmoil he had stirred up, in our conviction that the orthodox creed which the holy fathers at Nicaea handed down and the holy council at Ephesus confirmed satisfies our needs. We repeatedly pressed the same most religious bishop to drop the inquiry, lest it be a cause of disturbance to the whole world, but he refused. Since we did not consider it without danger for such an inquiry into the faith to be put in motion without reference to your holy council and all the presidents of the holy churches, we deemed it necessary for your holinesses to assemble, so that, by investigating the inquiry that has been put in motion and the attendant proceedings, you could excise every diabolical root, expel from the holy churches the promoters and supporters of the impious blasphemy of Nestorius, and decree the preservation of the orthodox faith, sure and sound, since all our hopes and the strength of our empire are founded on orthodox faith in God and your holy prayers.

(Theodosius II, *Letter to the bishops at Ephesus* (449),
quoted in the *Acts of Chalcedon* 1.51)

The Second Council of Ephesus (Ephesus II) was directed by Dioscorus, defended Eutyches, and condemned Flavian of Constantinople. This verdict was immediately disputed both by Flavian and by Leo, bishop of Rome (440–461). Leo memorably branded the council as a *latrocinium* or 'den of thieves', hence the nickname 'the Robber Synod'. The only Latin theologian actively involved in the fifth-century controversies, Leo had already composed his own judgement in support of Flavian and against Eutyches. His work, the *Tome of Leo*, was ignored at Ephesus II but became the definitive western statement on the two natures of Christ.

With the distinctive character of each nature being preserved and coming together into one person, lowliness was assumed by divinity, impotence by power, mortality by immortality; and for the payment of the debt owed by our nature the divine nature was united to the passible nature, so that – this fitting our cure – one and the same, being 'the mediator between God and men, the man Christ Jesus' [1 Timothy 2.5], would be able to die in respect of the one and would not be able to expire in respect of the other. Therefore in the pure and perfect nature of true man, true God was born, complete in what is His own and complete in what is ours. We call ours that which the Creator deposited in us from the beginning and which He received back again to restore; for that which the deceiver introduced in addition – and the man, being deceived, sinned – did not have any trace in the Saviour. Nor because He entered into a share in human weakness did He in consequence become a sharer also in our sins. For He assumed the form of a servant without any defilement of sin, augmenting the human without lessening the divine, since that emptying through which the invisible made Himself visible, and the Maker and Master of the universe chose to become one among men, was a condescension of compassion and not a deficiency of power. Therefore the one who while remaining in the form of God created man, Himself in the form of a servant became man; for each nature preserves without any loss its own distinctive character, and just as the form of God does not destroy the form of the servant, so the forming of the servant did not diminish the form of God.

(The *Tome of Leo*, quoted in the *Acts of Chalcedon* 2.22)

The controversies over Eutyches, Leo's *Tome* and Ephesus II still raged when Theodosius II died in 450 after a riding accident. His successor, Marcian (450–457), summoned the Church to yet another great council, this time at Chalcedon on the eastern coast of the Bosporus opposite Constantinople. In October 451, some 370 bishops approved a new definition of the Christian faith. The creeds proclaimed at the councils of Nicaea (325) and Constantinople (381) were read and agreed, and the bishops at Chalcedon then declared:

The council sets itself against those who attempt to dissolve the mystery of the dispensation into a duality of sons, and it removes from the list of priests those who dare to say that the Godhead of the only-begotten is passible; it opposes those who imagine a mixing or confusion in the case of the two natures of Christ, it expels those who rave that the form of a servant which He took from us was heavenly or of some other substance, and it anathematizes those who invent two natures of the Lord before the union and imagine one nature after the union.

Following, therefore, the holy fathers, we all in harmony teach confession of one and the same Son our Lord Jesus Christ, the same perfect in Godhead and the same perfect in manhood, truly God and the same truly man, of a rational soul and body, consubstantial with the Father in respect of the Godhead, and the same consubstantial with us in respect of the manhood, like us in all things apart from sin, begotten from the Father before the ages in respect of the Godhead, and the same in the last days for us and for our salvation from the Virgin Mary the *Theotokos* in respect of the manhood, one and the same Christ, Son, Lord, only-begotten, acknowledged in two natures without confusion, change, division, or separation (the difference of the natures being in no way destroyed by the union, but rather the distinctive character of each nature being preserved and coming together into one person and one *hypostasis*), not parted or divided into two persons, but one and the same Son, only-begotten, God, Word, Lord, Jesus Christ, even as the prophets from of old and Jesus Christ Himself taught us about Him and the symbol of the fathers has handed down to us.

(The Chalcedonian Definition, *Acts of Chalcedon* 5.34)

The Chalcedonian Definition sought a theological middle ground, compatible with the teachings of Cyril, Leo, and the Formula of Reunion while condemning the more extreme ideas associated with Nestorius and Eutyches. Christ was acknowledged as two natures united in one person and one *hypostasis*. For the Greek Orthodox Church and the major western Churches this has remained the traditional orthodox statement of the Incarnation, and Chalcedon is upheld by those Churches as the fourth ecumenical council. Even at the time of the Definition, however, the claim that this faith was taught by all in harmony was false. Many eastern Christians regarded Chalcedon's emphasis on Christ's two natures as a betrayal of Cyril's legacy, a view particularly strong in Egypt (unsurprisingly) and in Syria. Those who rejected Chalcedon and taught that the incarnate Christ had only one nature (in Greek *mia phusis*) became known as the Miaphysites or Monophysites.

Over the century that followed, recurring efforts were made to reconcile the supporters and opponents of the Chalcedonian Definition. On 28 June 482, the emperor Zeno (474–491) issued a decree called the Henotikon. The decree sidelined Chalcedon and sought to unify all eastern Christians around the Nicene Creed (the faith of the 318 fathers) and the condemnation of Nestorius and Eutyches.

Knowing that neither the holy and orthodox churches of God everywhere, nor the priests beloved of God who are in charge of them, nor our empire, have tolerated or tolerate a different creed or definition of faith contrary to the aforesaid holy teaching, let us unite ourselves with no hesitation. We have written this not in order to make innovations in the faith but so as to reassure you. But we anathematize anyone who has thought, or thinks, any other opinion, either now or at any time, whether at Chalcedon or at any synod whatsoever, and especially the aforesaid Nestorius and Eutyches and those who hold their opinions. Accordingly, join with the Church, the spiritual mother, enjoying the same sacred communion in it as us, in accordance with the aforesaid one and only definition of the faith of the 318 holy fathers. For our all-holy mother the Church is eagerly awaiting to embrace you as legitimate sons, and yearns to hear your sweet and long-awaited voice. Therefore hasten yourselves, for in doing this you will both attract to yourselves the goodwill of our Lord God and Saviour Jesus Christ and be praised by our imperial rule.

(The Henotikon of Zeno, quoted in Evagrius, *Ecclesiastical History* 3.14)

Like so many attempted compromises, the vague language of the Henotikon failed to satisfy either side in the debate. Yet the emperors remained deeply concerned to reunite the eastern Church, both to avert the divine wrath that Christian divisions might inspire and to maintain the bonds between imperial Constantinople, which was predominantly Chalcedonian, and the wealthy provinces of Syria and Egypt with their strong Miaphysite populations. The greatest efforts were made under Justinian (527–565). In 532 Justinian hosted 'Conversations' between Chalcedonian and Miaphysite bishops in Constantinople, seeking common ground. This was followed by Justinian's condemnation of the 'Three Chapters' in 544/5. These were the writings of three men – Theodore of Mopsuestia, Theodoret of Cyrrhus and Ibas of Edessa – who had been associated with Nestorius. Justinian hoped that Chalcedonians and Miaphysites alike could unite in condemnation of their common 'Nestorian' enemies. The emperor's plans culminated in the Council of Constantinople of 553, which opened with the reading of a letter by Justinian laying down his vision to the assembled bishops.

When, according to His mercy the Lord God entrusted the government of the state to us, we made it the start and foundation of our reign to unite the divided priests of the holy churches of God from east to west, and in order to suppress all the contention that the followers of the impious Eutyches and Nestorius were stirring up against the holy Council of Chalcedon, we made the same holy council to be proclaimed in the churches of God together with the aforesaid three other holy councils, knowing for certain that its teaching on the faith accords in all respects with the three other holy councils. We convinced many who had been contradicting the same holy council, while others who continued to contradict the same holy council we expelled from the holy churches of God and the venerable monasteries, with the result that, through the firm preservation of the concord and peace of the most holy churches and their priests, the one and the same faith professed by the holy four councils is preached in the holy churches of God.

When through the good will of God these measures for strengthening the holy four councils had been taken by us and prevailed in the holy church of God, the followers of Nestorius, wishing to impose their own impiety on the holy church of God and not being able to do this by means of Nestorius, endeavoured to introduce it by means of Theodore of Mopsuestia, the teacher of Nestorius, who had uttered far worse blasphemies than Nestorius and in addition to his other innumerable blasphemies against Christ our Lord had said that God the Word was someone other than Christ, and also by means of the impious writings of Theodoret, those he issued against the orthodox faith, the holy First Council of Ephesus and against Cyril of holy memory and his Twelve Chapters, and in addition through the criminal letter that Ibas is said to have written to Mari the Persian, which is replete with all the impiety of Theodore and Nestorius . . . We therefore, following the holy fathers, and wishing to proclaim the orthodox and immaculate faith in the churches of God and to frustrate the attempts of the impious, first of all consulted you residing in your churches about the aforesaid impious Three Chapters, and you made known to us your wishes, for which we also commended you, when without hesitation and with all alacrity you professed the orthodox faith and condemned the one that is impious. But because, even after the condemnation you issued, certain persons continued on the same course, defending the same impious Three Chapters, for this reason we have summoned you to the imperial city, exhorting you as you assemble together to declare again your will in this matter.

(Acts of Constantinople 1.7.7–9, abridged)

Justinian's Council of Constantinople, although hailed in Chalcedonian tradition as the fifth ecumenical council, was in all practical terms a failure. The attack on the Three Chapters did not resolve the underlying theological divisions between Chalcedonians and Miaphysites, and even as Justinian launched that attack more significant developments were occurring elsewhere. In 542/3 a man named Jacob Baradeus was ordained Miaphysite bishop of Edessa. Over the next thirty years Jacob in turn carried out numerous Miaphysite episcopal ordinations, an achievement celebrated by one of those bishops, John of Ephesus.

> He armed himself with divine strength, and went out to the work of his ministry, while he thenceforth began to pour out the priesthood derived from him copiously over the regions in all the eastern districts, like a great river in the days of Nisan, having entered upon the high road of heroism at a vigorous spiritual pace without ceasing or resting night and day, while in accordance with the saying of the Apostle he clothed himself in the breastplate of righteousness, and girded his loins with the perfection of faith, and took hold of the shield of salvation [Ephesians 6.14–17], while he was at all times carrying on a contest on behalf of the truth 'on the right hand and on the left, in glory and in dishonour' [2 Corinthians 6.7–8]. And so in the upper and lower countries, while he was running the vigorous course of heroism without ceasing from the Persian frontier even as far as the royal city of Constantinople, and Alexandria and all the countries, and fulfilling the work of the ministry to all the orthodox believers, not only by organizing the clergy and the giving of the priesthood, but also by consoling and comforting and edifying and strengthening and teaching all the party of the believers everywhere; so that consequently his fame was carried over all quarters, and in every country and city; so that all the synodite bishops from all sides were exasperated, and made threats against him to arrest him and tear him in pieces.
>
> (John of Ephesus, *Lives of the Eastern Saints* 49)

The ordination of increasing numbers of Miaphysite bishops by Jacob Baradeus and others laid the basis for a separate Church structure independent of imperial Greek Christianity. Previously, both Chalcedonians and Miaphysites had held to the ideal of a single united Church, with the point of controversy focused upon the teachings that this Church would hold as orthodox. From the sixth century onwards the Miaphysite or Oriental Orthodox Churches emerged. They included the Coptic Church of Egypt, the Syrian Orthodox Church (sometimes rather inaccurately identified as the Jacobite Church from Jacob Baradeus), and the Churches of Ethiopia and Armenia. All these Churches continue to exist today, alongside the Church of the East and the Greek Orthodox (Chalcedonian) Church. The Christological controversies of the fifth and sixth centuries thus left a profound and lasting legacy. The deep divisions within eastern Christianity contributed to the success of the seventh-century Islamic Conquests, which for some Christian writers hailed the coming of the end.

The blessed Apostle said: 'Not all who belong to Israel are Israel' [Romans 9.6], nor are all those who are called Christians Christians. For in the days of the prophet Elijah only 7000 of the Israelites were left who worshipped the Lord God, but through them the whole of Israel was saved. So too at the time of chastisement by these tyrants a few people out of many will remain as Christians, as our Saviour shows us in the Holy Gospel when He says, 'When the Son of Man shall come, will He find faith on earth?' [Luke 18.8]. Even those who are perfect in the countries will be disheartened during those days of chastisement. Many people who were members of the Church will deny the true Faith of the Christians, along with the holy Cross and the awesome Mysteries: without being subjected to any compulsion, or lashings or blows, they will deny Christ, putting themselves on a par with the unbelievers. For this reason the Apostle, too, proclaimed concerning them, 'At the latter times people will leave the Faith and go after unclean spirits, and after demonic teaching' [1 Timothy 4.1]; they will be rebels and accusers, haughty, hating anything good, traitors and savages. All who are false and weak in the faith will be tested and recognized during that chastisement: they will separate themselves of their own will from the Christian assembly, for the occasion itself will invite them to go after its defilement. As for the humble, the gentle, kind, quiet, truthful, noble, wise and elect, such people will not be sought out at that time, for they will be rejected and despised.

(Pseudo-Methodius, *Apocalypse* 12.1–6)

Copyright Acknowledgements

Acts of Chalcedon
Translated in R. Price and M. Gaddis, *The Acts of the Council of Chalcedon* (Liverpool 2005), by permission of Liverpool University Press

Acts of Constantinople
Translated in R. Price, *The Acts of the Council of Constantinople of 553, with related texts on the Three Chapters Controversy* (Liverpool 2009), by permission of Liverpool University Press

Cyril of Alexandria, *Second Letter to Nestorius*
Formula of Reunion
Translated in R. Price and M. Gaddis, *The Acts of the Council of Chalcedon* (Liverpool 2005), by permission of Liverpool University Press

Evagrius, *Ecclesiastical History*
Translated in M. Whitby, *The Ecclesiastical History of Evagrius Scholasticus* (Liverpool 2000), by permission of Liverpool University Press

John of Ephesus, *Lives of the Eastern Saints*
Translated in E. W. Brooks, *John of Ephesus: Lives of the Eastern Saints* (Patrologia Orientalis XVIII, Paris 1924), by permission of Brepols Publishers

Pseudo-Methodius, *Apocalypse*
Translated in A. Palmer with S. P. Brock and R. G. Hoyland, *The Seventh Century in the West-Syrian Chronicles* (Liverpool 1993), by permission of Liverpool University Press

Further Reading

A. S. Atiya, *A History of Eastern Christianity* (London 1968)

S. P. Brock and D. G. K. Taylor (eds), *The Hidden Pearl: The Syrian Orthodox Church and Its Ancient Aramaic Heritage*, 4 volumes (Rome 2001)

J. F. Coakley and K. Parry (eds), *The Church of the East: Life and Thought* (Manchester 1996)

W. H. C. Frend, *The Rise of the Monophysite Movement: Chapters in the History of the Church in the Fifth and Sixth Centuries* (Cambridge 1972)

P. T. R. Gray, *The Defense of Chalcedon in the East (451–553)* (Leiden 1979)

A. Grillmeier, *Christ in Christian Tradition*, vol. 1, *From the Apostolic Age to Chalcedon (AD 451)*, 2nd edition (London 1975)

J. McGuckin, *Saint Cyril of Alexandria and the Christological Controversy* (Crestwood, New York 2004)

V. L. Menze, *Justinian and the Making of the Syrian Orthodox Church* (Oxford 2008)

J. Meyendorff, *Imperial Unity and Christian Divisions: The Church 450–680 AD* (Crestwood, New York 1989)

R. A. Norris (ed.), *The Christological Controversy* (Philadelphia 1980)

R. Price and M. Gaddis, *The Acts of the Council of Chalcedon*, 3 volumes (Liverpool 2005)

S. Wessel, *Cyril of Alexandria and the Nestorian Controversy: The Making of a Saint and of a Heretic* (Oxford 2004)

F. M. Young, *From Nicaea to Chalcedon: A Guide to the Literature and its Background* (Philadelphia 1983)

20

Christianity and the Barbarian Invasions

In the middle of the fourth century the Later Roman empire stood supreme. From Gaul and Spain to Egypt and Syria, the empire dominated the ancient Graeco-Roman world as it had since before the birth of Christ. Barely a hundred years later, in AD 476, the last western Roman emperor Romulus Augustulus was deposed and the western Roman empire ceased to exist. Roman rule survived in the east, centred upon the new imperial city of Constantinople. In the west, Germanic kingdoms emerged, ruled over by Goths (Italy, Spain), Vandals (North Africa), Franks (Gaul) and other invading peoples. And yet throughout this time of crisis Christianity continued to expand. The survival of Roman Christianity combined with the conversion of the Germanic tribes laid the foundations for medieval Christendom and left the Church the only institution that still united the former western empire.

The first Germanic people to settle in large numbers within Late Roman territory were the Goths. Two Gothic tribes, the Tervingi and Greuthungi, arrived on the Roman Danube river frontier in 376 fleeing the advance of the Huns. Christianity had already reached the Goths several decades earlier, chiefly through the efforts of the missionary Ulfila (see Chapter 17). By the standards of later orthodoxy Ulfila's teachings belonged to the 'Arian' heresy, creating a recurring source of tension between Roman and Germanic Christians. But he played a key role in promoting Christianity among the tribes beyond the Roman frontier.

At this time [c.347/8] Ulfila led a large body of the Scythians from those living across the Danube (the people whom in olden times they called Getae, but now call Goths) to the land of the Romans, driven through piety from their own homes. Now this people became Christian in the following way. In the reigns of Valerian [253–260] and Gallienus [253–268], a large number of Scythians from beyond the Danube crossed into Roman territory and overran much of Europe. Crossing also into Asia, they reached as far as Galatia and Cappadocia. They took many prisoners, including some who were members of the clergy, and went home with a great quantity of booty. Now the pious band of prisoners, living as they did among the barbarians, converted many of them to the way of piety and persuaded them to adopt the Christian faith instead of the pagan. Among these prisoners were the ancestors of Ulfila; they were Cappadocians by nationality, from a village near the city of Parnassus called Sadagolthina. It was this Ulfila who led the exodus of the pious ones, being the first bishop appointed among them.

(Philostorgius, *Ecclesiastical History* 2.5)

After crossing the Danube, the Tervingi and Greuthungi Goths defeated and killed the eastern Roman emperor Valens at the Battle of Adrianople in 378. The Goths settled briefly in the Balkans, then invaded Italy under the leadership of Alaric and in August 410 sacked the city of Rome. Far away in the Holy Land, the Christian writer Jerome lamented:

When the bright light of all the world was put out, or rather, when the Roman empire was decapitated and, to speak more correctly, the whole world perished in one city.

(Jerome, *Preface to Ezekiel*)

The Goths who sacked Rome were themselves Christians, however, and protected the churches as places of sanctuary. Jerome acknowledged this in a letter recounting the experiences of two female friends, the ascetics Principia and Marcella.

The blood-stained victors found their way into Marcella's house. 'Be it mine to say what I have heard' [Virgil, *Aeneid* 6.266], or rather to relate what those holy men saw who were present and who say that you too, Principia, were with her in the hour of danger. When the soldiers entered she is said to have received them without alarm, and when they asked her for gold she pointed to her coarse dress to show that she had no hidden treasure. However, they would not believe in her self-chosen poverty, but scourged her and beat her with sticks. She is said to have felt no pain but to have thrown herself at their feet and to have pleaded with tears for you, that you might not be taken from her or, owing to your youth, have to endure what she as an old woman had no occasion to fear. Christ softened their hard hearts and even among blood-stained swords natural affection found a place. The barbarians escorted both her and you to the basilica of the apostle Paul, that you might find there either a place of safety or a tomb.

(Jerome, *Letter* 127.13, to Principia)

Alaric died shortly after the Sack of Rome and his followers eventually settled in southern Gaul in 418, founding the Visigothic kingdom of Aquitaine. The Gothic attacks on Italy had also allowed other Germanic tribes to enter the empire, notably the Vandals who crossed the Rhine river frontier in December 406 and advanced across Spain to invade North Africa. Some Roman Christians regarded the Germanic invasions as fitting punishment for their own sins. Writing in c.440, Salvian of Marseille contrasted Roman vice with Germanic virtue.

As for the way of life among the Goths and Vandals, in what single respect can we consider ourselves superior to them, or even worthy of comparison? Let me speak first of their affection and charity, which the Lord teaches us are the chief of virtues, and which He commends not only through the sacred Scriptures but also in His own words, when He says 'By this shall all men know that you are my disciples, if you love one another' [John 13.35]. Now almost all barbarians, at least those who belong to one tribe, under one king's rule, love one another, whereas almost all the Romans are at strife with one another. What citizen is there who does not envy his fellows? Who shows complete charity to his neighbours? All are indeed far from their neighbours in affection, however near in place; though living side by side, they are far apart in spirit.

While this is a most grievous wrong, I wish it were true only of citizens and neighbours. But the situation is still more serious, for not even relations preserve the bonds of kinship. Who renders a brotherly service for his next of kin? Who pays to family affection the debt he knows is due to the name he bears? Who is as closely related by his affections as by blood? Who is not fired with a dark passion of ill-will? Whose emotions are not the prey of envy? Who does not look on another's good fortune as his own punishment? Who does not reckon another's good as his own evil? Who finds his own good fortune so ample that he is willing that another should be fortunate also? Most men are now suffering a strange and incalculable evil, in that it is not enough for any man to be happy himself unless another is thereby made wretched. What a situation is this, how savage, how rooted in the same impiety we deplore, how alien to barbarians and familiar to Romans.

(Salvian of Marseille, *On the Governance of God* 5.4)

Salvian's younger contemporary Sidonius Apollinaris took a less pessimistic view. A Gallo-Roman aristocrat and later bishop, Sidonius lived through the crucial years of transition from Roman to Germanic rule in southern Gaul. He left a flattering description of the Visigothic king Theoderic II (453–466), glossing over the king's 'Arian' Christianity to praise his nobility.

You have often begged a description of Theoderic the Gothic king, whose gentle breeding fame commends to every nation; you want him in his quantity and quality, in his person, and the manner of his existence. I gladly accede, as far as the limits of my page allow, and highly approve so fine and ingenuous a curiosity. He is a man worth knowing, even by those who cannot enjoy his close acquaintance, so happily have providence and nature joined to endow him with the perfect gifts of fortune; his way of life is such that not even the envy which lies in wait for kings can rob him of his proper praise.

Before daybreak he goes with a very small suite to attend the service of his priests. He prays with assiduity, but, if I may speak in confidence, one may suspect more of habit than conviction in this piety. Administrative duties of the kingdom take up the rest of the morning. Armed nobles stand about the royal seat; the mass of guards in their garb of skins are admitted that they may be within call, but kept at the threshold for quiet's sake; only a murmur of them comes in from their post at the doors, between the curtain and the outer barrier. And now the foreign envoys are introduced. The king hears them out, and says little; if a thing needs more discussion he puts it off, but accelerates matters ripe for dispatch. The second hour arrives; he rises from the throne to inspect his treasure-chamber or stable.

When inclined for a board-game, he is quick to gather up the dice, examines them with care, shakes the box with expert hand, throws rapidly, humorously apostrophizes them, and patiently waits the issue. Silent at a good throw, he makes merry over a bad, annoyed by neither fortune and always the philosopher.

He is too proud to ask or to refuse a revenge; he disdains to avail himself of one if offered; and if it is opposed will quietly go on playing. You effect recovery of your men without obstruction on his side; he recovers his without collusion upon yours. You see the strategist when he moves the pieces; his one thought is victory. Yet at play he puts off a little of his kingly rigour, inciting all to good fellowship and the freedom of the game: I think he is afraid of being feared. Vexation in the man whom he beats delights him; he will never believe that his opponents have not let him win unless their annoyance proves him really victor. You would be surprised how often the pleasure born of these little happenings may favour the march of great affairs. Petitions that some wrecked influence had left derelict come unexpectedly to port; I myself am gladly beaten by him when I have a favour to ask, since the loss of my game may mean the gaining of my cause.

(Sidonius Apollinaris, *Letter* 1.2.1–8 (abridged))

Not all our Roman sources were so impressed by Germanic virtue or willing to collaborate with heretical barbarian kings. North Africa fell to the Vandals in 439. The Vandal king Gaiseric (428–477) was one of the most successful early Germanic leaders, and despite the later use of their name the 'Vandals' were probably no more destructive than any other Germanic people. Our perspective is somewhat distorted by our major source for Vandal North Africa, the fifth-century catholic bishop Victor of Vita who described in exaggerated detail the destruction attributed to the 'Arian' barbarians.

Finding a province which was at peace and enjoying quiet, the whole land beautiful and flowering on all sides, they set to work on it with their wicked forces, laying it waste by devastation and bringing everything to ruin with fire and murders. They did not even spare the fruit-bearing orchards, in case people who had hidden in the caves of mountains or steep places or any remote areas would be able to eat the foods produced by them after they had passed. So it was that no place remained safe from being contaminated by them, as they raged with great cruelty, unchanging and relentless. In particular, they gave vent to their wicked ferocity with great strength against the churches and basilicas of the saints, cemeteries and monasteries, so that they burned houses of prayer with fires greater than those they used against the cities and all the towns. When they happened to find the doors of a sacred building closed they were keen to open up a way with the blows of their hatchets, so that of them it could then rightly be said: 'They broke its doors in pieces with their axes as if they were in a forest of trees, they cast it down with axe and hatchet. They set your sanctuary on fire; they cast the tabernacle of your name to the ground and defiled it' [Psalm 74.5–7].

(Victor of Vita, *History of the Vandal Persecution* 1.3–4)

When Romulus Augustulus, the last western Roman emperor, was deposed in 476, almost the entire western empire had already been lost. Imperial power was restricted solely to Italy, which after Romulus' fall came under the rule of the Germanic general Odovacer. Then in 489–493 another wave of Gothic invaders entered Italy from the Balkans. Known as the Ostrogoths ('eastern Goths') to distinguish them from the Visigoths ('western Goths') who had settled in southern Gaul, the invaders created the Ostrogothic kingdom of Italy under Theoderic the Great (493–526). Theoderic was the most powerful Germanic king of his generation. Although like most Goths an 'Arian' Christian, he even intervened successfully in a disputed papal election, a feat celebrated in a letter sent to Rome in the name of his grandson and successor Athalaric (526–534).

Your response to the decision of the glorious lord my grandfather over the episcopal election gives, I declare, great satisfaction to my mind. For it was right to obey the judgement of a good prince: taking thought with prudent deliberation, although about an alien faith, he evidently chose such a pontiff [Pope Felix IV] as should displease no worthy man. You may thus appreciate that he specially desired that religion in all churches should flourish with good priests. You have, therefore, accepted a man who has been worthily formed by divine grace and praised by royal scrutiny. No one should still be engaged in the old rivalry. He whose hopes the prince has overcome should not feel the shame of defeat. Indeed, if he loves the new pontiff without guile, he makes him his own. For why grieve, when the rival's partisan finds in this man the same qualities he hoped for? These contests are civil ones, wars without weapons, quarrels without hatred; this affair is carried on by acclamations not lamentations. For although one person has been debarred still the faithful have lost nothing, seeing that the longed-for bishopric is occupied.

(Athalaric to the Senate of Rome (526), quoted in Cassiodorus, *Variae* 8.15)

Theoderic's efforts to unite his Gothic and Italian subjects, however, failed to resolve the differences between Romans and barbarians and between catholic and 'Arian' Christians. The final years of his reign saw increasing conflict, and Theoderic's kingdom did not long survive him. One hostile source compared Theoderic's death to that of the heresiarch Arius whose teachings he allegedly followed.

> [On Wednesday, 26 August 526, Theoderic ordered] that on the following Sabbath the Arians would take possession of the catholic basilicas. But He who does not allow His faithful worshippers to be oppressed by unbelievers soon brought upon Theoderic the same punishment that Arius, the founder of his religion, had suffered. For the king was seized with diarrhoea, and after three days of open bowels lost both his throne and his life on the very same day on which he rejoiced to attack the churches.
>
> (Anonymous Valesianus, *History of King Theoderic* 16.94–95)

Both the Vandals in North Africa and the Ostrogoths in Italy were swept away in the mid-sixth century by the armies of Justinian (eastern emperor 527–565), who temporarily at least restored imperial rule over those regions. By this stage the Visigoths had also been driven from their original kingdom in southern Gaul, and had established their power in Spain. Here too tensions arose between the 'Arian' Visigoths and their Roman subjects, particularly during the reign of king Leovigild (568–586) who fought to unite the Iberian peninsula under his control. Bishop Masona of Merida led resistance to the 'Arian' king, and refused to surrender the relics of his city's patron saint Eulalia (a victim of the Great Persecution).

> When he [Masona] came to the city of Toledo and stood in the presence of the vile tyrant, the king – provoking him with all manner of insults and pressing him with many threats – strove with all the force of his depraved plan to drag him into the Arian heresy. But when the man of God had willingly put up with all the insults directed at him and bore everything with equanimity, he began to answer without delay but with all gentleness the things that the rabid dog snarled at him and, while paying no heed to the insults directed at himself yet aggrieved at the injury done to the catholic faith, boldly resisted the tyrant. The mad king was tormented more and more by his constancy and so redoubled the rabid yelpings of his foaming mouth against the servant of God. He began to threaten him in terrible ways to hand over the tunic of the most holy virgin Eulalia in order that he might hang it in the basilica dedicated to Arian depravity there in Toledo. To

this the man of God replied, 'Know that I shall never soil my heart with the filth of Arian superstition, that I shall never befuddle my wits with its perverted dogma, and that I shall never hand over the tunic of my lady Eulalia to be polluted by the hands or even the fingertips of heretics. You shall never have it however long you try'.

(Anonymous, *The Lives of the Fathers of Merida* 5.6.9–13)

Leovigild's son and successor Reccared (586–601) adopted a very different policy to that of his father. Upon his accession Reccared embraced catholic Christianity, the first major Germanic ruler to convert away from 'Arian' teachings. He announced the conversion of his kingdom at the Third Council of Toledo in 589. Despite some Gothic resistance, Reccared's religious policy proved successful and helped to secure Visigothic rule over Spain until the Arab Conquest of the peninsula began in 711.

In the third year of the emperor Maurice [582–602], after Leovigild had died, his son Reccared was crowned king. He was a devout man, very different from his father in his way of life. For while the one was irreligious and had a very warlike disposition, the other was pious and outstanding in peace; while the one was increasing the dominion of the Gothic people through the arts of war, the other was gloriously elevating the same people by the victory of the faith. For in the very beginning of his reign, Reccared adopted the catholic faith, recalling all the peoples of the entire Gothic nation to the observance of the correct faith and removing the ingrained stain of their error. Reccared then convoked a synod of bishops from various provinces of Spain and Gallia Narbonensis to condemn the Arian heresy. This most religious ruler attended the council himself and confirmed its deeds with his presence and signature. He abjured, along with all of his subjects, the false teaching of Arius, which the people of the Goths had held up to that time. He then proclaimed the unity of the three persons in God, the Son born consubstantially from the Father, and the Holy Spirit proceeding inseparably from the Father and Son and being the one Spirit of them both, making them all one. With the help of his newly received faith, Reccared gloriously waged war against hostile peoples.

(Isidore of Seville, *History of the Kings of the Goths* 52–54)

The Visigoths had been driven from Gaul by the most successful of all the early Germanic peoples: the Franks. From their original heartland around the northern banks of the Rhine, the Franks expanded to conquer the region that now bears their name. Uniquely among the leading tribes of the post-Roman west, the Franks under king Clovis (c.481–c.511) converted directly to catholic Christianity without ever adopting 'Arian' beliefs (see Chapter 17). It was Clovis who defeated the Visigothic king Alaric II at the Battle of Vouille in 507, confirming Frankish superiority over Gaul. Gregory of Tours, our chief source for early Frankish history, offers a strongly pro-catholic account of that campaign which presents Clovis as an anti-Arian crusader who also showed due reverence for Martin, the patron saint of Tours.

'I find it hard to go on seeing these Arians occupy a part of Gaul', said Clovis to his ministers. 'With God's help let us invade them. When we have beaten them, we will take over their territory'. They all agreed to this proposal. An army was assembled and Clovis marched on Poitiers. Some of his troops passed through land belonging to Tours. In respect for Saint Martin, Clovis ordered that they should requisition nothing in this neighbourhood except fodder and water. One of the soldiers found some hay belonging to a poor man. 'The king commanded that nothing should be requisitioned except fodder, didn't he?', said this man. 'Well, this is fodder. We shan't be disobeying his orders if we take it'. He laid hands on the poor man and took his hay by main force. This was reported to Clovis. He drew his sword and killed the soldier on the spot. 'It is no good expecting to win this fight if we offend Saint Martin', said he. This was enough to ensure that the army took nothing else from this region.

The king sent messengers to the church of Saint Martin. 'Off with you', he said, 'and see if you can bring me some good tidings from God's house'. He loaded them with gifts which they were to offer to the church. 'Lord God', said he, 'if you are on my side and if you have decreed that this people of unbelievers, who have always been hostile to you, are to be delivered into my hands, deign to show me a propitious sign as these men enter Saint Martin's church, so that I may know that you will support your servant Clovis'. The messengers set out on their journey and came to Tours as Clovis had commanded. As they entered the church, it happened that the precentor was just beginning to intone this antiphon: 'For you have girded me with strength unto the battle; you have subdued under me those that rose up against me. You have also given me the necks of mine enemies, that I might destroy them that hate me' [Psalm 18.39–40]. When the messengers heard this psalm, they gave thanks to God. They made their vows to the saint and went happily back to report to the king.

(Gregory of Tours, *History of the Franks* 2.37)

Clovis and his descendants, the Merovingian dynasty, ruled over Francia for three hundred years. Their adoption of catholic Christianity was a major factor in their success, making possible the unification of Franks and Romans to a degree never achieved in the 'Arian' Gothic kingdoms. Yet over time, while Frankish society flourished, the power of their Merovingian kings declined. The last Merovingian, Childeric III, was deposed in 752 with the assistance of the papacy and secured in a monastery. His successor was Pepin the Short, who had held the office of Mayor of the Palace. Pepin was the son of Charles Martel, who had defeated Arab attacks on Francia in the 730s, and the first king of the Carolingian dynasty of Charlemagne.

It was the Mayor of the Palace who took responsibility for the administration of the realm and all matters which had to be done or planned at home or abroad. At the time of Childeric III's deposition, Pepin the Short, the father of Charlemagne, was already performing this duty as if by hereditary right. Charles Martel, the father of Pepin the Short, had performed the same office with great success, inheriting it in his turn from his own father Pepin of Herstal. It was Charles Martel who had crushed the despots who were claiming dominion for themselves throughout the whole land of the Franks. It was he, too, who had conquered the Saracens, when they were striving to occupy Gaul, in two battles – one in Aquitaine, near the city of Poitiers, and the other by the river Berre near Narbonne. In this way he compelled them to withdraw into Spain.

(Einhard, *Life of Charlemagne* 1.1–2)

Across the former territories of the western empire, from Italy and North Africa to Spain and Gaul, the newly emerging Germanic kingdoms preserved both Christianity and considerable elements of Roman culture. The collapse of Roman imperial authority did not mark a complete break with the past, and indeed for the Christian Church offered an opportunity for increased power and prestige. The Church, led by the papacy, was now the only institution that extended throughout western Europe, and bishops were figures of religious, political and social importance (see further Chapter 8). Thus in 595 Gregory the Great (bishop of Rome 590–604) could appoint Virgilius of Arles as his episcopal representative in Gaul, and remind the bishops of Francia of their chain of command.

The provision of the divine dispensation has decided that there should be diverse grades and distinct orders, so that, while inferiors show reverence to the more powerful, and the more powerful bestow love on their inferiors, one harmony of concord may emerge from diversity and the administration of all the individual offices may be properly carried out. Nor indeed could the whole [Church] otherwise survive, except that a great order of different offices hold it together. Indeed, that creation itself cannot be governed or exist in a state of absolute equality we are taught by the example of the heavenly hosts, since there are angels and also archangels and it is manifest that they are not equal, but as you know one differs from the other in power and rank. If therefore among these who are without sin there is evidently this distinction, who among men can refuse to submit himself willingly to this order of things which he knows that even angels obey? For thus peace and charity mutually embrace each other, and the sincerity of harmony remains firm in the reciprocal love which is well pleasing to God.

Since each single duty is beneficially fulfilled when there is one person who may be recognised as president, we have therefore perceived it to be opportune, in the churches that are under the dominion of our most excellent son king Childebert [the Merovingian Childebert II (575–595)], according to ancient custom, to give our vicariate jurisdiction to our brother Virgilius, bishop of the city of Arles, so that the integrity of the catholic faith, that is of the four holy synods, may be preserved under the protection of God with attentive devotion, and so that, if any contention should by chance arise among our brethren and fellow-priests, he may resolve it with discreet moderation by the rigour of his authority as representing the Apostolic See. We have also charged him that, if such a dispute should arise over any cases that require the presence of others, he should assemble our brethren and fellow-bishops in sufficient number, discuss the matter appropriately with due regard to equity, and decide it with canonical integrity. But if a contention (which may the Divine power avert) should happen to arise on matters of faith, or any business come up about which there may perhaps be serious doubt, and he should be in need of the judgment of the Apostolic See because of its significance, we have directed him that he should diligently enquire into the truth and then he should take care to bring the question to our attention by his report, so that it may be terminated by a suitable sentence so as to remove all doubt.

(Gregory the Great, *Letter* 5.59, to all the bishops of Gaul who are under the rule of Childebert)

The great exception to the pattern of religious and cultural survival in the former western Roman empire was Britain. Abandoned earlier than the other provinces, Britain was left to its own devices with the withdrawal of imperial support at the time of the Sack of Rome in 410. The Anglo-Saxons who settled in Britain from the fifth century onwards were far less influenced by Roman culture than the Goths, Vandals or Franks, and had little experience of Christianity. In c.540 Gildas the monk composed a lament for British decline, condemning alike kings and priests for their roles in *The Ruin of Britain*.

Britain has kings, but they are tyrants; she has judges, but they are wicked. They often plunder and terrorize the innocent; they defend and protect the guilty and thieving. They have many wives, who are whores and adulteresses. They constantly swear false oaths; they make vows but almost at once tell lies. They wage wars, civil and unjust. They chase thieves energetically all over the country, but love and even reward the thieves who sit with them at table. They distribute alms profusely, but pile up an immense mountain of crime for all to see. They take their seats as judges, but rarely seek out the rules of right judgement. They despise the harmless and humble, but exalt to the stars, so far as they can, their military companions – bloody, proud and murderous men, adulterers and enemies of God – if chance, as they say, so allows: men who should have been rooted out vigorously, name and all. They keep many prisoners in their jails, who are more often loaded with chafing chains because of intrigue than because they deserve punishment. They hang around the altars swearing oaths, then shortly afterwards scorn them as though they were dirty stones.

Britain has priests, but they are fools; very many ministers, but they are shameless; clerics, but they are treacherous grabbers. They are called shepherds, but they are wolves all ready to slaughter souls. They do not look to the good of their people, but to the filling of their own bellies. They have church buildings, but go to them for the sake of base profit. They teach the people but by giving them the worst of examples, vice and bad character. Rarely do they sacrifice and never do they stand with pure heart amid the altars. They do not reprimand the people for their sins; indeed they do the same things themselves. They make mock of the precepts of Christ, and all their prayers are directed to the fulfilment of their lustful desires. They usurp with unclean feet the seat of the apostle Peter, yet thanks to their greed they fall into the pestilential chair of the traitor Judas. They hate truth as an enemy, and love lies like favourite brothers. They look askance at the just poor as though they were dreadful snakes; and, showing no regard for shame, they respect the wicked rich as though they were angels from heaven.

(Gildas, *The Ruin of Britain* 27 and 66)

Yet all hope was not lost. Knowledge of Christianity and classical culture in the British Isles survived, particularly in Ireland, and at the end of the sixth century the mission of Augustine of Canterbury brought renewed ties with Rome and the continent. When Bede completed his *Ecclesiastical History of the English People* in 731 he looked to the future with hope and with trust in God.

The Picts now have a treaty of peace with the English and rejoice to share in the catholic peace and truth of the Church universal. The Irish who live in Britain are content with their own territories and devise no plots or treachery against the English. Though, for the most part, the Britons oppose the English through their inbred hatred, and the whole state of the catholic Church by their incorrect Easter and their evil customs, yet being opposed by the power of God and man alike, they cannot obtain what they want in either respect. For although they are partly their own masters, yet they have also been brought partly under the rule of the English. In these favourable times of peace and prosperity, many of the Northumbrian race, both noble and simple, have laid aside their weapons and taken the tonsure, preferring that they and their children should take monastic vows rather than train themselves in the art of war. What the result will be, a later generation will discover. This is the state of the whole of Britain at the present time, about 285 years after the coming of the English to Britain, in the year of our Lord 731. Let the earth rejoice in His perpetual kingdom and let Britain rejoice in His faith and let the multitude of isles be glad and give thanks at the remembrance of His holiness.

(Bede, *Ecclesiastical History of the English People* 5.23)

Copyright Acknowledgements

Anonymous, *The Lives of the Fathers of Merida*
Translated in A. T. Fear, *Lives of the Visigothic Fathers* (Liverpool 1997), by permission of Liverpool University Press

Bede, *Ecclesiastical History of the English People*
Translated in J. McClure and R. Collins, *Bede: The Ecclesiastical History of the English People* (Oxford and New York 1994), by permission of Oxford University Press

Cassiodorus, *Variae*
Translated in S. J. B. Barnish, *Cassiodorus: Selected Variae* (Liverpool 1992), by permission of Liverpool University Press

Einhard, *Life of Charlemagne*
Translated in L. Thorpe, *Einhard and Notker the Stammerer: Two Lives of Charlemagne* (London 1969), by permission of Penguin Books Ltd

Gildas, *The Ruin of Britain*
Translated in M. Winterbottom, *Gildas: The Ruin of Britain and other works* (London and Chichester 1978)

Gregory of Tours, *History of the Franks*
Translated in L. Thorpe, *Gregory of Tours: The History of the Franks* (Harmondsworth 1974), by permission of Penguin Books Ltd

Isidore of Seville, *History of the Kings of the Goths*
Translated in K. B. Wolf, *Conquerors and Chroniclers of Early Medieval Spain*, 2nd edition (Liverpool 1999), by permission of Liverpool University Press

Philostorgius, *Ecclesiastical History*
Translated in P. Heather and J. Matthews, *The Goths in the Fourth Century* (Liverpool 1991), by permission of Liverpool University Press

Victor of Vita, *History of the Vandal Persecution*
Translated in J. Moorhead, *Victor of Vita: History of the Vandal Persecution* (Liverpool 1992), by permission of Liverpool University Press

Further Reading

T. Charles-Edwards (ed.), *Short Oxford History of the British Isles: After Rome* (Oxford 2003)
J. Harries, *Sidonius Apollinaris and the Fall of Rome, AD 407–485* (Oxford 1994)
P. Heather, *Goths and Romans 332–489* (Oxford 1991)
P. Heather, *The Fall of the Roman Empire: A New History* (London 2005)
R. A. Markus, *Gregory the Great and his World* (Cambridge 1997)
A. H. Merrills and R. Miles, *The Vandals* (Oxford 2010)
J. Moorhead, *Theoderic in Italy* (Oxford 1992)
J. J. O'Donnell, *The Ruin of the Roman Empire* (London 2009)
R. Stocking, *Bishops, Councils, and Consensus in the Visigothic Kingdom, 589–633* (Ann Arbor 2000)
B. Ward-Perkins, *The Fall of Rome and the End of Civilization* (Oxford 2005)
C. J. Wickham, *Framing the Early Middle Ages: Europe and the Mediterranean 400–800* (Oxford 2005)
S. Williams and G. Friell, *The Rome that did not Fall: The Survival of the East in the Fifth Century* (London 1999)
I. Wood, *The Merovingian Kingdoms 450–571* (London 1994)

Epilogue: The Dawn of Medieval Christendom

The centuries covered by this sourcebook represent a fundamental period of transformation for both Christianity and the Later Roman world. At the beginning of the fourth century, a single Roman empire united the lands surrounding the Mediterranean Sea and beyond. It was an empire still dominated by the religion and culture of ancient Greece and Rome, with the Christian Church a threatened but expanding minority. Christian resistance to the Great Persecution was rewarded by the conversion of Constantine and the dramatic changes that imperial favour brought to the Church. By AD 400 Christianity was firmly established as the official religion of the empire, and Christian values influenced every aspect of Roman life and society. Yet the triumph of Christianity changed not only the empire but Christianity itself. The imperial Church sought to impose uniformity on the diverse customs of the early Christians, from the clerical hierarchy and the canon of Scripture to the doctrines of the Trinity and the Incarnation. At the same time new elements emerged, shaped above all by the rise of the ascetic movement and the cults of holy men and women. Later generations would look back on the fourth and fifth centuries as the golden age of the Christian patristic tradition and the crucible in which medieval Christendom was forged.

The years of Christian triumph also marked the beginning of the 'Decline and Fall' of the western Roman empire. The Germanic invasions of the fifth century shattered the unity of the ancient Mediterranean world. To the east the empire endured, centred upon the new imperial city of Constantinople. The former western provinces were replaced by a mosaic of constantly shifting kingdoms as Goths, Vandals, Franks and others struggled for supremacy. Christianity, however, not only survived the collapse of Roman imperial power in the west but flourished. The Germanic peoples embraced the Christian faith, and the bishops of Rome gained prestige in the vacuum left by the disappearance of the western emperors. By AD 600, as classical antiquity gave way to the Middle Ages, the Church was the only institution that still connected Egypt and Spain, Greece and Italy, Gaul and Britain. Unlike the Later Roman empire from which it emerged, Medieval Christendom was united not by a single state but by a single religion, which would define European history for the next millennium.

Three closing passages draw together east and west at the dawn of medieval Christendom. In the eastern Roman or Byzantine empire, imperial Christianity remained strong. The magnificent church of Hagia Sophia, dedicated by the emperor Justinian in 537, became the symbol of Christian Constantinople and still stands today in what is now Istanbul.

> The emperor, disregarding all questions of expense, eagerly pressed on to begin the work of construction and began to gather all the artisans from the whole world. And Anthemius of Tralles, the most learned man in the skilled craft which is known as the art of building, not only of all his contemporaries but also when compared with those who had lived long before him, ministered to the emperor's enthusiasm. He duly regulated the tasks of the various artisans, preparing in advance designs of the future construction, and associated with him another master-builder, Isidorus by name, a Milesian by birth, a man who was intelligent and worthy to assist the emperor Justinian. Indeed this also was an indication of the honour in which God held the emperor, that He had already provided the men who would be most serviceable to him in the tasks which were waiting to be carried out. And one might with good reason marvel at the discernment of the emperor himself, in that out of the whole world he was able to select the men who were most suitable for the most important of his enterprises. So the church has become a spectacle of marvellous beauty, overwhelming to those who see it, but to those who know it by hearsay altogether incredible. For it soars to a height to match the sky, and as if surging up from amongst the other buildings it stands on high and looks down upon the rest of the city, adorning it, because it is a part of it, but glorying in its own beauty, because, though a part of the city it dominates, it at the same time towers above it to such a height that the whole city is viewed from there as from a watch-tower. Both its breadth and its length have been so carefully proportioned, that it may not improperly be said to be exceedingly long and at the same time unusually broad. And it exults in an indescribable beauty.
>
> (Procopius, *Buildings* 1.1.23–28)

In Rome there was no emperor, only the bishop. At the end of the sixth century, Pope Gregory the Great was the single most influential voice in the post-Roman west. His *Pastoral Rule* expressed Gregory's concerns both for the duties of those in authority and for the corrupting effects of power, concerns that became ever more compelling with the rise of the medieval Papal Monarchy.

The ruler should be a humble companion of those who live good lives and firm through the zeal of righteousness against the vices of evil-doers; so that in nothing should he prefer himself to the good and yet when the fault of the bad requires it he should at once be conscious of the power of his position. Thus, while among subordinates who live well he may downplay his rank and count them as his equals, but he must not fear to execute the laws of rectitude towards the perverse. For, as I remember saying in my book on morals, it is clear that nature produced all men as equals, yet through the variation in the order of their merits, sin sets some below others. But this very diversity which has accrued from vice is ordered by divine judgment, so that, since all men cannot stand on an equal footing, one should be ruled by another. Thus all who preside over others ought to consider not the authority of their rank but the equality of their condition, and rejoice not to rule over others but to do them good. For indeed our ancient fathers are said to have been not kings of men, but shepherds of flocks.

All too often, however, a ruler is puffed up with pride from the very fact of his being pre-eminent over others. While all things serve his need, while his commands are quickly executed according to his desire, while all his subjects extol with praises what he has done well but have no authority to speak against what he has done wrong, and while they commonly praise even what they should have rebuked, so his mind, seduced by what is offered in abundance from below, is lifted up above itself. And so, while outwardly surrounded by unbounded favour, inside he loses his sense of truth. Forgetful of who he is, he scatters himself among the voices of other men and believes himself to be what outwardly he hears himself called rather than such as he ought inwardly to have judged himself to be. He looks down on those who are under him, nor does he acknowledge them as his equals in the order of nature; and those whom he has surpassed in the accident of power he believes himself to have transcended also in the merits of his life. He esteems himself wiser than all whom he sees himself to excel in power.

(Gregory the Great, *Pastoral Rule* 2.6, abridged)

To the north of Italy, the Franks ruled over the greatest of the early Germanic kingdoms. And it was from Francia that the first western ruler would arise to claim the imperial title as heir to Constantine and the Christian Roman emperors, with the coronation of Charlemagne in Rome in the church of St Peter's Vatican on Christmas Day 800.

Throughout the whole period of his reign nothing was ever nearer to his heart than that, by his own efforts and exertion, the city of Rome should regain its former proud position. His ambition was not merely that the church of Saint Peter should remain safe and protected thanks to him, but that by means of his wealth it should be more richly adorned and endowed than any other church. However much he thought of Rome, it still remains true that throughout his whole reign of 47 years he went there only four times to fulfil his vows and to offer up his prayers. These were not the sole reasons for Charlemagne's last visit to Rome. The truth is that the inhabitants of Rome had violently attacked Pope Leo [Leo III, bishop 795–816], (almost) putting out his eyes and cutting off his tongue, and had forced him to flee to the king for help. Charlemagne really came to Rome to restore the Church, which was in a very bad state indeed, but in the end he spent the whole winter there. It was on this occasion that he received the title of Emperor and Augustus. At first he was far from wanting this. He made it clear that he would not have entered the cathedral that day at all, although it was the greatest of all the festivals of the Church, if he had known in advance what the Pope was planning to do. Once he had accepted the title, he endured with great patience the jealousy of the so-called Roman emperors [in the east], who were most indignant at what had happened. He overcame their hostility only by the sheer strength of his personality, which was much more powerful than theirs. He was for ever sending messengers to them, and in his dispatches he called them his brothers.

(Einhard, *Life of Charlemagne* 3.27–28)

Copyright Acknowledgements

Einhard, *Life of Charlemagne*
Translated in L. Thorpe, *Einhard and Notker the Stammerer: Two Lives of Charlemagne* (London 1969), by permission of Penguin Books Ltd

General Bibliography

P. Brown, *The World of Late Antiquity* (London 1971)

P. Brown, *The Rise of Western Christendom: Triumph and Diversity* AD *200–1000*, 2nd edition (Oxford 2003)

P. Brown, *Through the Eye of a Needle: Wealth, the Fall of Rome, and the Making of Christianity in the West, 350–550* AD (Princeton 2012)

V. Burrus (ed.), *Late Ancient Christianity: A People's History of Christianity*, Volume II (Minneapolis 2005)

Av. Cameron, *The Mediterranean World in Late Antiquity,* AD *395–700*, 2nd edition (London 2011)

H. Chadwick, *The Church in Ancient Society: From Galilee to Gregory the Great* (Oxford 2001)

G. Clark, *Christianity and Roman Society* (Cambridge 2004)

J. Elsner, *Imperial Rome and Christian Triumph: The Art of the Roman Empire* AD *100–450* (Oxford 1998)

G. Fowden, *Empire to Commonwealth: Consequences of Monotheism in Late Antiquity* (Princeton 1993)

S. A. Harvey and D. G. Hunter (eds), *The Oxford Handbook of Early Christian Studies* (Oxford 2008)

P. Heather, *The Fall of the Roman Empire: A New History* (London 2005)

J. Herrin, *The Formation of Christendom* (London 1987)

M. Innes, *Introduction to Early Medieval Western Europe 300–900: The Sword, the Plough and the Book* (London 2007)

S. F. Johnson (ed.), *The Oxford Handbook of Late Antiquity* (Oxford 2012)

A. H. M. Jones, *The Later Roman Empire 284–602: A Social, Economic, and Administrative Survey*, 3 volumes (Oxford 1964)

J. K. Knight, *The End of Antiquity: Archaeology, Society and Religion* AD *235–700*, revised edition (Stroud 2007)

R. A. Markus, *The End of Ancient Christianity* (Cambridge 1990)

S. Mitchell, *A History of the Later Roman Empire* AD *284–641* (Malden and Oxford 2006)

P. Rousseau (ed.), *A Companion to Late Antiquity* (Malden and Oxford 2009)

J. M. H. Smith, *Europe after Rome: A New Cultural History 500–1000* (Oxford 2005)

B. Ward-Perkins, *The Fall of Rome and the End of Civilization* (Oxford 2005)

C. J. Wickham, *Framing the Early Middle Ages: Europe and the Mediterranean 400–800* (Oxford 2005)

Index of Authors and Texts

Index of Scriptural Citations

General Index

Adam and Eve 92, 178, 189–90, 194–7, 215, 243, 248
Alaric 123, 264–5
Alexander of Alexandria 65–8, 70, 176
Alexandria 65, 105, 129, 165, 227, 259
 ecclesiastical authority of 105–7, 248–9
 Jews in 176–7
Altar of Victory 146–7, 149
Ambrose of Milan 87, 90–1, 109–10, 113, 146–7, 194, 218–19, 239–40
 and Theodosius I 121–3, 147, 174–5, 214
Anglo-Saxons 151, 209, 231–3, 274–5
Antioch 71, 98–9, 105, 144–5, 203
 ecclesiastical authority of 105–7, 248–9
Antony 127–30, 131, 134, 138, 199–201, 202
Apollinaris of Laodicea 157–8, 248, 250, 252
Apollo 43, 144–5, 150, 162
 Constantine's vision of 28–9, 33
'Arian Controversy' 65–79, 90, 120, 129, 202
 Germanic 'Arianism' 62–3, 76, 78–9, 230–1, 263, 266–72
Arius 65–71, 73, 248, 250, 269, 270
asceticism 50, 127–38, 159–62, 179, 190–5, 199–210, 277
Athanasius of Alexandria 70, 107–8, 110, 227, 247–8, 252, 253
 and the 'Arian Controversy' 70–3, 74, 77, 112, 247–8
 on asceticism 127–9, 134–5, 195, 199–201
 on Scripture 83–4
 Life of Antony 127–9, 199–201
Attila 114, 207–8
Augustine of Canterbury 209, 232, 275
Augustine of Hippo 90, 95–6, 137, 186, 194, 204, 237–44
 and the Donatist Schism 53, 60–2, 240
 and Manichaeism 179–80, 238–9, 240

 on classical culture 160–1, 162, 163–4, 165, 238
 on religious violence 60–2
 Confessions 186, 237–40
 City of God 123–4, 237, 241–4
Augustus 1–2, 118–19, 146

baptism 34–5, 78, 81, 92–7, 188, 225, 237–8, 240
 infant baptism 93–4, 95–6, 216, 237–8
Basil of Cappadocian Caesarea 76
 on asceticism 131–2, 133, 136, 137
 on classical culture 158–9, 162
Bede 100, 151, 209–10, 232–3, 275
Bethlehem 48, 98, 192, 214
bishops 46, 59–60, 62, 71, 78, 88, 103–15, 119–23, 125, 134–5, 152, 189–90, 194–5, 259
 Constantine's benefits to 40, 42–3, 45–7, 50, 54–5, 57, 105, 119, 152
 hierarchy of 103–7, 111–15, 248–9, 259
 in the post-Roman west 110–11, 152, 231, 232, 266–70, 272–3
Britain 27, 151, 208, 231–3, 273–5, 277
 Christianity in 12, 21, 46, 97, 208–10, 219, 232, 240, 274–5
 Gregorian mission to 114, 209, 232–3, 274–5
Byzantium 34, 125, 166–7, 278, 280

Caecilian of Carthage 40, 42, 46, 54–8
calendar 81, 96–9, 175
Chalcedonian Definition 255–6
charity 5–7, 9, 89, 128, 130, 144, 149–50, 170, 265
 clerical support for 8–9, 40, 43, 107, 111
 women and 7, 8–9, 185, 193, 195, 203, 208
Charlemagne 36, 115, 125, 165–6, 272, 279–80
China 179, 180, 233–4, 251
Christmas 81, 91, 98–9, 122, 152, 279